VOL **2**

- **KEEP UP YOUR** -

Biblical Greek

IN TWO MINUTES A DAY

THE TWO MINUTES A DAY
BIBLICAL LANGUAGE SERIES
INCLUDES:

Keep Up Your Biblical Greek in Two Minutes a Day
Volume 1
365 Selections for Easy Review

Keep Up Your Biblical Greek in Two Minutes a Day
Volume 2
365 More Selections for Easy Review

Keep Up Your Biblical Hebrew in Two Minutes a Day
Volume 1
365 Selections for Easy Review

Keep Up Your Biblical Hebrew in Two Minutes a Day
Volume 2
365 More Selections for Easy Review

Keep Up Your Biblical Aramaic in Two Minutes a Day
365 Selections for Easy Review

VOL **2**

─── **KEEP UP YOUR** ───

Biblical Greek

IN TWO MINUTES A DAY

365 MORE SELECTIONS FOR EASY REVIEW

Compiled and edited by
Jonathan G. Kline

HENDRICKSON
PUBLISHERS

Keep Up Your Biblical Greek in Two Minutes a Day, Volume 2

© 2017 by Hendrickson Publishers Marketing, LLC
P. O. Box 3473
Peabody, Massachusetts 01961-3473
www.hendrickson.com

ISBN 978-1-68307-057-3

Book cover and jacket design by Maria Poulopoulos

Printed in the United States of America

First Printing—November 2017

Library of Congress Cataloging-in-Publication Data

A catalog record for this title is available from the Library of Congress
Hendrickson Publishers Marketing, LLC ISBN 978-1-68307-057-3

Contents

Preface

Keep Up Your Biblical Greek in Two Minutes a Day: Volume 2 has been specially designed to help you build on your previous study of Greek by reading a small amount of the New Testament in its original language every day in an easy, manageable, and spiritually enriching way. This book does not do away with the need to consult traditional textbooks and to review paradigms and the fundamentals of Greek grammar, which are essential tasks for developing an enduring ability to read and understand Greek well. Rather, this book complements such grammatical study by enabling you to build a robust vocabulary base and by encouraging you to work with the biblical text and review morphology and syntax in a largely inductive manner.

In order to help you reconnect with Greek in a direct and efficient way, this book contains no grammatical jargon or extraneous material—only verses from the New Testament, in Greek and English, carefully selected and presented (along with brief vocabulary entries) in a manner intended to facilitate rapid and enjoyable learning. The book is designed to be used on a daily basis (ideally), or in any case with some measure of consistency. The page for each day includes the following:

- one new vocabulary word, with transliteration and meanings, and two review words from earlier in the book or from *Keep Up Your Biblical Greek in Two Minutes a Day: Volume 1*
- the English text of a New Testament verse, with these three Greek words embedded in it, as they appear in the verse
- the Greek text of the verse, in full and then divided into phrases or clauses, with the corresponding English phrases or clauses next to them

To encourage you to spend a little time with Greek on a regular basis, each page is labeled with a day number (from 1 to 365), a date (from January 1 to December 31), and a week number (from Week 1 to Week 52). The book is thus designed so that you can work through it in a calendar year (whether starting on January 1 or any other date), though of course you need not use it according to this scheme. What is important, in any event, is not perfection or following a rigid schedule, but regular practice. There is no reason to feel bad if you miss a day or two, for example; the next time you have a chance to use the book, you can simply pick up where you left off, or skip to the page for the current date.

As the title *Keep Up Your Biblical Greek in Two Minutes a Day* indicates, spending at least two minutes with each day's page is recommended. Yet glancing at the page for a given day for even ten or fifteen seconds can still provide real benefits; and in any case this is better than not opening the book at all. Here are some suggestions for different ways you might wish to use this book, depending on how much time you have on a particular day:

10 seconds to 1 minute. *Activity:* Read the daily Bible verse in English, noticing the Greek words in parentheses. *Benefit:* You have read a Bible verse in English and have been quickly reminded of what a few Greek words mean and perhaps of an aspect or two of Greek grammar. *Alternate activity:* Look at the Greek word for the day and read its definitions. *Benefit:* You have been reminded of the basic range of meaning of a Greek word that occurs with a relatively high frequency in the New Testament.

2 to 5 minutes. *Activity:* Read the daily Bible verse in English, noticing the Greek words in parentheses. Next, look at the Greek word for the day and its meanings. Finally, read the Greek text as best you can, perhaps only in the phrase/clause section on the lower half of the page, simply ignoring what you don't understand. *Benefit:* You have read a Bible verse in English and (as much as you are able) in Greek. You have been reminded of what at least a few, and perhaps many, Greek words mean, and also of certain principles of Greek morphology and syntax.

10 to 20 minutes. *Activity:* Every day of a given week, look at all seven pages for the present week, spending whatever amount of time you desire on each page (perhaps skimming some pages and spending more time on others). *Benefit:* After the week is over, you will likely have developed a deep familiarity with the week's biblical texts and a lasting knowledge of the week's vocabulary words. You will also have deepened your familiarity with various principles of Greek morphology and syntax.

As these suggestions indicate, although this book has been designed to provide substantial benefits if you use it for only two minutes a day, mulling over (and, as need be, puzzling through) its contents for longer periods of time can help you even further along the journey toward achieving a lasting mastery of Greek.

Another interesting and helpful way to use this book—one that is especially suited for more advanced users—is to review vocabulary by means of a "chain" method. For example, pick a day in the book, perhaps at random and preferably toward the end (say, Day 363), and read the page. Then, pick one of the two review words for the day (e.g., πεινάω), go to the page on which that word is the new word for the day (Day 203), and read that page. Next, pick one of the review words on this new page (e.g., ἀναγινώσκω), go to the page on which it is the new word for the day (Day 67), and read that page.

You can repeat this process as many times as you want, until you get as close as possible to the beginning of the book. (If you have a copy of *Keep Up Your Biblical Greek in Two Minutes a Day: Volume 1*, this process would lead you back to that book when you reached a page in the present volume whose two review words were from *Volume 1*.)

If the verse for a particular day is one that you would like to internalize or try to memorize in Greek, feel free to temporarily suspend your regular reading of a new page each day and instead spend several days, or perhaps even a week, reading the same page every day. By doing so, you may notice new things about the grammar or syntax of the verse, and at least some, if not all, of the verse will likely remain in your mind and heart for a long time to come. If you take the time to meditate on a verse in this way, you may also wish to look up the verse in a technical commentary or two to see what scholars have said about it; or you may choose to look up the verse in the index of an intermediate or advanced Greek grammar in order to learn about the morphology of the words the verse contains or about its syntax. Meditating on or memorizing even two or three Greek verses in this way over the course of a year can go a long way toward helping you internalize and become proficient in the language.

As the foregoing discussion indicates, the benefits you derive from using this book will obviously depend on how much time you spend with it and how often, the specific ways you choose to use it, your current level of Greek proficiency, and your ability to learn inductively. Nevertheless, I have done my best to design the book so that it can help you make substantial and enduring gains in learning even if you are able to use it for only short periods of time at most sittings and even if your Greek is at a rudimentary level when you begin.

The Vocabulary

This book's precursor, *Keep Up Your Biblical Greek in Two Minutes a Day: Volume 1*, presents, one day at a time and in order of descending frequency, the 365 most frequently occurring words in the New Testament. *Volume 2* presents the next 365 most frequently occurring words—that is, those that occur between 41 and 16 times (including about half of the words that occur 41 times and about a third of those that occur 16 times). If you master the 365 daily words presented in *Volume 1* and about the first quarter of the words presented in *Volume 2*, you will know the lexical form lying behind every Greek word that *The Greek New Testament: A Reader's Edition* assumes knowledge of (i.e., all the words that that volume does not gloss in its apparatus). Another encouraging—and somewhat startling—fact is that although the 730 lexemes (dictionary forms) presented in volumes 1 and 2 of *Keep Up Your Biblical Greek in Two Minutes a Day* account for only 4 percent of the total number of unique lexemes that occur in the New Testament, *88 percent of the actual words found in the New Testament* are forms of the 730 words found in these volumes. Learning the details of morphology is essential, of course, for identifying which words in the biblical text are forms of which lexical forms presented in these books; but mastering the core vocabulary found in these books is an important first step for gaining proficiency in reading the New Testament in Greek.

I created the initial list of 365 core review words for this book by comparing the main frequency list of vocabulary found in Warren C. Trenchard's *Complete Vocabulary Guide to the Greek New Testament* (Zondervan) and a similar list generated using the computer program BibleWorks. I checked the frequency data from these sources against those found in an unpublished database created by Mark House and Maurice Robinson for Hendrickson Publishers and then made my own decisions regarding which words should be included in this book's list and their frequencies. In general, though not invariably, the frequency I provide for each day's vocabulary word (found to the right of the gray box containing the word's gloss(es) and followed by an "x") is based on the number of times the word occurs in the Westcott-Hort edition of the Greek New Testament (on which see further below). For interested readers, I have also included the Strong's number for each daily vocabulary word (prefixed with an "S" and found below each day's frequency number).

In order to facilitate rapid review—and as a reflection of the fact that *Keep Up Your Biblical Greek in Two Minutes a Day* is intended primarily as a resource for review and skill building, not as a tool for scientific research—I have almost invariably presented lexical forms in as pared down a form as possible. For example, I have generally not provided the genitive forms of nouns or the feminine or neuter forms of adjectives. On occasion, however, I have made an exception to such rules and have included more than one lexical form—for example, for lexemes that do not have straightforward inflections.

The Glosses

I generated the initial list of glosses for each day's vocabulary word by abridging the entries in Hendrickson's *Compact Greek-English Lexicon of the New Testament*, a 2008 revision by Mark House of an earlier pocket dictionary created by Alexander Souter. In a good number of cases I further modified an entry after consulting a standard modern lexicon of the Greek New Testament or, occasionally, by looking in detail at the contexts in which a word occurs.

As with the lexical forms, I have intentionally kept the glosses basic and brief so that you can quickly grasp a word's essential or most common meaning(s). The glosses are not exhaustive. For more comprehensive and nuanced glosses or definitions, please consult a standard Greek lexicon or vocabulary guide.

Likewise, and again to facilitate rapid and easy review, I have kept grammatical information in the glosses to an absolute minimum. For example, I have not indicated which meanings of a preposition accompany which noun cases, and I have almost never indicated which of a verb's meanings are attested in which voice (the active, middle, or passive). The only exception I made to this latter rule is in the case of the verb ἅπτω (Day 26), whose meanings in the middle ("to touch") and active ("to light, kindle") are so distinct that I thought noting the voices would be helpful.

Finally, and contrary to standard practice, I have glossed all verbs as infinitives rather than as first-person singulars (even though, of course, the lexical form presented is the first-person singular present form). My hope is that this will allow you to quickly focus on a verb's meanings.

The Verses

In this book I have attempted to present an interesting variety of verses from the New Testament, in terms of both content and grammar. The process by which I chose the verses was an organic and creative one that was guided by grammatical, theological, aesthetic, and—above all—pedagogical concerns. I have included verses from nearly every book of the New Testament and of varying lengths and difficulties. The verses contain content that is inspiring, comforting, challenging, and thought provoking. This allows you, if you wish, to use the book as a kind of daily devotional. Whether you think of the book in this way or not, my goal in creating it has been not only to help you improve your knowledge of Greek for its own sake, but also—and more importantly—to help you engage closely with, meditate on, wrestle with, be challenged by, and find solace and hope in the words of the New Testament writers.

The Phrases and Clauses

In breaking up each day's verse into phrases and/or clauses, I have done my best to help you see the correspondence between brief elements in the day's Greek text and English translation. Naturally, however, a one-to-one correspondence does not always exist (and in a technical sense never completely exists) between a Greek word, phrase, or clause and its English translation. For this reason, you may occasionally find the way that I have matched up parts of the Greek and English verses to be slightly forced. It goes without saying that the correspondences shown are not meant to be completely scientific or precise in every case; rather, they are a pedagogical tool intended to help you work through each day's verse little by little and in a short amount of time, in order to arrive at a basic understanding of the grammar and syntax of the Greek.

Correlatively, in an attempt to be sensitive to the unique content of each day's verse and to help you understand it as well as possible, I have sometimes divided syntactically or grammatically identical structures found in different verses in different ways. Such inconsistencies are intentional and, again, are always the result of my trying to present the parts of a given day's verse in the way that I thought would be most helpful, as well as in a way that makes the most sense in light of the specific English translation used for the day in question. By breaking up the verses in different ways, in fact, I hope to have made the point that there is no rigid or single system that one ought to use for analyzing a Greek sentence's grammar in order to achieve understanding.

The Words in Bold Type

On each day's page there are three Greek words embedded in the English verse, with the English equivalents marked in bold type. In keeping with the minimalist approach I have used for the lexical forms and glosses, I have kept the number of English words in bold type to a minimum, especially for non-verbs, since this formatting is intended primarily to remind you of a word's basic meaning, not (as a rule) to convey syntactic information communicated by the word in question. Thus, for example, if a Greek noun appears in the dative (e.g., σαββάτῳ, "on the sabbath," in Luke 14:1, quoted on Day 27), I have put only the word that reflects the noun's basic meaning ("sabbath") in bold type. Similarly, if the best way to render a participle in a certain instance is by means of a phrase beginning with an English word such as "while" or "because" (e.g., εἰδότες, "because you know," in Jas 3:1, quoted on Day 137), I have not put such conjunctions in bold type; rather, I have placed in bold only what I judged to be the more basic information conveyed by the participle ("you know"). As this example indicates, for participles—and also for finite verbal forms—I have normally placed in bold the relevant English pronoun (if one is present) and any information conveying tense or aspect. When a Greek personal pronoun accompanies a finite verbal form, I have not put the English pronoun in bold type—in order to draw your attention to the presence of the Greek pronoun.

Such details as the foregoing, which may occasionally result in apparent inconsistencies in formatting, reflect the fact, again, that a one-to-one correspondence does not exist between Greek and English (or, of course, between any two languages). I have done my best to be as consistent as possible in how I have formatted the text, and I was always guided by what I thought would be most helpful to you, the reader. As with the way I have broken up the text into phrases and clauses, the bold type is meant not to reflect a "scientific" analysis of the Greek text but simply to help you quickly understand what the words mean.

Sources Used

The Greek text quoted in this book is taken from the edition of the New Testament prepared by B. F. Westcott and F. J. A. Hort, which is in the public domain. The differences between the Westcott-Hort edition and more modern scholarly ones such as the Nestle-Aland and UBS editions are generally of little significance for those who are not professional practitioners of textual criticism, and this is especially true of the small number of such differences found in the verses quoted in *Keep Up Your Greek in Two Minutes a Day: Volume 2*. Here are two illustrations, to give you a sense of their minor nature: (1) In 1 Cor 1:4 (the verse for Day 30 of this book), Westcott-Hort contains the reading "I thank God," whereas the Nestle-Aland editions read "I thank my God." In this case I have used curly brackets to set off a Greek word, μου, that is present in the Nestle-Aland editions and translated in the English version used but absent from Westcott-Hort. (2) Another text-critical issue is found in Matt 17:15 (the verse for Day 318), which in Westcott-Hort reads "he is ill" (lit., "he has [ἔχει] badly") but which in the Nestle-Aland editions reads "he suffers [πάσχει] badly." (The latter reading is, however, listed as a variant in the margin of the Westcott-Hort text.)

In their original work, Westcott and Hort marked substitutions, additions to, and omissions from their text found in New Testament manuscripts by means of various sigla. In order to help you read an unencumbered text, in this book I have retained only their siglum for omissions (i.e., square brackets). The substitutions and additions Westcott and Hort marked can be found in the apparatus of Hendrickson's 2007 edition of their text, published under the title *The Greek New Testament*. (For the interested reader, this apparatus also notes all the differences between the Westcott-Hort text and one of the recent Nestle-Aland editions, as well as the variant readings attested in a scholarly reconstruction of the Byzantine text tradition.)

The following English translations are used in this book: NRSV, ESV, NASB, NIV, HCSB, CSB, and MLB. I chose these seven translations because most of them are widely used, and I wanted to help provide a sense of different ways in which Greek can be rendered in English. Another reason I chose these particular translations is because most of them—especially the NASB, ESV, and NRSV—tend to be rather "literal" renderings; one indication of this is that their syntax often corresponds closely to that of the Greek, making it relatively easy to show which parts of the English text parallel which parts of the Greek text (a key feature of this book). The other translations used here—the NIV, HCSB, CSB, and MLB—are often relatively literal but, in contrast to the NASB, ESV, and NRSV, they usually lie further toward the "dynamic equivalence" end of the translation spectrum. I hope that by seeing how each of these translations deals with a sampling of verses, you will grow in your familiarity with and appreciation of the translation philosophies that underlie them.

In addition to embedding three Greek words in each day's English translation, I have made a number of minor modifications to the punctuation and formatting of the translations for the sake of clarity and consistency of presentation. The most common changes include the following: the change of a comma or semicolon at the end of a verse to a period; the insertion of an opening or closing quotation mark when a quotation is carried on from the previous verse or carries on into the next verse; and the capitalization of a lowercase letter at the beginning of a verse. When a verse constitutes a complete quotation, I have removed the quotation marks at the beginning and end of the verse. I have also removed the italics from words in the NASB that mark English words that do not explicitly correspond to a word in the Greek.

For the most part, I have cited entire verses. Occasionally, however, in order to make all the text fit on the page for the day, it was necessary to omit material. Material omitted from the middle of a verse is always marked with ellipses, but material omitted from the beginning or end of a verse is generally not marked. Occasionally I have used ellipses at the end or beginning of a verse not to indicate omitted material but to signal that the text that has been quoted constitutes an incomplete sentence.

In a few instances, I have inserted one or more words in brackets in the English Bible translation to indicate a word (or more than one) that is present in the Greek but not reflected in the translation. On a greater number of occasions, I have inserted a more literal rendering in brackets, prefixing it with "lit."

Because both the English and Greek verses quoted in this book are presented in isolation, I encourage you, as often as you are able, to look at them in their original contexts in order to gain a better understanding of their meaning and how they function in the passages from which they have been excerpted.

* * * * *

I offer this book with empathy and in friendship to everyone who has spent countless hours studying Greek but who has experienced difficulty, principally on account of a lack of time, in keeping up with the language. May you receive encouragement, challenge, hope, joy, and peace from the time you spend with the biblical texts on these pages.

—Jonathan G. Kline, PhD

Give (δὸς) us **today (σήμερον)** our daily **bread (ἄρτον).** (MLB)

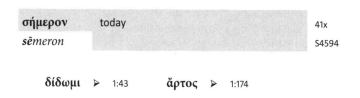

σήμερον	today	41x
sēmeron		S4594

δίδωμι ▷ 1:43   ἄρτος ▷ 1:174

Τὸν **ἄρτον** ἡμῶν τὸν ἐπιούσιον **δὸς** ἡμῖν **σήμερον·**

Give us	δὸς ἡμῖν
today	σήμερον
our daily bread	Τὸν ἄρτον ἡμῶν τὸν ἐπιούσιον

And this good news of the kingdom **will be proclaimed**
(κηρυχθήσεται) **throughout** (ἐν ὅλῃ) the world, as a testimony to
all the nations; and then the **end** (τέλος) will come. (NRSV)

τέλος *telos*	end, result, culmination, fulfillment	41x S5056

ὅλος ▷ 1:156　　　κηρύσσω ▷ 1:265

καὶ **κηρυχθήσεται** τοῦτο τὸ εὐαγγέλιον τῆς βασιλείας ἐν **ὅλῃ**
τῇ οἰκουμένῃ εἰς μαρτύριον πᾶσιν τοῖς ἔθνεσιν, καὶ τότε ἥξει τὸ
τέλος.

And this good news of the kingdom	καὶ . . . τοῦτο τὸ εὐαγγέλιον τῆς βασιλείας
will be proclaimed	**κηρυχθήσεται**
throughout the world	ἐν **ὅλῃ** τῇ οἰκουμένῃ
as a testimony	εἰς μαρτύριον
to all the nations	πᾶσιν τοῖς ἔθνεσιν
and then	καὶ τότε
the **end** will come	ἥξει τὸ **τέλος**

Now to the King of the **ages (αἰώνων)**, immortal, invisible, the **only (μόνῳ)** God, be **honor (τιμὴ)** and glory forever and ever [lit., for the **ages (αἰῶνας)** of the **ages (αἰώνων)**]. Amen. (MLB)

| τιμή | honor, price | 41x |
| *timē* | | S5092 |

αἰών ➤ 1:136   μόνος ➤ 1:323

Τῷ δὲ βασιλεῖ τῶν **αἰώνων**, ἀφθάρτῳ, ἀοράτῳ, **μόνῳ** θεῷ, **τιμὴ** καὶ δόξα εἰς τοὺς **αἰῶνας** τῶν **αἰώνων**· ἀμήν.

Now to the King of the **ages**	Τῷ δὲ βασιλεῖ τῶν **αἰώνων**
immortal	ἀφθάρτῳ
invisible	ἀοράτῳ
the **only** God	**μόνῳ** θεῷ
be **honor**	**τιμὴ**
and glory	καὶ δόξα
forever and ever [lit., for the **ages** of the **ages**]	εἰς τοὺς **αἰῶνας** τῶν **αἰώνων**
Amen	ἀμήν

But he **took (κρατήσας)** her by the hand and **called out (ἐφώνησεν)**, "Child, **get up (ἔγειρε)**!" (NRSV)

| φωνέω | to shout, call, summon, invite, address | 41x |
| phōneō | | S5455 |

ἐγείρω ➤ 1:118   **κρατέω** ➤ 1:321

αὐτὸς δὲ **κρατήσας** τῆς χειρὸς αὐτῆς **ἐφώνησεν** λέγων Ἡ παῖς, **ἔγειρε**.

But he **took** her by the hand	αὐτὸς δὲ **κρατήσας** τῆς χειρὸς αὐτῆς
and **called out**	**ἐφώνησεν** λέγων
Child	Ἡ παῖς
get up!	**ἔγειρε**

I was once alive **apart from (χωρὶς)** the law, but when the
commandment (ἐντολῆς) came (ἐλθούσης), sin came alive and
I died. (ESV)

χωρίς *chōris*	apart from, separate from, without, separately	41x S5565

ἔρχομαι ➤ 1:30 **ἐντολή** ➤ 1:239

ἐγὼ δὲ ἔζων **χωρὶς** νόμου ποτέ· **ἐλθούσης** δὲ τῆς **ἐντολῆς** ἡ
ἁμαρτία ἀνέζησεν, ἐγὼ δὲ ἀπέθανον

I was once alive	ἐγὼ δὲ ἔζων . . . ποτέ
apart from the law	**χωρὶς** νόμου
but when the **commandment came**	**ἐλθούσης** δὲ τῆς **ἐντολῆς**
sin came alive	ἡ ἁμαρτία ἀνέζησεν
and I died	ἐγὼ δὲ ἀπέθανον

So **he questioned (ἐπηρώτα)** him at some length [lit., with **considerable (ἱκανοῖς)** words], but he **made** no **answer (ἀπεκρίνατο)**. (ESV)

ἱκανός	sufficient, considerable	40x
hikanos		S2425

ἀποκρίνομαι ➤ 1:68   **ἐπερωτάω** ➤ 1:286

ἐπηρώτα δὲ αὐτὸν ἐν λόγοις **ἱκανοῖς·** αὐτὸς δὲ οὐδὲν **ἀπεκρίνατο** αὐτῷ.

So **he questioned** him	**ἐπηρώτα** δὲ αὐτὸν
at some length [lit., with **considerable** words]	ἐν λόγοις **ἱκανοῖς**
but he **made** no **answer**	αὐτὸς δὲ οὐδὲν **ἀπεκρίνατο** αὐτῷ

Come (Ἄγε) now (νῦν), you rich people, **weep (κλαύσατε)** and wail over the miseries that are coming on you. (CSB)

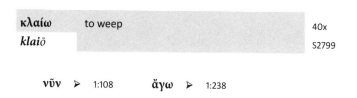

| **κλαίω** | to weep | 40x |
| *klaiō* | | S2799 |

νῦν ▷ 1:108   ἄγω ▷ 1:238

Ἄγε νῦν οἱ πλούσιοι, **κλαύσατε** ὀλολύζοντες ἐπὶ ταῖς ταλαιπωρίαις ὑμῶν ταῖς ἐπερχομέναις.

Come now	**Ἄγε νῦν**
you rich people	οἱ πλούσιοι
weep	**κλαύσατε**
and wail	ὀλολύζοντες
over the miseries that are coming on you	ἐπὶ ταῖς ταλαιπωρίαις ὑμῶν ταῖς ἐπερχομέναις

[It] does not act unbecomingly; **it does** not **seek (ζητεῖ) its
own (ἑαυτῆς)**, is not provoked, **does** not **take into account
(λογίζεται)** a wrong suffered. (NASB)

λογίζομαι	to count, reckon, number, consider	40x
logizomai		S3049

ἑαυτοῦ ➤ 1:55   ζητέω ➤ 1:150

οὐκ ἀσχημονεῖ, **οὐ ζητεῖ τὰ ἑαυτῆς**, οὐ παροξύνεται, **οὐ λογίζεται
τὸ κακόν**,

[It] does not act unbecomingly	οὐκ ἀσχημονεῖ
it does not **seek its own**	**οὐ ζητεῖ τὰ ἑαυτῆς**
is not provoked	οὐ παροξύνεται
does not **take into account** a wrong suffered	**οὐ λογίζεται** τὸ κακόν

And you will be **hated (μισούμενοι)** by everyone, because of My name. But whoever perseveres to the **end (τέλος) will be saved (σωθήσεται)**. (MLB)

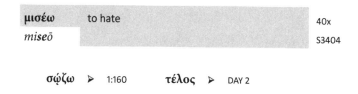

| μισέω | to hate | 40x |
| *miseō* | | S3404 |

σῴζω ➤ 1:160   **τέλος** ➤ DAY 2

καὶ ἔσεσθε **μισούμενοι** ὑπὸ πάντων διὰ τὸ ὄνομά μου. ὁ δὲ ὑπομείνας εἰς **τέλος** οὗτος **σωθήσεται**.

And you will be **hated**	καὶ ἔσεσθε **μισούμενοι**
by everyone	ὑπὸ πάντων
because of My name	διὰ τὸ ὄνομά μου
But whoever perseveres	ὁ δὲ ὑπομείνας
to the **end**	εἰς **τέλος**
will be saved	οὗτος **σωθήσεται**

You yourselves like living **stones (λίθοι) are being built up (οἰκοδομεῖσθε)** as a spiritual house, to be a **holy (ἅγιον)** priesthood, to offer spiritual sacrifices acceptable to God through Jesus Christ. (ESV)

οἰκοδομέω	to build, build up, edify	40x
oikodomeō		S3618

ἅγιος ➤ 1:67   **λίθος** ➤ 1:270

καὶ αὐτοὶ ὡς **λίθοι** ζῶντες **οἰκοδομεῖσθε** οἶκος πνευματικὸς εἰς ἱεράτευμα **ἅγιον**, ἀνενέγκαι πνευματικὰς θυσίας εὐπροσδέκτους θεῷ διὰ Ἰησοῦ Χριστοῦ·

You yourselves . . . **are being built up**	καὶ αὐτοὶ . . . **οἰκοδομεῖσθε**
like living **stones**	ὡς **λίθοι** ζῶντες
as a spiritual house	οἶκος πνευματικὸς
to be a **holy** priesthood	εἰς ἱεράτευμα **ἅγιον**
to offer spiritual sacrifices	ἀνενέγκαι πνευματικὰς θυσίας
acceptable to God	εὐπροσδέκτους θεῷ
through Jesus Christ	διὰ Ἰησοῦ Χριστοῦ

Hence, too, He is able **to save (σώζειν)** to the uttermost those **who come (προσερχομένους)** to God through Him, because He **always (πάντοτε)** lives to intercede for them. (MLB)

πάντοτε *pantote*	always, at all times	40x S3842

σώζω ➤ 1:160   **προσέρχομαι** ➤ 1:197

ὅθεν καὶ **σώζειν** εἰς τὸ παντελὲς δύναται τοὺς **προσερχομένους** δι᾽ αὐτοῦ τῷ θεῷ, **πάντοτε** ζῶν εἰς τὸ ἐντυγχάνειν ὑπὲρ αὐτῶν.

Hence, too	ὅθεν καὶ
He is able **to save**	**σώζειν** . . . δύναται
to the uttermost	εἰς τὸ παντελὲς
those **who come**	τοὺς **προσερχομένους**
to God	τῷ θεῷ
through Him	δι᾽ αὐτοῦ
because He **always** lives	**πάντοτε** ζῶν
to intercede for them	εἰς τὸ ἐντυγχάνειν ὑπὲρ αὐτῶν

But the things which God announced beforehand by the **mouth** (στόματος) of all the prophets, that His Christ **would suffer** (παθεῖν), He has thus **fulfilled** (ἐπλήρωσεν). (NASB)

πάσχω	to experience, suffer	40x
paschō		S3958

πληρόω ➤ 1:200   **στόμα** ➤ 1:216

ὁ δὲ θεὸς ἃ προκατήγγειλεν διὰ **στόματος** πάντων τῶν προφητῶν **παθεῖν** τὸν χριστὸν αὐτοῦ **ἐπλήρωσεν** οὕτως.

But the things which God announced beforehand	ὁ δὲ θεὸς ἃ προκατήγγειλεν
by the **mouth** of all the prophets	διὰ **στόματος** πάντων τῶν προφητῶν
that His Christ **would suffer**	**παθεῖν** τὸν χριστὸν αὐτοῦ
He has thus **fulfilled**	**ἐπλήρωσεν** οὕτως

Then some people came, **bringing (φέροντες)** to him a paralyzed man, **carried (αἰρόμενον)** by **four (τεσσάρων)** of them. (NRSV)

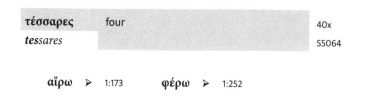

| τέσσαρες | four | | 40x |
| *tess*ares | | | S5064 |

αἴρω ▷ 1:173   φέρω ▷ 1:252

καὶ ἔρχονται **φέροντες** πρὸς αὐτὸν παραλυτικὸν **αἰρόμενον** ὑπὸ **τεσσάρων**.

Then some people came	καὶ ἔρχονται
bringing to him a paralyzed man	**φέροντες** πρὸς αὐτὸν παραλυτικὸν
carried by **four** of them	**αἰρόμενον** ὑπὸ **τεσσάρων**

And to the one **who does** not **work (ἐργαζομένῳ)** but believes in him **who justifies (δικαιοῦντα)** the ungodly, his faith **is counted (λογίζεται)** as righteousness. (ESV)

| δικαιόω | to make righteous, justify, acquit | 39x |
| dikaioō | | S1344 |

ἐργάζομαι ➤ 1:361   **λογίζομαι** ➤ DAY 8

τῷ δὲ μὴ **ἐργαζομένῳ**, πιστεύοντι δὲ ἐπὶ τὸν **δικαιοῦντα** τὸν ἀσεβῆ, **λογίζεται** ἡ πίστις αὐτοῦ εἰς δικαιοσύνην,

And to the one **who does** not **work**	τῷ δὲ μὴ **ἐργαζομένῳ**
but believes in him **who justifies** the ungodly	πιστεύοντι δὲ ἐπὶ τὸν **δικαιοῦντα** τὸν ἀσεβῆ
his faith **is counted**	**λογίζεται** ἡ πίστις αὐτοῦ
as righteousness	εἰς δικαιοσύνην

So **they went** (ἀπελθόντες) and **found** (εὗρον) everything as
he had told them; and **they prepared** (ἡτοίμασαν) the Passover
meal. (NRSV)

| ἑτοιμάζω | to prepare, make ready | 39x |
| *hetoimazō* | | S2090 |

εὑρίσκω ➤ 1:93   **ἀπέρχομαι** ➤ 1:143

ἀπελθόντες δὲ **εὗρον** καθὼς εἰρήκει αὐτοῖς, καὶ **ἡτοίμασαν** τὸ
πάσχα.

So **they went**	**ἀπελθόντες** δὲ
and **found** everything	**εὗρον**
as he had told them	καθὼς εἰρήκει αὐτοῖς
and **they prepared**	καὶ **ἡτοίμασαν**
the Passover meal	τὸ πάσχα

Strive **to enter (εἰσελθεῖν)** through the narrow **door (θύρας)**. For many, I tell you, **will seek (ζητήσουσιν) to enter (εἰσελθεῖν)** and will not be able. (ESV)

| θύρα | door | 39x |
| *thura* | | S2374 |

εἰσέρχομαι ➢ 1:82   ζητέω ➢ 1:150

Ἀγωνίζεσθε **εἰσελθεῖν** διὰ τῆς στενῆς **θύρας**, ὅτι πολλοί, λέγω ὑμῖν, **ζητήσουσιν εἰσελθεῖν** καὶ οὐκ ἰσχύσουσιν,

Strive **to enter**	Ἀγωνίζεσθε **εἰσελθεῖν**
through the narrow **door**	διὰ τῆς στενῆς **θύρας**
For many	ὅτι πολλοί
I tell you	λέγω ὑμῖν
will seek to enter	**ζητήσουσιν εἰσελθεῖν**
and will not be able	καὶ οὐκ ἰσχύσουσιν

And coming out of the **tombs (μνημείων)** after His resurrection
they entered the holy **city (πόλιν)** and appeared to **many
(πολλοῖς)**. (NASB)

μνημεῖον	tomb, monument	39x
mnēmeion		S3419

    πολύς ➤ 1:45   **πόλις** ➤ 1:96

καὶ ἐξελθόντες ἐκ τῶν **μνημείων** μετὰ τὴν ἔγερσιν αὐτοῦ
εἰσῆλθον εἰς τὴν ἁγίαν **πόλιν** καὶ ἐνεφανίσθησαν **πολλοῖς**.

And coming out of the **tombs**	καὶ ἐξελθόντες ἐκ τῶν **μνημείων**
after His resurrection	μετὰ τὴν ἔγερσιν αὐτοῦ
they entered the holy **city**	εἰσῆλθον εἰς τὴν ἁγίαν **πόλιν**
and appeared to **many**	καὶ ἐνεφανίσθησαν **πολλοῖς**

Because (ἐν ᾧ) he himself **suffered** (**πέπονθεν**) when **he was tempted** (**πειρασθείς**), he is able to help those **who are being tempted** (**πειραζομένοις**). (NIV)

| πειράζω | to test, tempt | 39x |
| *peirazō* | | S3985 |

ὅς, ἥ, ὅ ▷ 1:12   πάσχω ▷ DAY 12

ἐν ᾧ γὰρ **πέπονθεν** αὐτὸς **πειρασθείς**, δύναται τοῖς **πειραζομένοις** βοηθῆσαι.

Because he himself **suffered**	ἐν ᾧ γὰρ **πέπονθεν** αὐτὸς
when **he was tempted**	**πειρασθείς**
he is able to help	δύναται . . . βοηθῆσαι
those **who are being tempted**	τοῖς **πειραζομένοις**

For I tell you, unless your righteousness exceeds [lit., **abounds (περισσεύσῃ)** more than] that of the **scribes (γραμματέων)** and Pharisees, you will never enter the **kingdom (βασιλείαν)** of heaven. (NRSV)

| περισσεύω | to abound, overflow, exceed | 39x |
| *perisseuō* | | S4052 |

βασιλεία ➤ 1:97   **γραμματεύς** ➤ 1:253

λέγω γὰρ ὑμῖν ὅτι ἐὰν μὴ **περισσεύσῃ** ὑμῶν ἡ δικαιοσύνη πλεῖον τῶν **γραμματέων** καὶ Φαρισαίων, οὐ μὴ εἰσέλθητε εἰς τὴν **βασιλείαν** τῶν οὐρανῶν.

For I tell you	λέγω γὰρ ὑμῖν ὅτι
unless	ἐὰν μὴ
your righteousness	ὑμῶν ἡ δικαιοσύνη
exceeds [lit., **abounds** more than]	**περισσεύσῃ** ... πλεῖον
that of the **scribes** and Pharisees	τῶν **γραμματέων** καὶ Φαρισαίων
you will never enter	οὐ μὴ εἰσέλθητε εἰς
the **kingdom** of heaven	τὴν **βασιλείαν** τῶν οὐρανῶν

And the devil who **had deceived (πλανῶν)** them **was thrown (ἐβλήθη)** into the lake of **fire (πυρὸς)** and sulfur, where the beast and the false prophet were, and they will be tormented day and night forever and ever. (NRSV)

| πλανάω | to lead astray, deceive, wander, err | 39x |
| *planaō* | | S4105 |

βάλλω ➤ 1:134   πῦρ ➤ 1:235

καὶ ὁ διάβολος ὁ **πλανῶν** αὐτοὺς **ἐβλήθη** εἰς τὴν λίμνην τοῦ **πυρὸς** καὶ θείου, ὅπου καὶ τὸ θηρίον καὶ ὁ ψευδοπροφήτης, καὶ βασανισθήσονται ἡμέρας καὶ νυκτὸς εἰς τοὺς αἰῶνας τῶν αἰώνων.

And the devil	καὶ ὁ διάβολος
who **had deceived** them	ὁ **πλανῶν** αὐτοὺς
was thrown into the lake of **fire** and sulfur	**ἐβλήθη** εἰς τὴν λίμνην τοῦ **πυρὸς** καὶ θείου
where the beast and the false prophet were	ὅπου καὶ τὸ θηρίον καὶ ὁ ψευδοπροφήτης
and they will be tormented	καὶ βασανισθήσονται
day and night	ἡμέρας καὶ νυκτὸς
forever and ever	εἰς τοὺς αἰῶνας τῶν αἰώνων

But Paul **shouted (ἐφώνησεν)** in a loud voice, "Do not harm
yourself [lit., do not **do (πράξῃς)** any **harm (κακόν)** to yourself],
for we are all here." (NRSV)

πράσσω	to do, act	39x
prassō		S4238

κακός ➤ 1:307   **φωνέω** ➤ DAY 4

ἐφώνησεν δὲ Παῦλος μεγάλη φωνῇ λέγων Μηδὲν **πράξῃς**
σεαυτῷ **κακόν**, ἅπαντες γάρ ἐσμεν ἐνθάδε.

But Paul **shouted**	**ἐφώνησεν** δὲ Παῦλος
in a loud voice	μεγάλη φωνῇ λέγων
Do not harm yourself [lit., do not **do** any **harm** to yourself]	Μηδὲν **πράξῃς** σεαυτῷ **κακόν**
for we are all here	ἅπαντες γάρ ἐσμεν ἐνθάδε

And the world with its **lust (ἐπιθυμία)** is passing away, but the one who does the **will (θέλημα)** of God **remains (μένει)** forever. (CSB)

ἐπιθυμία	desire, passion, lust	38x
epithumia		S1939

μένω ➤ 1:139   **θέλημα** ➤ 1:287

καὶ ὁ κόσμος παράγεται καὶ ἡ **ἐπιθυμία** [αὐτοῦ], ὁ δὲ ποιῶν τὸ **θέλημα** τοῦ θεοῦ **μένει** εἰς τὸν αἰῶνα.

And the world . . . is passing away	καὶ ὁ κόσμος παράγεται
with its **lust**	καὶ ἡ **ἐπιθυμία** [αὐτοῦ]
but the one who does the **will** of God	ὁ δὲ ποιῶν τὸ **θέλημα** τοῦ θεοῦ
remains forever	**μένει** εἰς τὸν αἰῶνα

And he has seen in a vision a **man (ἄνδρα)** named Ananias come in and **lay (ἐπιθέντα)** his hands on him **so that (ὅπως)** he might regain his sight. (ESV)

ἐπιτίθημι	to lay on, place upon	38x
epitithēmi		S2007

ἀνήρ ➤ 1:73   ὅπως ➤ 1:298

καὶ εἶδεν **ἄνδρα** [ἐν ὁράματι] Ἀνανίαν ὀνόματι εἰσελθόντα καὶ **ἐπιθέντα** αὐτῷ [τὰς] χεῖρας **ὅπως** ἀναβλέψῃ.

And he has seen in a vision	καὶ εἶδεν . . . [ἐν ὁράματι]
a **man** named Ananias	**ἄνδρα** . . . Ἀνανίαν ὀνόματι
come in	εἰσελθόντα
and **lay** his hands on him	καὶ **ἐπιθέντα** αὐτῷ [τὰς] χεῖρας
so that he might regain his sight	**ὅπως** ἀναβλέψῃ

They answered, "We have nothing **here (ὧδε)** except **five (πέντε) loaves (ἄρτους)** and two fish." (MLB)

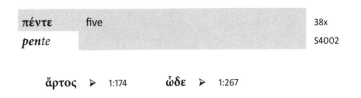

| πέντε | five | 38x |
| *pente* | | S4002 |

ἄρτος ➤ 1:174   **ὧδε** ➤ 1:267

οἱ δὲ λέγουσιν αὐτῷ Οὐκ ἔχομεν **ὧδε** εἰ μὴ **πέντε ἄρτους** καὶ δύο ἰχθύας.

They answered	οἱ δὲ λέγουσιν αὐτῷ
We have nothing **here**	Οὐκ ἔχομεν **ὧδε**
except	εἰ μὴ
five loaves	**πέντε ἄρτους**
and two fish	καὶ δύο ἰχθύας

Be submissive (ὑποτασσόμενοι) to one another (ἀλλήλοις) out of **reverence (φόβῳ)** for Christ. (MLB)

ὑποτάσσω	to subject, put into subjection, submit	38x
hupotassō		S5293

ἀλλήλων ➤ 1:168　　　**φόβος** ➤ 1:326

ὑποτασσόμενοι ἀλλήλοις ἐν **φόβῳ** Χριστοῦ.

Be submissive	ὑποτασσόμενοι
to **one another**	ἀλλήλοις
out of **reverence** for Christ	ἐν **φόβῳ** Χριστοῦ

Or what woman having ten silver coins, if she loses one of them,
does not **light (ἅπτει)** a lamp, sweep the **house (οἰκίαν)**, and
search carefully **until (ἕως)** she finds it? (NRSV)

| **ἅπτω** | (middle) to touch; (active) to light, kindle | 37x |
| *haptō* | | S680 + S681 |

ἕως ▷ 1:111   **οἰκία** ▷ 1:178

Ἦ τίς γυνὴ δραχμὰς ἔχουσα δέκα, ἐὰν ἀπολέσῃ δραχμὴν μίαν,
οὐχὶ **ἅπτει** λύχνον καὶ σαροῖ τὴν **οἰκίαν** καὶ ζητεῖ ἐπιμελῶς **ἕως** οὗ
εὕρῃ;

Or what woman	Ἦ τίς γυνὴ
having ten silver coins	δραχμὰς ἔχουσα δέκα
if she loses one of them	ἐὰν ἀπολέσῃ δραχμὴν μίαν
does not **light** a lamp	οὐχὶ **ἅπτει** λύχνον
sweep the **house**	καὶ σαροῖ τὴν **οἰκίαν**
and search carefully	καὶ ζητεῖ ἐπιμελῶς
until she finds it?	**ἕως** οὗ εὕρῃ;

On one occasion when Jesus [lit., he] was going to the house of a
leader (ἀρχόντων) of the Pharisees **to eat (φαγεῖν)** a meal on the
sabbath (σαββάτῳ), they were watching him closely. (NRSV)

ἄρχων	ruler, governor, leader	37x
archōn		S758

ἐσθίω ➢ 1:100　　　σάββατον ➢ 1:246

Καὶ ἐγένετο ἐν τῷ ἐλθεῖν αὐτὸν εἰς οἶκόν τινος τῶν **ἀρχόντων**
[τῶν] Φαρισαίων **σαββάτῳ φαγεῖν** ἄρτον καὶ αὐτοὶ ἦσαν
παρατηρούμενοι αὐτόν.

On one occasion	Καὶ ἐγένετο
when Jesus [lit., he] was going	ἐν τῷ ἐλθεῖν αὐτὸν
to the house of a **leader** of the Pharisees	εἰς οἶκόν τινος τῶν **ἀρχόντων** [τῶν] Φαρισαίων
to eat a meal	**φαγεῖν** ἄρτον
on the **sabbath**	**σαββάτῳ**
they were watching him closely	καὶ αὐτοὶ ἦσαν παρατηρούμενοι αὐτόν

Then they also will answer, "Lord, when was it that **we saw
(εἴδομεν)** you hungry or thirsty or a stranger or naked or sick or
in **prison (φυλακῇ)**, and **did** not **take care of (διηκονήσαμέν)**
you?" (NRSV)

διακονέω	to serve	37x
diakoneō		S1247

ὁράω ➤ 1:40   **φυλακή** ➤ 1:332

τότε ἀποκριθήσονται καὶ αὐτοὶ λέγοντες Κύριε, πότε σε **εἴδομεν**
πεινῶντα ἢ διψῶντα ἢ ξένον ἢ γυμνὸν ἢ ἀσθενῆ ἢ ἐν **φυλακῇ** καὶ
οὐ **διηκονήσαμέν** σοι;

Then they also will answer	τότε ἀποκριθήσονται καὶ αὐτοὶ λέγοντες
Lord	Κύριε
when was it that	πότε
we saw you	σε **εἴδομεν**
hungry or thirsty	πεινῶντα ἢ διψῶντα
or a stranger or naked	ἢ ξένον ἢ γυμνὸν
or sick or in **prison**	ἢ ἀσθενῆ ἢ ἐν **φυλακῇ**
and **did** not **take care of** you?	καὶ οὐ **διηκονήσαμέν** σοι;

So then, I **thought (ἔδοξα)** to **myself (ἐμαυτῷ)** that I had **to do (πρᾶξαι)** many things hostile to the name of Jesus of Nazareth.
(NASB)

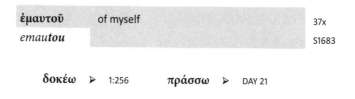

| ἐμαυτοῦ | of myself | 37x |
| *emautou* | | S1683 |

δοκέω ➤ 1:256   πράσσω ➤ DAY 21

Ἐγὼ μὲν οὖν **ἔδοξα ἐμαυτῷ** πρὸς τὸ ὄνομα Ἰησοῦ τοῦ Ναζωραίου δεῖν πολλὰ ἐναντία **πρᾶξαι**·

So then, I **thought** to **myself** that	Ἐγὼ μὲν οὖν **ἔδοξα ἐμαυτῷ**
I had **to do** many things hostile	δεῖν πολλὰ ἐναντία **πρᾶξαι**
to the name of Jesus of Nazareth	πρὸς τὸ ὄνομα Ἰησοῦ τοῦ Ναζωραίου

I give thanks (Εὐχαριστῶ) to my God **always (πάντοτε)** for you because of the **grace (χάριτι)** of God that has been given you in Christ Jesus. (NRSV)

εὐχαριστέω	to give thanks	37x
eucharisteō		S2168

χάρις ➤ 1:106   **πάντοτε** ➤ DAY 11

Εὐχαριστῶ τῷ θεῷ {μου} **πάντοτε** περὶ ὑμῶν ἐπὶ τῇ **χάριτι** τοῦ θεοῦ τῇ δοθείσῃ ὑμῖν ἐν Χριστῷ Ἰησοῦ,

I give thanks	**Εὐχαριστῶ**
to my God	τῷ θεῷ {μου}
always	**πάντοτε**
for you	περὶ ὑμῶν
because of the **grace** of God	ἐπὶ τῇ **χάριτι** τοῦ θεοῦ
that has been given you	τῇ δοθείσῃ ὑμῖν
in Christ Jesus	ἐν Χριστῷ Ἰησοῦ

Both **Judas** (Ἰούδας) and Silas, **who were** (ὄντες) also prophets themselves, **encouraged** (παρεκάλεσαν) the brothers and sisters and strengthened them with a long message. (CSB)

Ἰούδας	Judah, Judas, Jude	37x
Ioudas		S2455

εἰμί ➤ 1:8   παρακαλέω ➤ 1:157

Ἰούδας τε καὶ Σίλας, καὶ αὐτοὶ προφῆται **ὄντες**, διὰ λόγου πολλοῦ **παρεκάλεσαν** τοὺς ἀδελφοὺς καὶ ἐπεστήριξαν·

Both **Judas** and Silas	Ἰούδας τε καὶ Σίλας
who were also prophets themselves	καὶ αὐτοὶ προφῆται **ὄντες**
encouraged the brothers and sisters	**παρεκάλεσαν** τοὺς ἀδελφοὺς
and strengthened them	καὶ ἐπεστήριξαν
with a long message	διὰ λόγου πολλοῦ

And not **only (μόνον)** that, but **we** also **boast (καυχώμεθα)** in our
sufferings (θλίψεσιν), knowing that **suffering (θλίψις)** produces
endurance. (NRSV)

καυχάομαι	to boast	37x
kauchaomai		S2744

μόνον　▷　1:244　　　　**θλῖψις**　▷　1:339

οὐ **μόνον** δέ, ἀλλὰ καὶ **καυχώμεθα** ἐν ταῖς **θλίψεσιν**, εἰδότες ὅτι ἡ
θλίψις ὑπομονὴν κατεργάζεται,

And not **only** that	οὐ **μόνον** δέ
but **we** also **boast**	ἀλλὰ καὶ **καυχώμεθα**
in our **sufferings**	ἐν ταῖς **θλίψεσιν**
knowing that	εἰδότες ὅτι
suffering produces endurance	ἡ **θλίψις** ὑπομονὴν κατεργάζεται

The chief priests and the **whole (ὅλον)** Sanhedrin **were looking for (ἐζήτουν) evidence (μαρτυρίαν)** against Jesus so that they could put him to death, but they did not find any. (NIV)

| **μαρτυρία** | witness, evidence, testimony | 37x |
| *marturia* | | S3141 |

    ζητέω ➤ 1:150   **ὅλος** ➤ 1:156

οἱ δὲ ἀρχιερεῖς καὶ **ὅλον** τὸ συνέδριον **ἐζήτουν** κατὰ τοῦ Ἰησοῦ **μαρτυρίαν** εἰς τὸ θανατῶσαι αὐτόν, καὶ οὐχ ηὕρισκον·

The chief priests	οἱ δὲ ἀρχιερεῖς
and the **whole** Sanhedrin	καὶ **ὅλον** τὸ συνέδριον
were looking for evidence	**ἐζήτουν** . . . **μαρτυρίαν**
against Jesus	κατὰ τοῦ Ἰησοῦ
so that they could put him to death	εἰς τὸ θανατῶσαι αὐτόν
but they did not find any	καὶ οὐχ ηὕρισκον

Now his **older (πρεσβύτερος)** son was in the **field (ἀγρῷ)**, and when he came and **approached (ἤγγισεν)** the house, he heard music and dancing. (NASB)

ἀγρός	field, country	36x
agros		S68

πρεσβύτερος ➤ 1:248   ἐγγίζω ➤ 1:352

ἦν δὲ ὁ υἱὸς αὐτοῦ ὁ **πρεσβύτερος** ἐν **ἀγρῷ**· καὶ ὡς ἐρχόμενος **ἤγγισεν** τῇ οἰκίᾳ, ἤκουσεν συμφωνίας καὶ χορῶν,

Now his **older** son	δὲ ὁ υἱὸς αὐτοῦ ὁ **πρεσβύτερος**
was in the **field**	ἦν . . . ἐν **ἀγρῷ**
and when he came	καὶ ὡς ἐρχόμενος
and **approached** the house	**ἤγγισεν** τῇ οἰκίᾳ
he heard music	ἤκουσεν συμφωνίας
and dancing	καὶ χορῶν

While he was saying these things to them, suddenly a **leader** (**ἄρχων**) of the synagogue came in and knelt before him, saying, "My daughter has **just (ἄρτι)** died; but come and **lay (ἐπίθες)** your hand on her, and she will live." (NRSV)

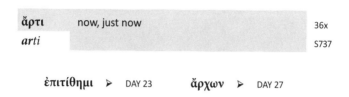

| ἄρτι | now, just now | 36x |
| *arti* | | S737 |

| ἐπιτίθημι | ⊳ DAY 23 | ἄρχων | ⊳ DAY 27 |

Ταῦτα αὐτοῦ λαλοῦντος αὐτοῖς ἰδοὺ **ἄρχων** [εἶς] προσελθὼν προσεκύνει αὐτῷ λέγων ὅτι Ἡ θυγάτηρ μου **ἄρτι** ἐτελεύτησεν· ἀλλὰ ἐλθὼν **ἐπίθες** τὴν χεῖρά σου ἐπ᾿ αὐτήν, καὶ ζήσεται.

While he was saying these things to them	Ταῦτα αὐτοῦ λαλοῦντος αὐτοῖς
suddenly a **leader** of the synagogue came in	ἰδοὺ **ἄρχων** [εἶς] προσελθὼν
and knelt before him	προσεκύνει αὐτῷ
saying	λέγων ὅτι
My daughter has **just** died	Ἡ θυγάτηρ μου **ἄρτι** ἐτελεύτησεν
but come	ἀλλὰ ἐλθὼν
and **lay** your hand on her	**ἐπίθες** τὴν χεῖρά σου ἐπ᾿ αὐτήν
and she will live	καὶ ζήσεται

He must (δεῖ) also have a good **reputation (μαρτυρίαν)** with outsiders, so that he will not fall into disgrace and into the **devil's (διαβόλου)** trap. (NIV)

διάβολος	slanderous, slanderer, devil	36x
diabolos		S1228

δεῖ ➤ 1:161   μαρτυρία ➤ DAY 33

δεῖ δὲ καὶ **μαρτυρίαν** καλὴν ἔχειν ἀπὸ τῶν ἔξωθεν, ἵνα μὴ εἰς ὀνειδισμὸν ἐμπέσῃ καὶ παγίδα τοῦ **διαβόλου**.

He must also have a good reputation	**δεῖ** δὲ καὶ **μαρτυρίαν** καλὴν ἔχειν
with outsiders	ἀπὸ τῶν ἔξωθεν
so that he will not fall into disgrace	ἵνα μὴ εἰς ὀνειδισμὸν ἐμπέσῃ
and into the **devil's** trap	καὶ παγίδα τοῦ **διαβόλου**

Truly I tell you, you will never get out **of there (ἐκεῖθεν)** until **you have paid (ἀποδῷς)** the **last (ἔσχατον)** penny. (CSB)

ἐκεῖθεν	thence, from that place	36x
ekeithen		S1564

ἔσχατος ➢ 1:300   **ἀποδίδωμι** ➢ 1:317

ἀμὴν λέγω σοι, οὐ μὴ ἐξέλθῃς **ἐκεῖθεν** ἕως ἂν **ἀποδῷς** τὸν **ἔσχατον** κοδράντην.

Truly I tell you	ἀμὴν λέγω σοι
you will never get out **of there**	οὐ μὴ ἐξέλθῃς **ἐκεῖθεν**
until **you have paid**	ἕως ἂν **ἀποδῷς**
the **last** penny	τὸν **ἔσχατον** κοδράντην

At once Jesus realized [in himself] that power had gone out from him. **He turned around (ἐπιστραφεὶς)** in the **crowd (ὄχλῳ)** and asked, "Who **touched (ἥψατο)** my clothes?" (NIV)

ἐπιστρέφω	to turn (back) to, return	36x
epistrephō		S1994

ὄχλος ▷ 1:90   **ἅπτω** ▷ DAY 26

καὶ εὐθὺς ὁ Ἰησοῦς ἐπιγνοὺς ἐν ἑαυτῷ τὴν ἐξ αὐτοῦ δύναμιν ἐξελθοῦσαν **ἐπιστραφεὶς** ἐν τῷ **ὄχλῳ** ἔλεγεν Τίς μου **ἥψατο** τῶν ἱματίων;

At once Jesus realized [in himself]	καὶ εὐθὺς ὁ Ἰησοῦς ἐπιγνοὺς ἐν ἑαυτῷ
that power had gone out from him	τὴν ἐξ αὐτοῦ δύναμιν ἐξελθοῦσαν
He turned around in the **crowd**	**ἐπιστραφεὶς** ἐν τῷ **ὄχλῳ**
and asked	ἔλεγεν
Who **touched** my clothes?	Τίς μου **ἥψατο** τῶν ἱματίων;

Pray (Προσεύχεσθε) for us, for **we are convinced (πειθόμεθα)** that we have a clear conscience, wanting to conduct ourselves **honorably (καλῶς)** in everything. (CSB)

καλῶς	well, nobly, honorably	36x
kalōs		S2573

προσεύχομαι ➤ 1:198   **πείθω** ➤ 1:303

Προσεύχεσθε περὶ ἡμῶν, **πειθόμεθα** γὰρ ὅτι καλὴν συνείδησιν ἔχομεν, ἐν πᾶσιν **καλῶς** θέλοντες ἀναστρέφεσθαι.

Pray for us	**Προσεύχεσθε** περὶ ἡμῶν
for **we are convinced** that	**πειθόμεθα** γὰρ ὅτι
we have a clear conscience	καλὴν συνείδησιν ἔχομεν
wanting to conduct ourselves	θέλοντες ἀναστρέφεσθαι
honorably in everything	ἐν πᾶσιν **καλῶς**

Beloved (ἀγαπητοί), never avenge yourselves, but leave **room** (τόπον) for the wrath of God [lit., for the **wrath (ὀργῇ)**]; for it is written, "Vengeance is mine, I will repay, says the Lord." (NRSV)

ὀργή	anger, wrath, passion	36x
orgē		S3709

τόπος ➤ 1:180   ἀγαπητός ➤ 1:261

μὴ ἑαυτοὺς ἐκδικοῦντες, **ἀγαπητοί**, ἀλλὰ δότε **τόπον** τῇ **ὀργῇ**, γέγραπται γάρ Ἐμοὶ ἐκδίκησις, ἐγὼ ἀνταποδώσω, λέγει Κύριος.

Beloved	ἀγαπητοί
never avenge yourselves	μὴ ἑαυτοὺς ἐκδικοῦντες
but leave **room**	ἀλλὰ δότε **τόπον**
for the wrath of God [lit., for the **wrath**]	τῇ **ὀργῇ**
for it is written	γέγραπται γάρ
Vengeance is mine	Ἐμοὶ ἐκδίκησις
I will repay	ἐγὼ ἀνταποδώσω
says the Lord	λέγει Κύριος

After Jesus **was born** (**γεννηθέντος**) in Bethlehem of **Judea** (**Ἰουδαίας**) in the days of King Herod, wise men from the east **arrived** (**παρεγένοντο**) in Jerusalem. (CSB)

| **παραγίνομαι** | to appear, come (on the scene), reach, arrive | 36x |
| *paraginomai* | | S3854 |

γεννάω ➤ 1:175   **Ἰουδαία** ➤ 1:340

Τοῦ δὲ Ἰησοῦ **γεννηθέντος** ἐν Βηθλεὲμ τῆς **Ἰουδαίας** ἐν ἡμέραις Ἡρῴδου τοῦ βασιλέως, ἰδοὺ μάγοι ἀπὸ ἀνατολῶν **παρεγένοντο** εἰς Ἱεροσόλυμα

After Jesus **was born**	Τοῦ δὲ Ἰησοῦ **γεννηθέντος**
in Bethlehem of **Judea**	ἐν Βηθλεὲμ τῆς **Ἰουδαίας**
in the days of King Herod	ἐν ἡμέραις Ἡρῴδου τοῦ βασιλέως
wise men from the east	ἰδοὺ μάγοι ἀπὸ ἀνατολῶν
arrived	**παρεγένοντο**
in Jerusalem	εἰς Ἱεροσόλυμα

Circumcision (περιτομὴ) is **nothing (οὐδέν)** and
uncircumcision is **nothing (οὐδέν)**. Keeping God's commands is
what counts [lit., but keeping God's **commands (ἐντολῶν)**]. (NIV)

περιτομή	circumcision	36x
peritomē		S4061

οὐδείς, οὐδεμία, οὐδέν ➤ 1:65   **ἐντολή** ➤ 1:239

ἡ **περιτομὴ οὐδέν** ἐστιν, καὶ ἡ ἀκροβυστία **οὐδέν** ἐστιν, ἀλλὰ
τήρησις **ἐντολῶν** θεοῦ.

Circumcision is nothing	ἡ περιτομὴ οὐδέν ἐστιν
and uncircumcision is **nothing**	καὶ ἡ ἀκροβυστία **οὐδέν** ἐστιν
Keeping God's commands is what counts [lit., but keeping God's **commands**]	ἀλλὰ τήρησις **ἐντολῶν** θεοῦ

How much more valuable is a person than a **sheep (προβάτου)**!
Therefore (ὥστε) it is lawful to do **good (καλῶς)** on the Sabbath.
(NIV)

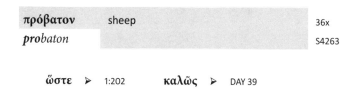

| **πρόβατον** | sheep | 36x |
| *probaton* | | S4263 |

ὥστε ➤ 1:202   καλῶς ➤ DAY 39

πόσῳ οὖν διαφέρει ἄνθρωπος **προβάτου**. **ὥστε** ἔξεστιν τοῖς
σάββασιν **καλῶς** ποιεῖν.

How much more valuable is a person than a **sheep**!	πόσῳ οὖν διαφέρει ἄνθρωπος **προβάτου**
Therefore it is lawful	**ὥστε** ἔξεστιν
to do **good**	**καλῶς** ποιεῖν
on the Sabbath	τοῖς σάββασιν

rejoicing in **hope** (ἐλπίδι), persevering in **tribulation** (θλίψει), devoted to **prayer** (προσευχῇ), . . . (NASB)

προσευχή	prayer	36x
proseuchē		S4335

ἐλπίς ➤ 1:296   θλῖψις ➤ 1:339

τῇ **ἐλπίδι** χαίροντες, τῇ **θλίψει** ὑπομένοντες, τῇ **προσευχῇ** προσκαρτεροῦντες,

rejoicing in **hope**	τῇ **ἐλπίδι** χαίροντες
persevering in **tribulation**	τῇ **θλίψει** ὑπομένοντες
devoted to **prayer**	τῇ **προσευχῇ** προσκαρτεροῦντες

He seized (ἐκράτησεν) the dragon, that ancient serpent, who is the Devil and **Satan (Σατανᾶς)**, and **bound (ἔδησεν)** him for a thousand years. (NRSV)

| Σατανᾶς | Satan | 36x |
| *Satanas* | | S4567 |

　　κρατέω　➤　1:321　　　　**δέω**　➤　1:346

καὶ **ἐκράτησεν** τὸν δράκοντα, ὁ ὄφις ὁ ἀρχαῖος, ὅς ἐστιν Διάβολος καὶ Ὁ **Σατανᾶς**, καὶ **ἔδησεν** αὐτὸν χίλια ἔτη,

He seized the dragon	καὶ **ἐκράτησεν** τὸν δράκοντα
that ancient serpent	ὁ ὄφις ὁ ἀρχαῖος
who is the Devil and **Satan**	ὅς ἐστιν Διάβολος καὶ Ὁ **Σατανᾶς**
and **bound** him	καὶ **ἔδησεν** αὐτὸν
for a thousand years	χίλια ἔτη

The crowds with one accord were giving attention to **what was said (λεγομένοις)** by **Philip (Φιλίππου)**, as they heard and saw the **signs (σημεῖα)** which he was performing. (NASB)

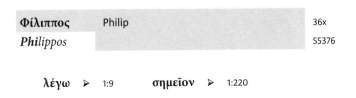

| Φίλιππος | Philip | 36x |
| *Philippos* | | S5376 |

λέγω   ➤   1:9   σημεῖον   ➤   1:220

προσεῖχον δὲ οἱ ὄχλοι τοῖς **λεγομένοις** ὑπὸ τοῦ **Φιλίππου** ὁμοθυμαδὸν ἐν τῷ ἀκούειν αὐτοὺς καὶ βλέπειν τὰ **σημεῖα** ἃ ἐποίει·

The crowds	δὲ οἱ ὄχλοι
with one accord were giving attention	προσεῖχον . . . ὁμοθυμαδὸν
to **what was said** by **Philip**	τοῖς **λεγομένοις** ὑπὸ τοῦ **Φιλίππου**
as they heard	ἐν τῷ ἀκούειν αὐτοὺς
and saw the **signs**	καὶ βλέπειν τὰ **σημεῖα**
which he was performing	ἃ ἐποίει

Nor was it to **offer (προσφέρῃ)** himself repeatedly, **as (ὥσπερ)** the high priest enters the **holy places (ἅγια)** every year with blood not his own. (ESV)

| ὥσπερ | as, even as | 36x |
| *hōsper* | | S5618 |

ἅγιος ➤ 1:67   προσφέρω ➤ 1:330

οὐδ᾽ ἵνα πολλάκις **προσφέρῃ** ἑαυτόν, **ὥσπερ** ὁ ἀρχιερεὺς εἰσέρχεται εἰς τὰ **ἅγια** κατ᾽ ἐνιαυτὸν ἐν αἵματι ἀλλοτρίῳ,

Nor was it to **offer** himself repeatedly	οὐδ᾽ ἵνα πολλάκις **προσφέρῃ** ἑαυτόν
as the high priest enters the **holy places**	**ὥσπερ** ὁ ἀρχιερεὺς εἰσέρχεται εἰς τὰ **ἅγια**
every year	κατ᾽ ἐνιαυτὸν
with blood not his own	ἐν αἵματι ἀλλοτρίῳ

And **Joseph** (Ἰωσὴφ), too, **went up** (Ἀνέβη) from Galilee out of the city of Nazareth to Judea, to the city of David **called** (**καλεῖται**) Bethlehem, because he was of the house and family of David. (MLB)

Ἰωσήφ	Joseph	35x
Iōsēph		S2501

καλέω ➤ 1:112   **ἀναβαίνω** ➤ 1:206

Ἀνέβη δὲ καὶ Ἰωσὴφ ἀπὸ τῆς Γαλιλαίας ἐκ πόλεως Ναζαρὲτ εἰς τὴν Ἰουδαίαν εἰς πόλιν Δαυεὶδ ἥτις **καλεῖται** Βηθλεέμ, διὰ τὸ εἶναι αὐτὸν ἐξ οἴκου καὶ πατριᾶς Δαυείδ,

And **Joseph**, too, **went up**	Ἀνέβη δὲ καὶ Ἰωσὴφ
from Galilee	ἀπὸ τῆς Γαλιλαίας
out of the city of Nazareth	ἐκ πόλεως Ναζαρὲτ
to Judea	εἰς τὴν Ἰουδαίαν
to the city of David	εἰς πόλιν Δαυεὶδ
called Bethlehem	ἥτις **καλεῖται** Βηθλεέμ
because he was	διὰ τὸ εἶναι αὐτὸν
of the house and family of David	ἐξ οἴκου καὶ πατριᾶς Δαυείδ

And let the one who is in the **field (ἀγρὸν)** not turn **back (εἰς τὰ ὀπίσω)** to take his **cloak (ἱμάτιον).** (ESV)

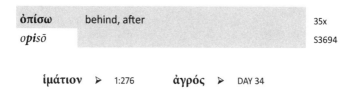

| ὀπίσω | behind, after | 35x |
| *opisō* | | S3694 |

ἱμάτιον ➤ 1:276   **ἀγρός** ➤ DAY 34

καὶ ὁ εἰς τὸν **ἀγρὸν** μὴ ἐπιστρεψάτω εἰς τὰ **ὀπίσω** ἆραι τὸ **ἱμάτιον** αὐτοῦ.

And let . . . not turn **back**	καὶ . . . μὴ ἐπιστρεψάτω εἰς τὰ **ὀπίσω**
the one who is in the **field**	ὁ εἰς τὸν **ἀγρὸν**
to take his **cloak**	ἆραι τὸ **ἱμάτιον** αὐτοῦ

What I tell you in the dark you must say in the **light (φωτί)**, and what you hear close to your **ear (οὖς) you must herald (κηρύξατε)** from the housetops. (MLB)

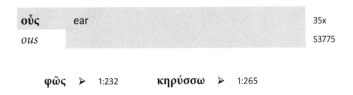

οὖς	ear	35x
ous		S3775

φῶς ➤ 1:232   **κηρύσσω** ➤ 1:265

ὃ λέγω ὑμῖν ἐν τῇ σκοτίᾳ, εἴπατε ἐν τῷ **φωτί**· καὶ ὃ εἰς τὸ **οὖς** ἀκούετε, **κηρύξατε** ἐπὶ τῶν δωμάτων.

What I tell you in the dark	ὃ λέγω ὑμῖν ἐν τῇ σκοτίᾳ
you must say in the **light**	εἴπατε ἐν τῷ **φωτί**
and what you hear close to your **ear**	καὶ ὃ εἰς τὸ **οὖς** ἀκούετε
you must herald from the housetops	**κηρύξατε** ἐπὶ τῶν δωμάτων

So husbands **ought (ὀφείλουσιν)** also to love **their own (ἑαυτῶν)**
wives as **their own (ἑαυτῶν) bodies (σώματα)**. He who loves **his
own (ἑαυτοῦ)** wife loves **himself (ἑαυτὸν)**. (NASB)

ὀφείλω	to owe, ought	35x
opheilō		S3784

ἑαυτοῦ ➢ 1:55	**σῶμα** ➢ 1:117	

οὕτως **ὀφείλουσιν** [καὶ] οἱ ἄνδρες ἀγαπᾶν τὰς **ἑαυτῶν** γυναῖκας
ὡς τὰ **ἑαυτῶν σώματα**· ὁ ἀγαπῶν τὴν **ἑαυτοῦ** γυναῖκα **ἑαυτὸν**
ἀγαπᾷ,

So husbands **ought** also	οὕτως **ὀφείλουσιν** [καὶ] οἱ ἄνδρες
to love	ἀγαπᾶν
their own wives	τὰς **ἑαυτῶν** γυναῖκας
as **their own bodies**	ὡς τὰ **ἑαυτῶν σώματα**
He who loves	ὁ ἀγαπῶν
his own wife	τὴν **ἑαυτοῦ** γυναῖκα
loves **himself**	**ἑαυτὸν** ἀγαπᾷ

And when all the **crowds** (ὄχλοι) that had gathered for this spectacle **saw** (θεωρήσαντες) what had occurred, **they went back** (ὑπέστρεφον), beating their breasts. (MLB)

ὑποστρέφω	to return, withdraw	35x
hupostrephō		S5290

ὄχλος ➤ 1:90   θεωρέω ➤ 1:297

καὶ πάντες οἱ συνπαραγενόμενοι **ὄχλοι** ἐπὶ τὴν θεωρίαν ταύτην, **θεωρήσαντες** τὰ γενόμενα, τύπτοντες τὰ στήθη **ὑπέστρεφον.**

And when all the **crowds** that had gathered	καὶ πάντες οἱ συνπαραγενόμενοι **ὄχλοι**
for this spectacle	ἐπὶ τὴν θεωρίαν ταύτην
saw what had occurred	**θεωρήσαντες** τὰ γενόμενα
they went back	**ὑπέστρεφον**
beating their breasts	τύπτοντες τὰ στήθη

Rolling up the **scroll (βιβλίον)** He handed it back to the attendant and **sat down (ἐκάθισεν)**. The **eyes (ὀφθαλμοὶ)** of everyone in the synagogue were fixed on Him. (MLB)

βιβλίον	scroll, book	34x
biblion		S975

ὀφθαλμός ➤ 1:169   **καθίζω** ➤ 1:327

καὶ πτύξας τὸ **βιβλίον** ἀποδοὺς τῷ ὑπηρέτῃ **ἐκάθισεν**· καὶ πάντων οἱ **ὀφθαλμοὶ** ἐν τῇ συναγωγῇ ἦσαν ἀτενίζοντες αὐτῷ.

Rolling up the **scroll**	καὶ πτύξας τὸ **βιβλίον**
He handed it back to the attendant	ἀποδοὺς τῷ ὑπηρέτῃ
and **sat down**	**ἐκάθισεν**
The **eyes** of everyone	καὶ πάντων οἱ **ὀφθαλμοὶ**
in the synagogue	ἐν τῇ συναγωγῇ
were fixed on Him	ἦσαν ἀτενίζοντες αὐτῷ

Then the high priest tore his **clothes (ἱμάτια)**, saying, "**He has blasphemed (Ἐβλασφήμησεν)**! What further **need (χρείαν)** do we have of witnesses? You have now heard His blasphemy." (MLB)

βλασφημέω	to blaspheme, speak evil about	34x
blasphēmeō		S987

ἱμάτιον ➤ 1:276   χρεία ➤ 1:316

τότε ὁ ἀρχιερεὺς διέρηξεν τὰ **ἱμάτια** αὐτοῦ λέγων **Ἐβλασφήμησεν**· τί ἔτι **χρείαν** ἔχομεν μαρτύρων; ἴδε νῦν ἠκούσατε τὴν βλασφημίαν·

Then the high priest tore his **clothes**	τότε ὁ ἀρχιερεὺς διέρηξεν τὰ **ἱμάτια** αὐτοῦ
saying	λέγων
He has blasphemed!	**Ἐβλασφήμησεν**
What further **need** do we have of witnesses?	τί ἔτι **χρείαν** ἔχομεν μαρτύρων;
You have now heard His blasphemy	ἴδε νῦν ἠκούσατε τὴν βλασφημίαν

I **should like (ἐβουλόμην)** to retain him for **myself (ἐμαυτὸν)**, so that **he might serve (διακονῇ)** me instead of you during my imprisonment for the sake of the good news. (MLB)

βούλομαι	to will, want	34x
boulomai		S1014

διακονέω ➤ DAY 28   **ἐμαυτοῦ** ➤ DAY 29

ὃν ἐγὼ **ἐβουλόμην** πρὸς **ἐμαυτὸν** κατέχειν, ἵνα ὑπὲρ σοῦ μοι **διακονῇ** ἐν τοῖς δεσμοῖς τοῦ εὐαγγελίου,

I **should like** to retain him	ὃν ἐγὼ **ἐβουλόμην** . . . κατέχειν
for **myself**	πρὸς **ἐμαυτὸν**
so that **he might serve** me	ἵνα . . . μοι **διακονῇ**
instead of you	ὑπὲρ σοῦ
during my imprisonment	ἐν τοῖς δεσμοῖς
for the sake of the good news	τοῦ εὐαγγελίου

And tell Archippus, "Pay attention to the **ministry (διακονίαν) you have received (παρέλαβες)** in the Lord, so that **you can accomplish (πληροῖς)** it." (CSB)

διακονία *diakonia*	service, ministry	34x S1248

πληρόω	➤	1:200	παραλαμβάνω	➤	1:313

καὶ εἴπατε Ἀρχίππῳ Βλέπε τὴν **διακονίαν** ἣν **παρέλαβες** ἐν κυρίῳ, ἵνα αὐτὴν **πληροῖς**.

And tell Archippus	καὶ εἴπατε Ἀρχίππῳ
Pay attention to the **ministry**	Βλέπε τὴν **διακονίαν**
you have received	ἣν **παρέλαβες**
in the Lord	ἐν κυρίῳ
so that **you can accomplish** it	ἵνα αὐτὴν **πληροῖς**

Then **He began (ἤρξατο)** to denounce the cities in which most of His **miracles (δυνάμεις)** were done, because **they did** not **repent (μετενόησαν)**. (NASB)

μετανοέω	to repent, change	34x
metanoeō		S3340

δύναμις ➢ 1:141　　　**ἄρχω** ➢ 1:201

Τότε **ἤρξατο** ὀνειδίζειν τὰς πόλεις ἐν αἷς ἐγένοντο αἱ πλεῖσται **δυνάμεις** αὐτοῦ, ὅτι οὐ **μετενόησαν·**

Then **He began**	Τότε **ἤρξατο**
to denounce	ὀνειδίζειν
the cities	τὰς πόλεις
in which most of His **miracles**	ἐν αἷς ... αἱ πλεῖσται **δυνάμεις** αὐτοῦ
were done	ἐγένοντο
because **they did** not **repent**	ὅτι οὐ **μετενόησαν**

Without father, without mother, without genealogy, having
neither (μήτε) beginning of days **nor (μήτε) end (τέλος)** of
life, but resembling the Son of God, **he remains (μένει)** a priest
forever. (NRSV)

μήτε	and not, neither, nor	34x
mēte		S3383

μένω ▷ 1:139   τέλος ▷ DAY 2

ἀπάτωρ, ἀμήτωρ, ἀγενεαλόγητος, **μήτε** ἀρχὴν ἡμερῶν **μήτε** ζωῆς
τέλος ἔχων, ἀφωμοιωμένος δὲ τῷ υἱῷ τοῦ θεοῦ, **μένει** ἱερεὺς εἰς
τὸ διηνεκές.

Without father	ἀπάτωρ
without mother	ἀμήτωρ
without genealogy	ἀγενεαλόγητος
having **neither** beginning of days	**μήτε** ἀρχὴν ἡμερῶν . . . ἔχων
nor end of life	**μήτε** ζωῆς **τέλος**
but resembling the Son of God	ἀφωμοιωμένος δὲ τῷ υἱῷ τοῦ θεοῦ
he remains a priest	**μένει** ἱερεὺς
forever	εἰς τὸ διηνεκές

He **who testifies (μαρτυρῶν)** to these things says, "**Yes (Ναί)**, **I am coming (ἔρχομαι)** quickly." Amen. **Come (ἔρχου)**, Lord Jesus.

(NASB)

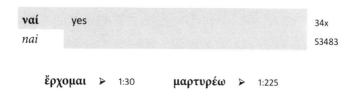

ναί	yes	34x
nai		S3483

ἔρχομαι ➤ 1:30   μαρτυρέω ➤ 1:225

Λέγει ὁ **μαρτυρῶν** ταῦτα **Ναί**· **ἔρχομαι** ταχύ. Ἀμήν· **ἔρχου**, κύριε Ἰησοῦ.

He **who testifies** to these things says	Λέγει ὁ **μαρτυρῶν** ταῦτα
Yes	**Ναί**
I am coming quickly	**ἔρχομαι** ταχύ
Amen	Ἀμήν
Come	**ἔρχου**
Lord Jesus	κύριε Ἰησοῦ

It is **good (καλὸν)** not to eat meat or **drink (πεῖν) wine (οἶνον)** or do anything that makes your brother or sister stumble. (NRSV)

οἶνος	wine	34x
oinos		S3631

καλός ▷ 1:165   πίνω ▷ 1:233

καλὸν τὸ μὴ φαγεῖν κρέα μηδὲ **πεῖν οἶνον** μηδὲ ἐν ᾧ ὁ ἀδελφός σου προσκόπτει·

It is **good**	**καλὸν**
not to eat meat	τὸ μὴ φαγεῖν κρέα
or **drink wine**	μηδὲ **πεῖν οἶνον**
or do anything that makes your brother or sister stumble	μηδὲ ἐν ᾧ ὁ ἀδελφός σου προσκόπτει

Now the **poor man (πτωχὸν) died (ἀποθανεῖν)** and was carried away by the **angels (ἀγγέλων)** to Abraham's bosom; and the rich man also **died (ἀπέθανεν)** and was buried. (NASB)

πτωχός	poor (person)	34x
ptōchos		S4434

     ἄγγελος ➤ 1:94   **ἀποθνήσκω** ➤ 1:148

ἐγένετο δὲ **ἀποθανεῖν** τὸν **πτωχὸν** καὶ ἀπενεχθῆναι αὐτὸν ὑπὸ τῶν **ἀγγέλων** εἰς τὸν κόλπον Ἀβραάμ· **ἀπέθανεν** δὲ καὶ ὁ πλούσιος καὶ ἐτάφη.

Now	ἐγένετο δὲ
the **poor man died**	**ἀποθανεῖν** τὸν **πτωχὸν**
and was carried away	καὶ ἀπενεχθῆναι αὐτὸν
by the **angels**	ὑπὸ τῶν **ἀγγέλων**
to Abraham's bosom	εἰς τὸν κόλπον Ἀβραάμ
and the rich man also **died**	**ἀπέθανεν** δὲ καὶ ὁ πλούσιος
and was buried	καὶ ἐτάφη

training us to **renounce (ἀρνησάμενοι)** godlessness and worldly **passions (ἐπιθυμίας)**, and to **live (ζήσωμεν)** self-controlled, upright, and godly lives in this present world. (MLB)

ἀρνέομαι	to deny, repudiate	33x
arneomai		S720

ζάω ➤ 1:121   **ἐπιθυμία** ➤ DAY 22

παιδεύουσα ἡμᾶς, ἵνα **ἀρνησάμενοι** τὴν ἀσέβειαν καὶ τὰς κοσμικὰς **ἐπιθυμίας** σωφρόνως καὶ δικαίως καὶ εὐσεβῶς **ζήσωμεν** ἐν τῷ νῦν αἰῶνι,

training us	παιδεύουσα ἡμᾶς
to **renounce**	ἵνα **ἀρνησάμενοι**
godlessness	τὴν ἀσέβειαν
and worldly **passions**	καὶ τὰς κοσμικὰς **ἐπιθυμίας**
and to **live** . . . lives	**ζήσωμεν**
self-controlled, upright, and godly	σωφρόνως καὶ δικαίως καὶ εὐσεβῶς
in this present world	ἐν τῷ νῦν αἰῶνι

So he came **again (πάλιν)** to Cana in Galilee, where he had made
the water **wine (οἶνον)**. And at Capernaum there was an official
whose son **was ill (ἠσθένει)**. (ESV)

| **ἀσθενέω** | to be sick, be weak | 33x |
| *astheneō* | | S770 |

πάλιν ➤ 1:120   **οἶνος** ➤ DAY 60

Ἦλθεν οὖν **πάλιν** εἰς τὴν Κανὰ τῆς Γαλιλαίας, ὅπου ἐποίησεν
τὸ ὕδωρ **οἶνον**. Καὶ ἦν τις βασιλικὸς οὗ ὁ υἱὸς **ἠσθένει** ἐν
Καφαρναούμ·

So he came **again**	Ἦλθεν οὖν **πάλιν**
to Cana in Galilee	εἰς τὴν Κανὰ τῆς Γαλιλαίας
where he had made the water **wine**	ὅπου ἐποίησεν τὸ ὕδωρ **οἶνον**
And at Capernaum	Καὶ . . . ἐν Καφαρναούμ
there was an official	ἦν τις βασιλικὸς
whose son **was ill**	οὗ ὁ υἱὸς **ἠσθένει**

Then God's temple in heaven **was opened (ἠνοίγη)**, and the ark of his **covenant (διαθήκης) was seen (ὤφθη)** within his temple; and there were flashes of lightning, rumblings, peals of thunder, an earthquake, and heavy hail. (NRSV)

διαθήκη *diathēkē*	covenant, testament, will	33x S1242

ὁράω ➤ 1:40   **ἀνοίγω** ➤ 1:221

καὶ **ἠνοίγη** ὁ ναὸς τοῦ θεοῦ ὁ ἐν τῷ οὐρανῷ, καὶ **ὤφθη** ἡ κιβωτὸς τῆς **διαθήκης** αὐτοῦ ἐν τῷ ναῷ αὐτοῦ· καὶ ἐγένοντο ἀστραπαὶ καὶ φωναὶ καὶ βρονταὶ καὶ σεισμὸς καὶ χάλαζα μεγάλη.

Then God's temple in heaven **was opened**	καὶ **ἠνοίγη** ὁ ναὸς τοῦ θεοῦ ὁ ἐν τῷ οὐρανῷ
and the ark of his **covenant**	καὶ . . . ἡ κιβωτὸς τῆς **διαθήκης** αὐτοῦ
was seen	**ὤφθη**
within his temple	ἐν τῷ ναῷ αὐτοῦ
and there were flashes of lightning	καὶ ἐγένοντο ἀστραπαὶ
rumblings, peals of thunder	καὶ φωναὶ καὶ βρονταὶ
an earthquake, and heavy hail	καὶ σεισμὸς καὶ χάλαζα μεγάλη

Immediately (εὐθέως) they left the **boat (πλοῖον)** and their father and **followed (ἠκολούθησαν)** him. (ESV)

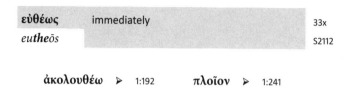

| εὐθέως | immediately | 33x |
| *eutheōs* | | S2112 |

ἀκολουθέω ➤ 1:192   πλοῖον ➤ 1:241

οἱ δὲ **εὐθέως** ἀφέντες τὸ **πλοῖον** καὶ τὸν πατέρα αὐτῶν **ἠκολούθησαν** αὐτῷ.

Immediately	εὐθέως
they left	οἱ δὲ . . . ἀφέντες
the **boat**	τὸ **πλοῖον**
and their father	καὶ τὸν πατέρα αὐτῶν
and **followed** him	**ἠκολούθησαν** αὐτῷ

If **you love** (ἀγαπᾶτε) those **who love** (ἀγαπῶντας) you, **what** (ποία) credit is that to you? For even **sinners** (ἁμαρτωλοὶ) **love** (ἀγαπῶσιν) those **who love** (ἀγαπῶντας) them. (NRSV)

ποῖος	what? of what sort?	33x
poios		S4169

ἀγαπάω ➤ 1:114   ἁμαρτωλός ➤ 1:320

καὶ εἰ **ἀγαπᾶτε** τοὺς **ἀγαπῶντας** ὑμᾶς, **ποία** ὑμῖν χάρις ἐστίν; καὶ γὰρ οἱ **ἁμαρτωλοὶ** τοὺς **ἀγαπῶντας** αὐτοὺς **ἀγαπῶσιν**.

If **you love**	καὶ εἰ **ἀγαπᾶτε**
those **who love** you	τοὺς **ἀγαπῶντας** ὑμᾶς
what credit is that to you?	**ποία** ὑμῖν χάρις ἐστίν;
For even **sinners**	καὶ γὰρ οἱ **ἁμαρτωλοὶ**
love	**ἀγαπῶσιν**
those **who love** them	τοὺς **ἀγαπῶντας** αὐτοὺς

And he was **returning (ὑποστρέφων)** and **sitting (καθήμενος)** in his chariot, and **was reading (ἀνεγίνωσκεν)** the prophet Isaiah.

(NASB)

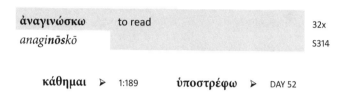

| ἀναγινώσκω | to read | 32x |
| *anaginōskō* | | S314 |

κάθημαι ➤ 1:189   **ὑποστρέφω** ➤ DAY 52

ἦν δὲ **ὑποστρέφων** καὶ **καθήμενος** ἐπὶ τοῦ ἅρματος αὐτοῦ καὶ **ἀνεγίνωσκεν** τὸν προφήτην Ἡσαΐαν.

And he was **returning**	ἦν δὲ **ὑποστρέφων**
and **sitting**	καὶ **καθήμενος**
in his chariot	ἐπὶ τοῦ ἅρματος αὐτοῦ
and **was reading**	καὶ **ἀνεγίνωσκεν**
the prophet Isaiah	τὸν προφήτην Ἡσαΐαν

Therefore take up the whole armor of God, that **you may be able** (δυνηθῆτε) to withstand in the evil day, and having done **all** (ἅπαντα), **to stand firm** (στῆναι). (ESV)

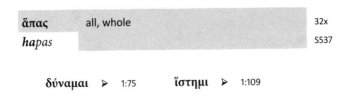

ἅπας	all, whole	32x
hapas		S537

δύναμαι ➤ 1:75   **ἵστημι** ➤ 1:109

διὰ τοῦτο ἀναλάβετε τὴν πανοπλίαν τοῦ θεοῦ, ἵνα **δυνηθῆτε** ἀντιστῆναι ἐν τῇ ἡμέρᾳ τῇ πονηρᾷ καὶ **ἅπαντα** κατεργασάμενοι **στῆναι**.

Therefore	διὰ τοῦτο
take up the whole armor of God	ἀναλάβετε τὴν πανοπλίαν τοῦ θεοῦ
that **you may be able** to withstand	ἵνα **δυνηθῆτε** ἀντιστῆναι
in the evil day	ἐν τῇ ἡμέρᾳ τῇ πονηρᾷ
and having done **all**	καὶ **ἅπαντα** κατεργασάμενοι
to stand firm	**στῆναι**

But Jesus looked at them and **said (εἶπεν)**, "**With (Παρὰ)** men this is impossible, but **with (παρὰ)** God all things are **possible (δυνατά)**." (MLB)

δυνατός	able, powerful, possible	32x
dunatos		S1415

λέγω ➤ 1:9   παρά ➤ 1:81

ἐμβλέψας δὲ ὁ Ἰησοῦς **εἶπεν** αὐτοῖς **Παρὰ** ἀνθρώποις τοῦτο ἀδύνατόν ἐστιν, **παρὰ** δὲ θεῷ πάντα **δυνατά**.

But Jesus looked at them and **said**	ἐμβλέψας δὲ ὁ Ἰησοῦς **εἶπεν** αὐτοῖς
With men	**Παρὰ** ἀνθρώποις
this is impossible	τοῦτο ἀδύνατόν ἐστιν
but **with** God	**παρὰ** δὲ θεῷ
all things are **possible**	πάντα **δυνατά**

All spoke well of him and **were amazed (ἐθαύμαζον)** at the gracious words that came [lit., **came forth (ἐκπορευομένοις)**] from his **mouth (στόματος)**. They said, "Is not this Joseph's son?" (NRSV)

| **ἐκπορεύομαι** | to come forth, journey out | 32x |
| *ekporeuomai* | | S1607 |

στόμα ➤ 1:216   **θαυμάζω** ➤ 1:348

καὶ πάντες ἐμαρτύρουν αὐτῷ καὶ **ἐθαύμαζον** ἐπὶ τοῖς λόγοις τῆς χάριτος τοῖς **ἐκπορευομένοις** ἐκ τοῦ **στόματος** αὐτοῦ, καὶ ἔλεγον Οὐχὶ υἱός ἐστιν Ἰωσὴφ οὗτος;

All spoke well of him	καὶ πάντες ἐμαρτύρουν αὐτῷ
and **were amazed**	καὶ **ἐθαύμαζον**
at the gracious words	ἐπὶ τοῖς λόγοις τῆς χάριτος
that came [lit., **came forth**] from his **mouth**	τοῖς **ἐκπορευομένοις** ἐκ τοῦ **στόματος** αὐτοῦ
They said	καὶ ἔλεγον
Is not this Joseph's son?	Οὐχὶ υἱός ἐστιν Ἰωσὴφ οὗτος;

And **he was ill (ἠσθένησεν)** indeed, even to the verge of death;
but God **took pity on (ἠλέησεν)** him, and not only on him but on
me as well, so that I might not experience [lit., **I might** not **have**
(σχῶ)] one grief after another. (MLB)

ἐλεέω	to have mercy, take pity on	32x
eleeō		S1653

ἔχω ➤ 1:23   **ἀσθενέω** ➤ DAY 63

καὶ γὰρ **ἠσθένησεν** παραπλήσιον θανάτου· ἀλλὰ ὁ θεὸς **ἠλέησεν**
αὐτόν, οὐκ αὐτὸν δὲ μόνον ἀλλὰ καὶ ἐμέ, ἵνα μὴ λύπην ἐπὶ λύπην
σχῶ.

And **he was ill** indeed	καὶ γὰρ **ἠσθένησεν**
even to the verge of death	παραπλήσιον θανάτου
but God **took pity on** him	ἀλλὰ ὁ θεὸς **ἠλέησεν** αὐτόν
and not only on him	οὐκ αὐτὸν δὲ μόνον
but on me as well	ἀλλὰ καὶ ἐμέ
so that I might not experience [lit., **I might** not **have**]	ἵνα μὴ . . . **σχῶ**
one grief after another	λύπην ἐπὶ λύπην

For many, of whom I have often told you and now tell you even with tears [lit., **weeping (κλαίων)**], **walk (περιπατοῦσιν)** as **enemies (ἐχθροὺς)** of the cross of Christ. (ESV)

ἐχθρός	enemy	32x
echthros		S2190

περιπατέω ➤ 1:179   **κλαίω** ➤ DAY 7

πολλοὶ γὰρ **περιπατοῦσιν** οὓς πολλάκις ἔλεγον ὑμῖν, νῦν δὲ καὶ **κλαίων** λέγω, τοὺς **ἐχθροὺς** τοῦ σταυροῦ τοῦ χριστοῦ,

For many	πολλοὶ γὰρ
of whom I have often told you	οὓς πολλάκις ἔλεγον ὑμῖν
and now tell you even with tears [lit., **weeping**]	νῦν δὲ καὶ **κλαίων** λέγω
walk	**περιπατοῦσιν**
as **enemies**	τοὺς **ἐχθροὺς**
of the cross of Christ	τοῦ σταυροῦ τοῦ χριστοῦ

Since **neither (μήτε) sun (ἡλίου) nor (μήτε)** stars appeared for many days, and no small storm was assailing us, from then on all hope of our **being saved (σώζεσθαι)** was gradually abandoned.
(NASB)

ἥλιος	sun	32x
hēlios		S2246

σώζω   ➤   1:160   μήτε   ➤   DAY 58

μήτε δὲ **ἡλίου μήτε** ἄστρων ἐπιφαινόντων ἐπὶ πλείονας ἡμέρας, χειμῶνός τε οὐκ ὀλίγου ἐπικειμένου, λοιπὸν περιῃρεῖτο ἐλπὶς πᾶσα τοῦ **σώζεσθαι** ἡμᾶς.

Since **neither sun**	**μήτε** δὲ **ἡλίου**
nor stars	**μήτε** ἄστρων
appeared	ἐπιφαινόντων
for many days	ἐπὶ πλείονας ἡμέρας
and no small storm was assailing us	χειμῶνός τε οὐκ ὀλίγου ἐπικειμένου
from then on	λοιπὸν
all hope of our **being saved**	ἐλπὶς πᾶσα τοῦ **σώζεσθαι** ἡμᾶς
was gradually abandoned	περιῃρεῖτο

Then I saw that the woman was drunk with the **blood (αἵματος)** of the saints and with the **blood (αἵματος)** of the **witnesses (μαρτύρων)** to Jesus. When I saw her, I was greatly astonished [lit., **I was amazed (ἐθαύμασα)** with a great amazement]. (CSB)

μάρτυς	witness, martyr	32x
martus		S3144

αἷμα ➤ 1:184   θαυμάζω ➤ 1:348

καὶ εἶδον τὴν γυναῖκα μεθύουσαν ἐκ τοῦ **αἵματος** τῶν ἁγίων καὶ ἐκ τοῦ **αἵματος** τῶν **μαρτύρων** Ἰησοῦ. Καὶ **ἐθαύμασα** ἰδὼν αὐτὴν θαῦμα μέγα·

Then I saw that the woman was drunk	καὶ εἶδον τὴν γυναῖκα μεθύουσαν
with the **blood** of the saints	ἐκ τοῦ **αἵματος** τῶν ἁγίων
and with the **blood** of the **witnesses** to Jesus	καὶ ἐκ τοῦ **αἵματος** τῶν **μαρτύρων** Ἰησοῦ
When I saw her	ἰδὼν αὐτὴν
I was greatly astonished [lit., **I was amazed** with a great amazement]	Καὶ **ἐθαύμασα** . . . θαῦμα μέγα

But now God **has placed (ἔθετο)** the **members (μέλη)**, each one of them, in the body, just as **He desired (ἠθέλησεν)**. (NASB)

| **μέλος**
 melos | member, part, limb | 32x
 S3196 |

θέλω ➤ 1:78 τίθημι ➤ 1:170

νῦν δὲ ὁ θεὸς **ἔθετο** τὰ **μέλη**, ἓν ἕκαστον αὐτῶν, ἐν τῷ σώματι καθὼς **ἠθέλησεν**.

But now	νῦν δὲ
God **has placed**	ὁ θεὸς **ἔθετο**
the **members**	τὰ **μέλη**
each one of them	ἓν ἕκαστον αὐτῶν
in the body	ἐν τῷ σώματι
just as **He desired**	καθὼς **ἠθέλησεν**

For you have **need (χρείαν)** of **endurance (ὑπομονῆς)**, so that
when you have done the will of God you may receive what is
promised [lit., the **promise (ἐπαγγελίαν)**]. (ESV)

ὑπομονή	endurance	32x
hupomonē		S5281

ἐπαγγελία ➤ 1:299   **χρεία** ➤ 1:316

ὑπομονῆς γὰρ ἔχετε χρείαν ἵνα τὸ θέλημα τοῦ θεοῦ ποιήσαντες
κομίσησθε τὴν ἐπαγγελίαν·

For you have **need** of **endurance**	ὑπομονῆς γὰρ ἔχετε χρείαν
so that when you have done the will of God	ἵνα τὸ θέλημα τοῦ θεοῦ ποιήσαντες
you may receive what is promised [lit., the **promise**]	κομίσησθε τὴν ἐπαγγελίαν

But looking at the **wind (ἄνεμον) he was afraid (ἐφοβήθη)** and, beginning to sink, **he cried (ἔκραξεν)**, "Lord, save me!" (MLB)

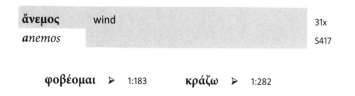

| ἄνεμος | wind | 31x |
| *anemos* | | S417 |

φοβέομαι ➤ 1:183   **κράζω** ➤ 1:282

βλέπων δὲ τὸν **ἄνεμον ἐφοβήθη**, καὶ ἀρξάμενος καταποντίζεσθαι **ἔκραξεν** λέγων Κύριε, σῶσόν με.

But looking at the **wind**	βλέπων δὲ τὸν **ἄνεμον**
he was afraid	**ἐφοβήθη**
and, beginning to sink	καὶ ἀρξάμενος καταποντίζεσθαι
he cried	**ἔκραξεν** λέγων
Lord	Κύριε
save me!	σῶσόν με

One thing more—**prepare (ἑτοίμαζέ)** a guest room for me, for **I am hoping (ἐλπίζω)** through your **prayers (προσευχῶν)** to be restored to you. (NRSV)

ἐλπίζω	to hope (for)	31x
elpizō		S1679

ἑτοιμάζω ➤ DAY 15   προσευχή ➤ DAY 44

ἅμα δὲ καὶ **ἑτοίμαζέ** μοι ξενίαν, **ἐλπίζω** γὰρ ὅτι διὰ τῶν **προσευχῶν** ὑμῶν χαρισθήσομαι ὑμῖν.

One thing more	ἅμα δὲ καὶ
prepare a guest room for me	**ἑτοίμαζέ** μοι ξενίαν
for **I am hoping**	**ἐλπίζω** γὰρ ὅτι
through your **prayers**	διὰ τῶν **προσευχῶν** ὑμῶν
to be restored to you	χαρισθήσομαι ὑμῖν

Heal **the sick (ἀσθενοῦντας); raise (ἐγείρετε)** the dead; **cleanse (καθαρίζετε)** lepers; expel demons. Freely you have received; freely give. (MLB)

| καθαρίζω | to cleanse, purify | 31x |
| *katharizō* | | S2511 |

ἐγείρω ➤ 1:118   ἀσθενέω ➤ DAY 63

ἀσθενοῦντας θεραπεύετε, νεκροὺς ἐγείρετε, λεπροὺς καθαρίζετε, δαιμόνια ἐκβάλλετε· δωρεὰν ἐλάβετε, δωρεὰν δότε.

Heal **the sick**	**ἀσθενοῦντας** θεραπεύετε
raise the dead	νεκροὺς **ἐγείρετε**
cleanse lepers	λεπροὺς **καθαρίζετε**
expel demons	δαιμόνια ἐκβάλλετε
Freely you have received	δωρεὰν ἐλάβετε
freely give	δωρεὰν δότε

Similarly (ὁμοίως), too, was not Rahab the harlot **accounted righteous (ἐδικαιώθη)** by her works, when she entertained the messengers and **sent** them **away (ἐκβαλοῦσα)** by a different road?
(MLB)

ὁμοίως	similarly, in the same way	31x
homoiōs		S3668

  ἐκβάλλω ➤ 1:207   **δικαιόω** ➤ DAY 14

ὁμοίως δὲ καὶ Ῥαὰβ ἡ πόρνη οὐκ ἐξ ἔργων **ἐδικαιώθη**,
ὑποδεξαμένη τοὺς ἀγγέλους καὶ ἑτέρᾳ ὁδῷ **ἐκβαλοῦσα**;

Similarly, too	**ὁμοίως** δὲ καὶ
was not Rahab the harlot **accounted righteous**	Ῥαὰβ ἡ πόρνη οὐκ . . . **ἐδικαιώθη**
by her works	ἐξ ἔργων
when she entertained the messengers	ὑποδεξαμένη τοὺς ἀγγέλους
and **sent** them **away** by a different road?	καὶ ἑτέρᾳ ὁδῷ **ἐκβαλοῦσα**;

Now such persons **we command (παραγγέλλομεν)** and **exhort (παρακαλοῦμεν)** in the Lord Jesus Christ to do their work quietly [lit., that, **working (ἐργαζόμενοι)** with quietness] and to earn their own living [lit., they eat their own food]. (NRSV)

| **παραγγέλλω** | to command, charge | 31x |
| *parangellō* | | S3853 |

παρακαλέω ➤ 1:157   **ἐργάζομαι** ➤ 1:361

τοῖς δὲ τοιούτοις **παραγγέλλομεν** καὶ **παρακαλοῦμεν** ἐν κυρίῳ Ἰησοῦ Χριστῷ ἵνα μετὰ ἡσυχίας **ἐργαζόμενοι** τὸν ἑαυτῶν ἄρτον ἐσθίωσιν.

Now such persons	τοῖς δὲ τοιούτοις
we command	**παραγγέλλομεν**
and **exhort**	καὶ **παρακαλοῦμεν**
in the Lord Jesus Christ	ἐν κυρίῳ Ἰησοῦ Χριστῷ
to do their work quietly [lit., that, **working** with quietness]	ἵνα μετὰ ἡσυχίας **ἐργαζόμενοι**
and to earn their own living [lit., they eat their own food]	τὸν ἑαυτῶν ἄρτον ἐσθίωσιν

I have said these things to you in figures of speech. The hour is coming when I will **no longer (οὐκέτι)** speak to you in figures of speech but **will tell (ἀπαγγελῶ)** you **plainly (παρρησίᾳ)** about the Father. (ESV)

| παρρησία | boldness, freedom, liberty | 31x |
| *parrēsia* | | S3954 |

οὐκέτι ▷ 1:324   ἀπαγγέλλω ▷ 1:343

Ταῦτα ἐν παροιμίαις λελάληκα ὑμῖν· ἔρχεται ὥρα ὅτε **οὐκέτι** ἐν παροιμίαις λαλήσω ὑμῖν ἀλλὰ **παρρησίᾳ** περὶ τοῦ πατρὸς **ἀπαγγελῶ** ὑμῖν.

I have said these things to you	Ταῦτα . . . λελάληκα ὑμῖν
in figures of speech	ἐν παροιμίαις
The hour is coming when	ἔρχεται ὥρα ὅτε
I will **no longer** speak to you	**οὐκέτι** . . . λαλήσω ὑμῖν
in figures of speech	ἐν παροιμίαις
but **will tell** you **plainly**	ἀλλὰ **παρρησίᾳ** . . . **ἀπαγγελῶ** ὑμῖν
about the Father	περὶ τοῦ πατρὸς

As Paul gathered a **bundle (πλῆθος)** of brushwood and **put (ἐπιθέντος)** it on the fire, a viper came out because of the heat and fastened itself on his **hand (χειρὸς)**. (CSB)

πλῆθος	crowd, multitude	31x
plēthos		S4128

χείρ   ➢   1:88   **ἐπιτίθημι**   ➢   DAY 23

συστρέψαντος δὲ τοῦ Παύλου φρυγάνων τι **πλῆθος** καὶ **ἐπιθέντος** ἐπὶ τὴν πυράν, ἔχιδνα ἀπὸ τῆς θέρμης ἐξελθοῦσα καθῆψε τῆς **χειρὸς** αὐτοῦ.

As Paul gathered	συστρέψαντος δὲ τοῦ Παύλου
a **bundle** of brushwood	φρυγάνων τι **πλῆθος**
and **put** it on the fire	καὶ **ἐπιθέντος** ἐπὶ τὴν πυράν
a viper came out	ἔχιδνα . . . ἐξελθοῦσα
because of the heat	ἀπὸ τῆς θέρμης
and fastened itself on his **hand**	καθῆψε τῆς **χειρὸς** αὐτοῦ

But (πλὴν) I tell you, **it will be (ἔσται)** more bearable for Tyre and Sidon on the day of **judgment (κρίσεως)** than for you. (NIV)

πλήν	but, only, however, nevertheless, except,	31x
plēn	apart from	S4133

εἰμί ➤ 1:8   κρίσις ➤ 1:322

πλὴν λέγω ὑμῖν, Τύρῳ καὶ Σιδῶνι ἀνεκτότερον **ἔσται** ἐν ἡμέρᾳ **κρίσεως** ἢ ὑμῖν.

But I tell you	πλὴν λέγω ὑμῖν
it will be more bearable	ἀνεκτότερον **ἔσται**
for Tyre and Sidon	Τύρῳ καὶ Σιδῶνι
on the day of **judgment**	ἐν ἡμέρᾳ **κρίσεως**
than for you	ἢ ὑμῖν

He was a burning and **shining (φαίνων)** lamp, and you **were willing (ἠθελήσατε)** to rejoice for a while [lit., an **hour (ὥραν)**] in his light. (NRSV)

φαίνω *phainō*	to shine, appear, become visible	31x S5316

θέλω ▷ 1:78   **ὥρα** ▷ 1:159

ἐκεῖνος ἦν ὁ λύχνος ὁ καιόμενος καὶ **φαίνων**, ὑμεῖς δὲ **ἠθελήσατε** ἀγαλλιαθῆναι πρὸς **ὥραν** ἐν τῷ φωτὶ αὐτοῦ·

He was a burning and **shining** lamp	ἐκεῖνος ἦν ὁ λύχνος ὁ καιόμενος καὶ **φαίνων**
and you **were willing**	ὑμεῖς δὲ **ἠθελήσατε**
to rejoice	ἀγαλλιαθῆναι
for a while [lit., an **hour**]	πρὸς **ὥραν**
in his light	ἐν τῷ φωτὶ αὐτοῦ

Now to Him who is able **to keep (φυλάξαι)** you from stumbling
and **to present (στῆσαι)** you faultless in the presence of His **glory
(δόξης)** with abounding joy, . . . (MLB)

φυλάσσω	to guard, protect, keep, observe	31x
phulassō		S5442

δόξα ➤ 1:95   **ἵστημι** ➤ 1:109

Τῷ δὲ δυναμένῳ **φυλάξαι** ὑμᾶς ἀπταίστους καὶ **στῆσαι**
κατενώπιον τῆς **δόξης** αὐτοῦ ἀμώμους ἐν ἀγαλλιάσει

Now to Him who is able	Τῷ δὲ δυναμένῳ
to keep you from stumbling	**φυλάξαι** ὑμᾶς ἀπταίστους
and **to present** you faultless	καὶ **στῆσαι** . . . ἀμώμους
in the presence of His **glory**	κατενώπιον τῆς **δόξης** αὐτοῦ
with abounding joy	ἐν ἀγαλλιάσει

Then one of the elders said to me, "Do not **weep (κλαῖε)**! See,
the Lion of the **tribe (φυλῆς)** of Judah, the Root of David, has
triumphed. He is able **to open (ἀνοῖξαι)** the scroll and its seven
seals." (NIV)

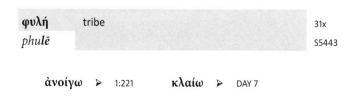

| **φυλή** | tribe | 31x |
| *phulē* | | S5443 |

ἀνοίγω   ➤   1:221   κλαίω   ➤   DAY 7

καὶ εἷς ἐκ τῶν πρεσβυτέρων λέγει μοι Μὴ **κλαῖε**· ἰδοὺ ἐνίκησεν ὁ
λέων ὁ ἐκ τῆς **φυλῆς** Ἰούδα, ἡ ῥίζα Δαυείδ, **ἀνοῖξαι** τὸ βιβλίον καὶ
τὰς ἑπτὰ σφραγῖδας αὐτοῦ.

Then one of the elders said to me	καὶ εἷς ἐκ τῶν πρεσβυτέρων λέγει μοι
Do not **weep**!	Μὴ **κλαῖε**
See	ἰδοὺ
the Lion of the **tribe** of Judah . . . has triumphed	ἐνίκησεν ὁ λέων ὁ ἐκ τῆς **φυλῆς** Ἰούδα
the Root of David	ἡ ῥίζα Δαυείδ
He is able **to open** the scroll	**ἀνοῖξαι** τὸ βιβλίον
and its seven seals	καὶ τὰς ἑπτὰ σφραγῖδας αὐτοῦ

But they all alike began to make excuses. The first said to him, "**I have bought (ἠγόρασα)** a field, and I must go out and **see (ἰδεῖν)** it. Please [lit., **I ask (ἐρωτῶ)** you,] have me excused." (ESV)

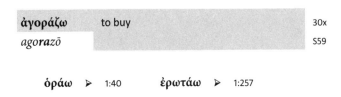

ἀγοράζω	to buy	30x
agorazō		S59

ὁράω ▷ 1:40   **ἐρωτάω** ▷ 1:257

καὶ ἤρξαντο ἀπὸ μιᾶς πάντες παραιτεῖσθαι. ὁ πρῶτος εἶπεν αὐτῷ Ἀγρὸν **ἠγόρασα** καὶ ἔχω ἀνάγκην ἐξελθὼν **ἰδεῖν** αὐτόν· **ἐρωτῶ** σε, ἔχε με παρητημένον.

But they . . . began to make excuses	καὶ ἤρξαντο . . . παραιτεῖσθαι
all alike	ἀπὸ μιᾶς πάντες
The first said to him	ὁ πρῶτος εἶπεν αὐτῷ
I have bought a field	Ἀγρὸν **ἠγόρασα**
and I must	καὶ ἔχω ἀνάγκην
go out	ἐξελθὼν
and **see** it	**ἰδεῖν** αὐτόν
Please [lit., **I ask** you,]	**ἐρωτῶ** σε
have me excused	ἔχε με παρητημένον

And **whenever (ὅταν)** the **unclean (ἀκάθαρτα)** spirits saw Him
they fell down before Him, **screaming (ἔκραζον)**, "You are the
Son of God!" (MLB)

ἀκάθαρτος	unclean, impure	30x
akathartos		S169

ὅταν ➤ 1:135 **κράζω** ➤ 1:282

καὶ τὰ πνεύματα τὰ **ἀκάθαρτα**, **ὅταν** αὐτὸν ἐθεώρουν,
προσέπιπτον αὐτῷ καὶ **ἔκραζον** λέγοντα ὅτι Σὺ εἶ ὁ υἱὸς τοῦ θεοῦ.

And **whenever** the **unclean** spirits saw Him	καὶ τὰ πνεύματα τὰ **ἀκάθαρτα**, **ὅταν** αὐτὸν ἐθεώρουν
they fell down before Him	προσέπιπτον αὐτῷ
screaming	καὶ **ἔκραζον** λέγοντα ὅτι
You are	Σὺ εἶ
the Son of God!	ὁ υἱὸς τοῦ θεοῦ

The city has no **need (χρείαν)** of the sun or of the moon to **shine (φαίνωσιν)** on it, because God's glory illumines it and the **Lamb (ἀρνίον)** is its light. (MLB)

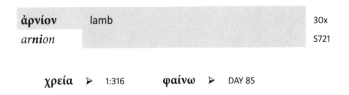

ἀρνίον	lamb	30x
arnion		S721

χρεία ▷ 1:316   φαίνω ▷ DAY 85

καὶ ἡ πόλις οὐ **χρείαν** ἔχει τοῦ ἡλίου οὐδὲ τῆς σελήνης, ἵνα **φαίνωσιν** αὐτῇ, ἡ γὰρ δόξα τοῦ θεοῦ ἐφώτισεν αὐτήν, καὶ ὁ λύχνος αὐτῆς τὸ **ἀρνίον**.

The city has no **need**	καὶ ἡ πόλις οὐ **χρείαν** ἔχει
of the sun	τοῦ ἡλίου
or of the moon	οὐδὲ τῆς σελήνης
to **shine** on it	ἵνα **φαίνωσιν** αὐτῇ
because God's glory	ἡ γὰρ δόξα τοῦ θεοῦ
illumines it	ἐφώτισεν αὐτήν
and the **Lamb**	καὶ . . . τὸ **ἀρνίον**
is its light	ὁ λύχνος αὐτῆς

Next the devil **took (παραλαμβάνει)** Him to a very high
mountain (ὄρος) and **showed (δείκνυσιν)** Him all the kingdoms
of the world and their splendor. (MLB)

δείκνυμι	to show, point out	30x
deiknumi		S1166

ὄρος ▹ 1:255   **παραλαμβάνω** ▹ 1:313

Πάλιν **παραλαμβάνει** αὐτὸν ὁ διάβολος εἰς **ὄρος** ὑψηλὸν λίαν,
καὶ **δείκνυσιν** αὐτῷ πάσας τὰς βασιλείας τοῦ κόσμου καὶ τὴν
δόξαν αὐτῶν,

Next	Πάλιν
the devil **took** Him	**παραλαμβάνει** αὐτὸν ὁ διάβολος
to a very high **mountain**	εἰς **ὄρος** ὑψηλὸν λίαν
and **showed** Him	καὶ **δείκνυσιν** αὐτῷ
all the kingdoms of the world	πάσας τὰς βασιλείας τοῦ κόσμου
and their splendor	καὶ τὴν δόξαν αὐτῶν

But I have **a few things (ὀλίγα)** against you. You have some there **who hold to (κρατοῦντας)** the **teaching (διδαχὴν)** of Balaam, who taught Balak to place a stumbling block in front of the Israelites: to eat meat sacrificed to idols and to commit sexual immorality. (CSB)

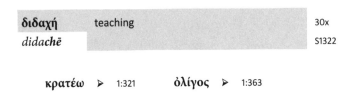

διδαχή	teaching	30x
didachē		S1322

κρατέω ➤ 1:321   **ὀλίγος** ➤ 1:363

ἀλλὰ ἔχω κατὰ σοῦ **ὀλίγα**, ὅτι ἔχεις ἐκεῖ **κρατοῦντας** τὴν **διδαχὴν** Βαλαάμ, ὃς ἐδίδασκεν τῷ Βαλὰκ βαλεῖν σκάνδαλον ἐνώπιον τῶν υἱῶν Ἰσραήλ, φαγεῖν εἰδωλόθυτα καὶ πορνεῦσαι·

But I have **a few things** against you	ἀλλὰ ἔχω κατὰ σοῦ **ὀλίγα**
You have . . . there	ὅτι ἔχεις ἐκεῖ
some . . . **who hold to** the **teaching** of Balaam	**κρατοῦντας** τὴν **διδαχὴν** Βαλαάμ
who taught Balak	ὃς ἐδίδασκεν τῷ Βαλὰκ
to place a stumbling block	βαλεῖν σκάνδαλον
in front of the Israelites	ἐνώπιον τῶν υἱῶν Ἰσραήλ
to eat meat sacrificed to idols	φαγεῖν εἰδωλόθυτα
and to commit sexual immorality	καὶ πορνεῦσαι

Then **they returned (ὑπέστρεψαν)** to Jerusalem from the mount called Olivet, which is **near (ἐγγὺς)** Jerusalem, a Sabbath day's journey away [lit., having a **journey (ὁδόν)** of a Sabbath]. (ESV)

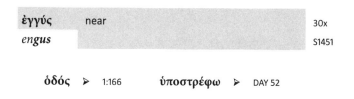

| ἐγγύς | near | 30x |
| *engus* | | S1451 |

ὁδός ➤ 1:166   ὑποστρέφω ➤ DAY 52

Τότε **ὑπέστρεψαν** εἰς Ἰερουσαλὴμ ἀπὸ ὄρους τοῦ καλουμένου Ἐλαιῶνος, ὅ ἐστιν **ἐγγὺς** Ἰερουσαλὴμ σαββάτου ἔχον **ὁδόν**.

Then **they returned**	Τότε **ὑπέστρεψαν**
to Jerusalem	εἰς Ἰερουσαλὴμ
from the mount	ἀπὸ ὄρους
called Olivet	τοῦ καλουμένου Ἐλαιῶνος
which is **near** Jerusalem	ὅ ἐστιν **ἐγγὺς** Ἰερουσαλὴμ
a Sabbath day's journey away [lit., having a **journey** of a Sabbath]	σαββάτου ἔχον **ὁδόν**

As **he was about to (Μέλλων)** be brought into the barracks, Paul said to the commander, "Am I allowed [lit., **is it permissible (ἔξεστίν)** for me] to say something to you?" He replied, "**You know (γινώσκεις)** how to speak Greek?" (CSB)

| ἔξεστι | it is permitted, allowed | 30x |
| *exesti* | | S1832 |

γινώσκω ➤ 1:70   μέλλω ➤ 1:152

Μέλλων τε εἰσάγεσθαι εἰς τὴν παρεμβολὴν ὁ Παῦλος λέγει τῷ χιλιάρχῳ Εἰ **ἔξεστίν** μοι εἰπεῖν τι πρὸς σέ; ὁ δὲ ἔφη Ἑλληνιστὶ **γινώσκεις**;

As **he was about to**	**Μέλλων** τε
be brought into the barracks	εἰσάγεσθαι εἰς τὴν παρεμβολὴν
Paul said to the commander	ὁ Παῦλος λέγει τῷ χιλιάρχῳ
Am I allowed [lit., **is it permissible** for me]	Εἰ **ἔξεστίν** μοι
to say something to you?	εἰπεῖν τι πρὸς σέ;
He replied	ὁ δὲ ἔφη
You know how to speak Greek?	Ἑλληνιστὶ **γινώσκεις**;

Then Festus, after he had conferred with his council, **replied** (ἀπεκρίθη), "You have appealed (ἐπικέκλησαι) to the emperor; to the emperor **you will go** (πορεύσῃ)." (NRSV)

ἐπικαλέω	to call (upon), appeal to, address	30x
epikaleō		S1941

ἀποκρίνομαι ▷ 1:68   πορεύομαι ▷ 1:105

τότε ὁ Φῆστος συνλαλήσας μετὰ τοῦ συμβουλίου **ἀπεκρίθη** Καίσαρα **ἐπικέκλησαι**, ἐπὶ Καίσαρα **πορεύσῃ**.

Then Festus	τότε ὁ Φῆστος
after he had conferred with his council	συνλαλήσας μετὰ τοῦ συμβουλίου
replied	**ἀπεκρίθη**
You have appealed to the emperor	Καίσαρα **ἐπικέκλησαι**
to the emperor **you will go**	ἐπὶ Καίσαρα **πορεύσῃ**

They came and woke him up, saying, "Master, Master, we're going to die!" Then he got up and **rebuked (ἐπετίμησεν)** the **wind (ἀνέμῳ)** and the raging waves [lit., the raging wave of **water (ὕδατος)**]. So they ceased, and there was a calm. (CSB)

ἐπιτιμάω	to rebuke, warn	30x
epitimaō		S2008

ὕδωρ ▷ 1:218   **ἄνεμος** ▷ DAY 77

προσελθόντες δὲ διήγειραν αὐτὸν λέγοντες Ἐπιστάτα ἐπιστάτα, ἀπολλύμεθα· ὁ δὲ διεγερθεὶς **ἐπετίμησεν** τῷ **ἀνέμῳ** καὶ τῷ κλύδωνι τοῦ **ὕδατος**, καὶ ἐπαύσαντο, καὶ ἐγένετο γαλήνη.

They came	προσελθόντες δὲ
and woke him up	διήγειραν αὐτὸν
saying	λέγοντες
Master, Master, we're going to die!	Ἐπιστάτα ἐπιστάτα, ἀπολλύμεθα
Then he got up	ὁ δὲ διεγερθεὶς
and **rebuked** the **wind**	**ἐπετίμησεν** τῷ **ἀνέμῳ**
and the raging waves [lit., the raging wave of **water**]	καὶ τῷ κλύδωνι τοῦ **ὕδατος**
So they ceased	καὶ ἐπαύσαντο
and there was a calm	καὶ ἐγένετο γαλήνη

as (**καθὼς**) he says also in **another place** (**ἑτέρῳ**), "You are a **priest** (**ἱερεὺς**) forever, according to the order of Melchizedek."
(NRSV)

ἱερεύς	priest	30x
hiereus		S2409

καθώς ➤ 1:87   **ἕτερος** ➤ 1:171

καθὼς καὶ ἐν **ἑτέρῳ** λέγει Σὺ **ἱερεὺς** εἰς τὸν αἰῶνα κατὰ τὴν τάξιν Μελχισεδέκ.

as he says also	**καθὼς** καὶ . . . λέγει
in **another place**	ἐν **ἑτέρῳ**
You are a **priest**	Σὺ **ἱερεὺς**
forever	εἰς τὸν αἰῶνα
according to the order of Melchizedek	κατὰ τὴν τάξιν Μελχισεδέκ

For as often as you eat this bread and drink the **cup (ποτήριον)**, you will proclaim the Lord's death **till (ἄχρι οὖ) He comes (ἔλθῃ)**.
(MLB)

ποτήριον	cup	30x
potērion		S4221

ἔρχομαι ➤ 1:30   **ἄχρι** ➤ 1:311

ὁσάκις γὰρ ἐὰν ἐσθίητε τὸν ἄρτον τοῦτον καὶ τὸ **ποτήριον** πίνητε, τὸν θάνατον τοῦ κυρίου καταγγέλλετε, **ἄχρι** οὖ **ἔλθῃ**.

For as often as	ὁσάκις γὰρ ἐὰν
you eat this bread	ἐσθίητε τὸν ἄρτον τοῦτον
and drink the **cup**	καὶ τὸ **ποτήριον** πίνητε
you will proclaim the Lord's death	τὸν θάνατον τοῦ κυρίου καταγγέλλετε
till He comes	**ἄχρι** οὖ **ἔλθῃ**

And when the sixth hour had come, there was **darkness (σκότος)** over the **whole (ὅλην)** land **until (ἕως)** the ninth hour. (ESV)

σκότος	darkness	30x
skotos		S4655

ἕως ➤ 1:111   **ὅλος** ➤ 1:156

Καὶ γενομένης ὥρας ἕκτης **σκότος** ἐγένετο ἐφ᾽ **ὅλην** τὴν γῆν **ἕως** ὥρας ἐνάτης.

And when the sixth hour had come	Καὶ γενομένης ὥρας ἕκτης
there was **darkness**	**σκότος** ἐγένετο
over the **whole** land	ἐφ᾽ **ὅλην** τὴν γῆν
until the ninth hour	**ἕως** ὥρας ἐνάτης

And at this sound the **multitude (πλῆθος) came together (συνῆλθε)**, and they were bewildered, because each one was hearing them speak in **his own (ἰδίᾳ)** language. (ESV)

συνέρχομαι *sunerchomai*	to accompany, go along with, come together	30x S4905

ἴδιος   ➢   1:151   **πλῆθος**   ➢   DAY 83

γενομένης δὲ τῆς φωνῆς ταύτης **συνῆλθε** τὸ **πλῆθος** καὶ συνεχύθη, ὅτι ἤκουσεν εἷς ἕκαστος τῇ **ἰδίᾳ** διαλέκτῳ λαλούντων αὐτῶν·

And at this sound	γενομένης δὲ τῆς φωνῆς ταύτης
the **multitude came together**	**συνῆλθε** τὸ **πλῆθος**
and they were bewildered	καὶ συνεχύθη
because each one was hearing them speak	ὅτι ἤκουσεν εἷς ἕκαστος . . . λαλούντων αὐτῶν
in **his own** language	τῇ **ἰδίᾳ** διαλέκτῳ

And so by your **knowledge (γνώσει)** this **weak person
(ἀσθενῶν) is destroyed (ἀπόλλυται)**, the brother for whom
Christ died. (ESV)

γνῶσις	knowledge	29x
gnōsis		S1108

ἀπόλλυμι	➤	1:190	ἀσθενέω	➤	DAY 63

ἀπόλλυται γὰρ ὁ **ἀσθενῶν** ἐν τῇ σῇ **γνώσει**, ὁ ἀδελφὸς δι᾽ ὃν
Χριστὸς ἀπέθανεν.

And so . . . this **weak person is destroyed**	**ἀπόλλυται** γὰρ ὁ **ἀσθενῶν**
by your **knowledge**	ἐν τῇ σῇ **γνώσει**
the brother	ὁ ἀδελφὸς
for whom Christ died	δι᾽ ὃν Χριστὸς ἀπέθανεν

But the others said, "**Hold on (Ἄφες)**! Let us see if **Elijah (Ἡλείας)** comes **to save (σώσων)** Him." (MLB)

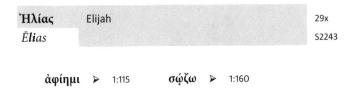

| Ἡλίας | Elijah | 29x |
| Ēlias | | S2243 |

ἀφίημι ➤ 1:115   σώζω ➤ 1:160

οἱ δὲ λοιποὶ εἶπαν Ἄφες ἴδωμεν εἰ ἔρχεται Ἡλείας σώσων αὐτόν.

But the others said	οἱ δὲ λοιποὶ εἶπαν
Hold on!	**Ἄφες**
Let us see	ἴδωμεν
if **Elijah** comes	εἰ ἔρχεται **Ἡλείας**
to save Him	**σώσων** αὐτόν

Look, I am coming soon, and my **reward (μισθός)** is with me **to repay (ἀποδοῦναι)** each person according to [lit., as is] his **work (ἔργον).** (CSB)

μισθός *misthos*	wages, pay, reward, recompense	29x S3408

ἔργον ➤ 1:92   **ἀποδίδωμι** ➤ 1:317

Ἰδοὺ ἔρχομαι ταχύ, καὶ ὁ **μισθός** μου μετ᾽ ἐμοῦ, **ἀποδοῦναι** ἑκάστῳ ὡς τὸ **ἔργον** ἐστὶν αὐτοῦ.

Look	Ἰδοὺ
I am coming soon	ἔρχομαι ταχύ
and my **reward** is with me	καὶ ὁ **μισθός** μου μετ᾽ ἐμοῦ
to repay each person	**ἀποδοῦναι** ἑκάστῳ
according to [lit., as is]	ὡς . . . ἐστὶν
his **work**	τὸ **ἔργον** . . . αὐτοῦ

If anyone **imagines (δοκεῖ)** that he knows something, he does **not yet (οὔπω)** know as he **ought (δεῖ)** to know. (ESV)

οὔπω	not yet	29x
oupō		S3768

δεῖ ➤ 1:161   **δοκέω** ➤ 1:256

εἴ τις **δοκεῖ** ἐγνωκέναι τι, **οὔπω** ἔγνω καθὼς **δεῖ** γνῶναι·

If anyone **imagines**	εἴ τις **δοκεῖ**
that he knows something	ἐγνωκέναι τι
he does **not yet** know	**οὔπω** ἔγνω
as he **ought** to know	καθὼς **δεῖ** γνῶναι

begging us earnestly [lit., with much **entreaty (παρακλήσεως)**] for the **privilege (χάριν)** of sharing in [lit., and the sharing of] this **ministry (διακονίας)** to the saints . . . (NRSV)

παράκλησις	encouragement, comfort, appeal, exhortation	29x
paraklēsis		S3874

χάρις	➤	1:106	διακονία ➤ DAY 56	

μετὰ πολλῆς **παρακλήσεως** δεόμενοι ἡμῶν, τὴν **χάριν** καὶ τὴν κοινωνίαν τῆς **διακονίας** τῆς εἰς τοὺς ἁγίους,

begging us	δεόμενοι ἡμῶν
earnestly [lit., with much **entreaty**]	μετὰ πολλῆς **παρακλήσεως**
for the **privilege**	τὴν **χάριν**
of sharing in [lit., and the sharing of]	καὶ τὴν κοινωνίαν
this **ministry**	τῆς **διακονίας**
to the saints	τῆς εἰς τοὺς ἁγίους

He went a little farther, **fell (ἔπιπτεν)** to the ground, and **prayed (προσηύχετο)** that if it were possible, the hour **might pass (παρέλθῃ)** from him. (CSB)

| παρέρχομαι | to pass (by), disappear, transgress, approach | 29x |
| *parerchomai* | | S3928 |

πίπτω ➤ 1:191   **προσεύχομαι** ➤ 1:198

καὶ προελθὼν μικρὸν **ἔπιπτεν** ἐπὶ τῆς γῆς, καὶ **προσηύχετο** ἵνα εἰ δυνατόν ἐστιν **παρέλθῃ** ἀπ᾽ αὐτοῦ ἡ ὥρα,

He went a little farther	καὶ προελθὼν μικρὸν
fell to the ground	**ἔπιπτεν** ἐπὶ τῆς γῆς
and **prayed**	καὶ **προσηύχετο**
that if it were possible	ἵνα εἰ δυνατόν ἐστιν
the hour **might pass**	**παρέλθῃ** . . . ἡ ὥρα
from him	ἀπ᾽ αὐτοῦ

You know that the **Passover (πάσχα)** takes place after two days,
and the Son of Man **will be handed over (παραδίδοται) to be
crucified (σταυρωθῆναι).** (CSB)

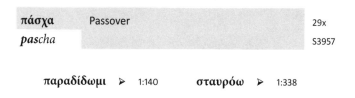

πάσχα	Passover	29x
pascha		S3957

παραδίδωμι ➤ 1:140　　　**σταυρόω** ➤ 1:338

Οἴδατε ὅτι μετὰ δύο ἡμέρας τὸ **πάσχα** γίνεται, καὶ ὁ υἱὸς τοῦ
ἀνθρώπου **παραδίδοται** εἰς τὸ **σταυρωθῆναι.**

You know that	Οἴδατε ὅτι
the **Passover** takes place	τὸ **πάσχα** γίνεται
after two days	μετὰ δύο ἡμέρας
and the Son of Man	καὶ ὁ υἱὸς τοῦ ἀνθρώπου
will be handed over	**παραδίδοται**
to be crucified	εἰς τὸ **σταυρωθῆναι**

The man answered and said to them, "Well, here is an amazing thing, that you do not know **where** He is **from (πόθεν)**, and yet **He opened (ἤνοιξέν)** my **eyes (ὀφθαλμούς)**." (NASB)

πόθεν	from where? from what place? how?	29x
pothen		S4159

ὀφθαλμός ➤ 1:169   ἀνοίγω ➤ 1:221

ἀπεκρίθη ὁ ἄνθρωπος καὶ εἶπεν αὐτοῖς Ἐν τούτῳ γὰρ τὸ θαυμαστόν ἐστιν ὅτι ὑμεῖς οὐκ οἴδατε **πόθεν** ἐστίν, καὶ **ἤνοιξέν** μου τοὺς **ὀφθαλμούς**.

The man answered	ἀπεκρίθη ὁ ἄνθρωπος
and said to them	καὶ εἶπεν αὐτοῖς
Well, here is an amazing thing	Ἐν τούτῳ γὰρ τὸ θαυμαστόν ἐστιν
that you do not know	ὅτι ὑμεῖς οὐκ οἴδατε
where He is **from**	**πόθεν** ἐστίν
and yet **He opened** my **eyes**	καὶ **ἤνοιξέν** μου τοὺς **ὀφθαλμούς**

But **only (μόνον)**, they kept hearing, "He **who once persecuted (διώκων . . . ποτὲ)** us is now preaching the faith which he **once (ποτε)** tried to destroy." (NASB)

| ποτέ
pote | once, formerly, ever, at one time, at some time, at any time | 29x
S4218 |

　　μόνον ▷ 1:244　　　**διώκω** ▷ 1:333

μόνον δὲ ἀκούοντες ἦσαν ὅτι Ὁ **διώκων** ἡμᾶς **ποτὲ** νῦν εὐαγγελίζεται τὴν πίστιν ἥν **ποτε** ἐπόρθει,

But **only**	**μόνον** δὲ
they kept hearing	ἀκούοντες ἦσαν ὅτι
He **who once persecuted** us	Ὁ **διώκων** ἡμᾶς **ποτὲ**
is now preaching the faith	νῦν εὐαγγελίζεται τὴν πίστιν
which he **once** tried to destroy	ἥν **ποτε** ἐπόρθει

It would be better for him if a millstone were hung around his neck and he were thrown into the **sea (θάλασσαν)**, than that **he would cause** one of these **little ones (μικρῶν)** to stumble **(σκανδαλίσῃ)**. (NASB)

σκανδαλίζω	to cause to stumble	29x
skandalizō		S4624

θάλασσα ➤ 1:188   **μικρός** ➤ 1:328

λυσιτελεῖ αὐτῷ εἰ λίθος μυλικὸς περίκειται περὶ τὸν τράχηλον αὐτοῦ καὶ ἔρριπται εἰς τὴν **θάλασσαν** ἢ ἵνα **σκανδαλίσῃ** τῶν **μικρῶν** τούτων ἕνα.

It would be better for him	λυσιτελεῖ αὐτῷ
if a millstone	εἰ λίθος μυλικὸς
were hung around his neck	περίκειται περὶ τὸν τράχηλον αὐτοῦ
and he were thrown into the **sea**	καὶ ἔρριπται εἰς τὴν **θάλασσαν**
than that **he would cause . . . to stumble**	ἢ ἵνα **σκανδαλίσῃ**
one of these **little ones**	τῶν **μικρῶν** τούτων ἕνα

I am telling the **truth** (Ἀλήθειαν) in Christ, I am not lying, my **conscience** (συνειδήσεώς) testifies with me in the Holy **Spirit** (πνεύματι). (NASB)

| συνείδησις | conscience | 29x |
| *suneidēsis* | | S4893 |

πνεῦμα ➤ 1:47   ἀλήθεια ➤ 1:154

Ἀλήθειαν λέγω ἐν Χριστῷ, οὐ ψεύδομαι, συνμαρτυρούσης μοι τῆς **συνειδήσεώς** μου ἐν **πνεύματι** ἁγίῳ,

I am telling the **truth**	Ἀλήθειαν λέγω
in Christ	ἐν Χριστῷ
I am not lying	οὐ ψεύδομαι
my **conscience**	τῆς **συνειδήσεώς** μου
testifies with me	συνμαρτυρούσης μοι
in the Holy **Spirit**	ἐν **πνεύματι** ἁγίῳ

He then said to the crowds **who came out (ἐκπορευομένοις)** to be baptized by him, "Brood of vipers! Who warned you **to flee (φυγεῖν)** from the **coming (μελλούσης)** wrath?" (CSB)

φεύγω	to flee, escape	29x
pheugō		S5343

μέλλω ➤ 1:152   **ἐκπορεύομαι** ➤ DAY 70

Ἔλεγεν οὖν τοῖς **ἐκπορευομένοις** ὄχλοις βαπτισθῆναι ὑπ᾽ αὐτοῦ Γεννήματα ἐχιδνῶν, τίς ὑπέδειξεν ὑμῖν **φυγεῖν** ἀπὸ τῆς **μελλούσης** ὀργῆς;

He then said	Ἔλεγεν οὖν
to the crowds **who came out**	τοῖς **ἐκπορευομένοις** ὄχλοις
to be baptized by him	βαπτισθῆναι ὑπ᾽ αὐτοῦ
Brood of vipers!	Γεννήματα ἐχιδνῶν
Who warned you	τίς ὑπέδειξεν ὑμῖν
to flee	**φυγεῖν**
from the **coming** wrath?	ἀπὸ τῆς **μελλούσης** ὀργῆς;

No one (οὐδεὶς) has **greater (μείζονα)** love than this, that someone would lay down his life for his **friends (φίλων)**. (HCSB)

φίλος	friend, friendly	29x
philos		S5384

μέγας ➤ 1:63   οὐδείς, οὐδεμία, οὐδέν ➤ 1:65

μείζονα ταύτης ἀγάπην **οὐδεὶς** ἔχει, ἵνα τις τὴν ψυχὴν αὐτοῦ θῇ ὑπὲρ τῶν **φίλων** αὐτοῦ.

No one has	**οὐδεὶς** ἔχει
greater love	**μείζονα** . . . ἀγάπην
than this	ταύτης
that someone	ἵνα τις
would lay down	θῇ
his life	τὴν ψυχὴν αὐτοῦ
for his **friends**	ὑπὲρ τῶν **φίλων** αὐτοῦ

To the church of God that **is (οὔσῃ)** in Corinth, to **those who are sanctified (ἡγιασμένοις)** in Christ Jesus, called to be saints, together with all those **who** in every place **call on (ἐπικαλουμένοις)** the name of our Lord Jesus Christ, both their Lord [lit., theirs] and ours: (NRSV)

ἁγιάζω	to sanctify, make holy	28x
hagiazō		S37

     εἰμί   ➤   1:8   ἐπικαλέω   ➤   DAY 95

τῇ ἐκκλησίᾳ τοῦ θεοῦ τῇ **οὔσῃ** ἐν Κορίνθῳ, **ἡγιασμένοις** ἐν Χριστῷ Ἰησοῦ, κλητοῖς ἁγίοις, σὺν πᾶσιν τοῖς **ἐπικαλουμένοις** τὸ ὄνομα τοῦ κυρίου ἡμῶν Ἰησοῦ Χριστοῦ ἐν παντὶ τόπῳ αὐτῶν καὶ ἡμῶν·

To the church of God	τῇ ἐκκλησίᾳ τοῦ θεοῦ
that **is** in Corinth	τῇ **οὔσῃ** ἐν Κορίνθῳ
to **those who are sanctified** in Christ Jesus	**ἡγιασμένοις** ἐν Χριστῷ Ἰησοῦ
called to be saints	κλητοῖς ἁγίοις
together with all those **who** . . . **call on**	σὺν πᾶσιν τοῖς **ἐπικαλουμένοις**
in every place	ἐν παντὶ τόπῳ
the name of our Lord Jesus Christ	τὸ ὄνομα τοῦ κυρίου ἡμῶν Ἰησοῦ Χριστοῦ
both their Lord [lit., theirs] and ours	αὐτῶν καὶ ἡμῶν

For Christ did not enter a **holy place (ἅγια)** made with hands, a mere copy of the **true one (ἀληθινῶν)**, but into heaven itself, now to appear in the **presence (προσώπῳ)** of God for us. (NASB)

ἀληθινός	true, genuine	28x
alēthinos		S228

    ἅγιος ➤ 1:67   **πρόσωπον** ➤ 1:231

οὐ γὰρ εἰς χειροποίητα εἰσῆλθεν **ἅγια** Χριστός, ἀντίτυπα τῶν **ἀληθινῶν**, ἀλλ᾽ εἰς αὐτὸν τὸν οὐρανόν, νῦν ἐμφανισθῆναι τῷ **προσώπῳ** τοῦ θεοῦ ὑπὲρ ἡμῶν·

For Christ did not enter	οὐ γὰρ εἰς . . . εἰσῆλθεν . . . Χριστός
a **holy place** made with hands	χειροποίητα . . . **ἅγια**
a mere copy of the **true one**	ἀντίτυπα τῶν **ἀληθινῶν**
but into heaven itself	ἀλλ᾽ εἰς αὐτὸν τὸν οὐρανόν
now to appear	νῦν ἐμφανισθῆναι
in the **presence** of God	τῷ **προσώπῳ** τοῦ θεοῦ
for us	ὑπὲρ ἡμῶν

Then after fourteen **years (ἐτῶν) I went up (ἀνέβην)** again to
Jerusalem with **Barnabas (Βαρνάβα)**, taking Titus along with me.
(ESV)

Βαρναβᾶς	Barnabas	28x
Barnabas		S921

ἀναβαίνω ➤ 1:206   ἔτος ➤ 1:312

Ἔπειτα διὰ δεκατεσσάρων **ἐτῶν** πάλιν **ἀνέβην** εἰς Ἱεροσόλυμα
μετὰ **Βαρνάβα**, συνπαραλαβὼν καὶ Τίτον·

Then	Ἔπειτα
after fourteen **years**	διὰ δεκατεσσάρων **ἐτῶν**
I went up again	πάλιν **ἀνέβην**
to Jerusalem	εἰς Ἱεροσόλυμα
with **Barnabas**	μετὰ **Βαρνάβα**
taking Titus along with me	συνπαραλαβὼν καὶ Τίτον

They were eating (ἤσθιον), they were drinking, **they were marrying (ἐγάμουν)**, they were being given in marriage, **until (ἄχρι)** the day that Noah entered the ark, and the flood came and destroyed them all. (NASB)

γαμέω	to marry	28x
gameō		S1060

ἐσθίω　➤　1:100　　　ἄχρι　➤　1:311

ἤσθιον, ἔπινον, **ἐγάμουν**, ἐγαμίζοντο, **ἄχρι** ἧς ἡμέρας εἰσῆλθεν Νῶε εἰς τὴν κιβωτόν, καὶ ἦλθεν ὁ κατακλυσμὸς καὶ ἀπώλεσεν πάντας.

They were eating	**ἤσθιον**
they were drinking	ἔπινον
they were marrying	**ἐγάμουν**
they were being given in marriage	ἐγαμίζοντο
until the day that	**ἄχρι** ἧς ἡμέρας
Noah entered the ark	εἰσῆλθεν Νῶε εἰς τὴν κιβωτόν
and the flood came	καὶ ἦλθεν ὁ κατακλυσμὸς
and destroyed them all	καὶ ἀπώλεσεν πάντας

who has made us competent to be **ministers (διακόνους)** of a
new **covenant (διαθήκης)**, not of letter but of spirit; for the letter
kills (ἀποκτείνει), but the Spirit gives life. (NRSV)

διάκονος	servant, minister, deacon	28x
diakonos		S1249

    ἀποκτείνω ➤ 1:226   **διαθήκη** ➤ DAY 64

ὃς καὶ ἱκάνωσεν ἡμᾶς **διακόνους** καινῆς **διαθήκης**, οὐ γράμματος
ἀλλὰ πνεύματος, τὸ γὰρ γράμμα **ἀποκτείνει**, τὸ δὲ πνεῦμα
ζωοποιεῖ.

who has made us competent	ὃς καὶ ἱκάνωσεν ἡμᾶς
to be **ministers**	**διακόνους**
of a new **covenant**	καινῆς **διαθήκης**
not of letter	οὐ γράμματος
but of spirit	ἀλλὰ πνεύματος
for the letter **kills**	τὸ γὰρ γράμμα **ἀποκτείνει**
but the Spirit gives life	τὸ δὲ πνεῦμα ζωοποιεῖ

But you are not to be that way. Instead, the **most prominent**
(**μείζων**) among you must be as the youngest, and the **leader**
(**ἡγούμενος**) as one **who serves** (**διακονῶν**). (MLB)

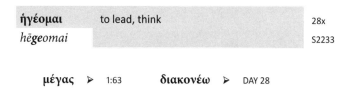

| **ἡγέομαι** | to lead, think | 28x |
| *hēgeomai* | | S2233 |

    μέγας ➤ 1:63   **διακονέω** ➤ DAY 28

ὑμεῖς δὲ οὐχ οὕτως, ἀλλ᾽ ὁ **μείζων** ἐν ὑμῖν γινέσθω ὡς ὁ
νεώτερος, καὶ ὁ **ἡγούμενος** ὡς ὁ **διακονῶν**·

But you	ὑμεῖς δὲ
are not to be that way	οὐχ οὕτως
Instead	ἀλλ᾽
the **most prominent** among you	ὁ **μείζων** ἐν ὑμῖν
must be	γινέσθω
as the youngest	ὡς ὁ νεώτερος
and the **leader**	καὶ ὁ **ἡγούμενος**
as one **who serves**	ὡς ὁ **διακονῶν**

When **Herod**'s (Ἡρῴδου) birthday celebration came, Herodias's
daughter (θυγάτηρ) danced before them [lit., in the **midst**
(μέσῳ)] and pleased **Herod** (Ἡρῴδῃ). (CSB)

θυγάτηρ	daughter	28x
thugatēr		S2364

μέσος ➤ 1:277   Ἡρῴδης ➤ 1:347

γενεσίοις δὲ γενομένοις τοῦ **Ἡρῴδου** ὠρχήσατο ἡ **θυγάτηρ** τῆς
Ἡρῳδιάδος ἐν τῷ **μέσῳ** καὶ ἤρεσεν τῷ **Ἡρῴδῃ**,

When **Herod**'s birthday celebration came	γενεσίοις δὲ γενομένοις τοῦ **Ἡρῴδου**
Herodias's **daughter** danced	ὠρχήσατο ἡ **θυγάτηρ** τῆς Ἡρῳδιάδος
before them [lit., in the **midst**]	ἐν τῷ **μέσῳ**
and pleased **Herod**	καὶ ἤρεσεν τῷ **Ἡρῴδῃ**

But even if I am being poured out as a libation over the **sacrifice** (**θυσία**) and the offering of your faith, **I am glad (χαίρω)** and rejoice with **all (πᾶσιν)** of you. (NRSV)

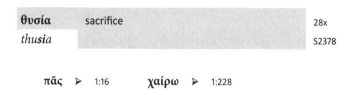

| **θυσία** | sacrifice | 28x |
| *thusia* | | S2378 |

πᾶς   ➤   1:16   χαίρω   ➤   1:228

Ἀλλὰ εἰ καὶ σπένδομαι ἐπὶ τῇ **θυσίᾳ** καὶ λειτουργίᾳ τῆς πίστεως ὑμῶν, **χαίρω** καὶ συνχαίρω **πᾶσιν** ὑμῖν·

But even if	Ἀλλὰ εἰ καὶ
I am being poured out as a libation	σπένδομαι
over the **sacrifice**	ἐπὶ τῇ **θυσίᾳ**
and the offering	καὶ λειτουργίᾳ
of your faith	τῆς πίστεως ὑμῶν
I am glad	**χαίρω**
and rejoice with **all** of you	καὶ συνχαίρω **πᾶσιν** ὑμῖν

You (Ὑμεῖς) are the salt of the earth; but if the salt has become tasteless, how can it be made salty again? **It is** no longer **good (ἰσχύει)** for anything, except **to be thrown (βληθὲν)** out and trampled under foot by men. (NASB)

ἰσχύω	to be strong, be able, have strength	28x
ischuō		S2480

σύ, (pl) ὑμεῖς   ➤   1:4   βάλλω   ➤   1:134

Ὑμεῖς ἐστε τὸ ἅλας τῆς γῆς· ἐὰν δὲ τὸ ἅλας μωρανθῇ, ἐν τίνι ἁλισθήσεται; εἰς οὐδὲν **ἰσχύει** ἔτι εἰ μὴ **βληθὲν** ἔξω καταπατεῖσθαι ὑπὸ τῶν ἀνθρώπων.

You are	Ὑμεῖς ἐστε
the salt of the earth	τὸ ἅλας τῆς γῆς
but if the salt has become tasteless	ἐὰν δὲ τὸ ἅλας μωρανθῇ
how	ἐν τίνι
can it be made salty again?	ἁλισθήσεται;
It is no longer **good** for anything	εἰς οὐδὲν **ἰσχύει** ἔτι
except **to be thrown** out	εἰ μὴ **βληθὲν** ἔξω
and trampled under foot by men	καταπατεῖσθαι ὑπὸ τῶν ἀνθρώπων

Who shall separate **us (ἡμᾶς)** from the love of Christ? Shall **trouble (θλίψις)** or hardship or persecution or famine or nakedness or danger or **sword (μάχαιρα)**? (NIV)

μάχαιρα	sword	28x
machaira		S3162

ἐγώ, (pl) ἡμεῖς ➤ 1:7   θλῖψις ➤ 1:339

τίς **ἡμᾶς** χωρίσει ἀπὸ τῆς ἀγάπης τοῦ χριστοῦ; **θλίψις** ἢ στενοχωρία ἢ διωγμὸς ἢ λιμὸς ἢ γυμνότης ἢ κίνδυνος ἢ **μάχαιρα**;

Who shall separate **us**	τίς **ἡμᾶς** χωρίσει
from the love of Christ?	ἀπὸ τῆς ἀγάπης τοῦ χριστοῦ;
Shall **trouble**	**θλίψις**
or hardship or persecution	ἢ στενοχωρία ἢ διωγμὸς
or famine or nakedness	ἢ λιμὸς ἢ γυμνότης
or danger or **sword**?	ἢ κίνδυνος ἢ **μάχαιρα**;

to whom God willed to make known what is the riches of the glory of this **mystery (μυστηρίου)** among the **Gentiles (ἔθνεσιν)**, which is Christ in you, the **hope (ἐλπὶς)** of glory. (NASB)

μυστήριον	secret, mystery	28x
mustērion		S3466

ἔθνος ➤ 1:98   **ἐλπίς** ➤ 1:296

οἷς ἠθέλησεν ὁ θεὸς γνωρίσαι τί τὸ πλοῦτος τῆς δόξης τοῦ **μυστηρίου** τούτου ἐν τοῖς **ἔθνεσιν**, ὅ ἐστιν Χριστὸς ἐν ὑμῖν, ἡ **ἐλπὶς** τῆς δόξης·

to whom God willed	οἷς ἠθέλησεν ὁ θεὸς
to make known	γνωρίσαι
what is the riches	τί τὸ πλοῦτος
of the glory	τῆς δόξης
of this **mystery**	τοῦ **μυστηρίου** τούτου
among the **Gentiles**	ἐν τοῖς **ἔθνεσιν**
which is Christ in you	ὅ ἐστιν Χριστὸς ἐν ὑμῖν
the **hope** of glory	ἡ **ἐλπὶς** τῆς δόξης

These things **I have spoken (λελάληκα)** to you, so that in Me you may have peace. In the world you have **tribulation (θλῖψιν)**, but take courage; I **have overcome (νενίκηκα)** the world. (NASB)

νικάω	to conquer	28x
nikaō		S3528

λαλέω ➤ 1:57   **θλῖψις** ➤ 1:339

ταῦτα **λελάληκα** ὑμῖν ἵνα ἐν ἐμοὶ εἰρήνην ἔχητε· ἐν τῷ κόσμῳ **θλῖψιν** ἔχετε, ἀλλὰ θαρσεῖτε, ἐγὼ **νενίκηκα** τὸν κόσμον.

These things **I have spoken** to you	ταῦτα **λελάληκα** ὑμῖν
so that in Me you may have peace	ἵνα ἐν ἐμοὶ εἰρήνην ἔχητε
In the world you have **tribulation**	ἐν τῷ κόσμῳ **θλῖψιν** ἔχετε
but take courage	ἀλλὰ θαρσεῖτε
I **have overcome** the world	ἐγὼ **νενίκηκα** τὸν κόσμον

And when Paul **had laid (ἐπιθέντος)** his hands on them, the
Holy Spirit came on them, and they began speaking in **tongues
(γλώσσαις)** and **prophesying (ἐπροφήτευον)**. (ESV)

προφητεύω	to prophesy, declare	28x
prophēteuō		S4395

γλῶσσα ▷ 1:318   ἐπιτίθημι ▷ DAY 23

καὶ **ἐπιθέντος** αὐτοῖς τοῦ Παύλου χεῖρας ἦλθε τὸ πνεῦμα τὸ ἅγιον
ἐπ᾽ αὐτούς, ἐλάλουν τε **γλώσσαις** καὶ **ἐπροφήτευον**.

And when Paul **had laid** his hands on them	καὶ **ἐπιθέντος** αὐτοῖς τοῦ Παύλου χεῖρας
the Holy Spirit came on them	ἦλθε τὸ πνεῦμα τὸ ἅγιον ἐπ᾽ αὐτούς
and they began speaking in **tongues**	ἐλάλουν τε **γλώσσαις**
and **prophesying**	καὶ **ἐπροφήτευον**

When Jesus had received [lit., **he had received (ἔλαβεν)**] the
sour wine, he [lit., Jesus] said, "**It is finished (Τετέλεσται)**." Then
bowing his head, **he gave up (παρέδωκεν)** his spirit. (CSB)

| τελέω | to end, complete, finish, accomplish, fulfill | 28x |
| *teleō* | | S5055 |

λαμβάνω ➤ 1:60　　　**παραδίδωμι** ➤ 1:140

ὅτε οὖν **ἔλαβεν** τὸ ὄξος [ὁ] Ἰησοῦς εἶπεν **Τετέλεσται**, καὶ κλίνας
τὴν κεφαλὴν **παρέδωκεν** τὸ πνεῦμα.

When Jesus had received [lit., **he had received**] the sour wine	ὅτε οὖν **ἔλαβεν** τὸ ὄξος
he [lit., Jesus] said	[ὁ] Ἰησοῦς εἶπεν
It is finished	**Τετέλεσται**
Then bowing his head	καὶ κλίνας τὴν κεφαλὴν
he gave up his spirit	**παρέδωκεν** τὸ πνεῦμα

He said: "A certain nobleman **went (ἐπορεύθη)** to a distant **land (χώραν)** to acquire a kingdom for himself and **to return (ὑποστρέψαι)**." (MLB)

χώρα	field, country, district, region	28x
chōra		S5561

πορεύομαι ▷ 1:105   **ὑποστρέφω** ▷ DAY 52

εἶπεν οὖν Ἄνθρωπός τις εὐγενὴς **ἐπορεύθη** εἰς **χώραν** μακρὰν λαβεῖν ἑαυτῷ βασιλείαν καὶ **ὑποστρέψαι**.

He said	εἶπεν οὖν
A certain nobleman	Ἄνθρωπός τις εὐγενὴς
went	**ἐπορεύθη**
to a distant **land**	εἰς **χώραν** μακρὰν
to acquire a kingdom for himself	λαβεῖν ἑαυτῷ βασιλείαν
and **to return**	καὶ **ὑποστρέψαι**

But Paul said, "I am **standing** (Ἑστὼς) before Caesar's tribunal, where I ought to be tried. To the Jews **I have done** no **wrong** (ἠδίκηκα), as **you** yourself **know** (ἐπιγινώσκεις) very well." (ESV)

ἀδικέω	to harm, injure, act unjustly	27x
adikeō		S91

ἵστημι   ▷   1:109   ἐπιγινώσκω   ▷   1:353

εἶπεν δὲ ὁ Παῦλος Ἑστὼς ἐπὶ τοῦ βήματος Καίσαρός εἰμι, οὗ με δεῖ κρίνεσθαι. Ἰουδαίους οὐδὲν **ἠδίκηκα**, ὡς καὶ σὺ κάλλιον **ἐπιγινώσκεις**.

But Paul said	εἶπεν δὲ ὁ Παῦλος
I am **standing**	Ἑστὼς . . . εἰμι
before Caesar's tribunal	ἐπὶ τοῦ βήματος Καίσαρός
where I ought to be tried	οὗ με δεῖ κρίνεσθαι
To the Jews **I have done** no **wrong**	Ἰουδαίους οὐδὲν **ἠδίκηκα**
as **you** yourself **know** very well	ὡς καὶ σὺ κάλλιον **ἐπιγινώσκεις**

He said this, not because he cared about the **poor (πτωχῶν)**, but because he was a thief, and having charge of the moneybag **he used to help himself to (ἐβάσταζεν)** what **was put (βαλλόμενα)** into it. (ESV)

βαστάζω	to bear, carry, take away	27x
bastazō		S941

    βάλλω ➤ 1:134   **πτωχός** ➤ DAY 61

εἶπεν δὲ τοῦτο οὐχ ὅτι περὶ τῶν **πτωχῶν** ἔμελεν αὐτῷ ἀλλ᾽ ὅτι κλέπτης ἦν καὶ τὸ γλωσσόκομον ἔχων τὰ **βαλλόμενα ἐβάσταζεν**.

He said this	εἶπεν δὲ τοῦτο
not because he cared	οὐχ ὅτι . . . ἔμελεν αὐτῷ
about the **poor**	περὶ τῶν **πτωχῶν**
but because he was a thief	ἀλλ᾽ ὅτι κλέπτης ἦν
and having charge of the moneybag	καὶ τὸ γλωσσόκομον ἔχων
he used to help himself to	ἐβάσταζεν
what **was put** into it	τὰ **βαλλόμενα**

As He entered a village, **ten (δέκα)** leprous **men (ἄνδρες)** who **stood (ἀνέστησαν)** at a distance met Him. (NASB)

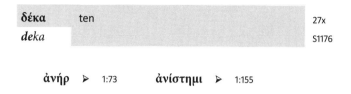

| δέκα | ten | 27x |
| *deka* | | S1176 |

ἀνήρ ➤ 1:73   **ἀνίστημι** ➤ 1:155

Καὶ εἰσερχομένου αὐτοῦ εἴς τινα κώμην ἀπήντησαν **δέκα** λεπροὶ **ἄνδρες**, οἳ **ἀνέστησαν** πόρρωθεν,

As He entered a village	Καὶ εἰσερχομένου αὐτοῦ εἴς τινα κώμην
ten leprous **men**	**δέκα** λεπροὶ **ἄνδρες**
who **stood** at a distance	οἳ **ἀνέστησαν** πόρρωθεν
met Him	ἀπήντησαν

And **hope (ἐλπὶς)** does not disappoint, because the love of God **has been poured out (ἐκκέχυται)** within our hearts through the Holy Spirit who **was given (δοθέντος)** to us. (NASB)

ἐκχέω	to pour out, shed	27x
ekcheō		S1632

     δίδωμι ➤ 1:43   **ἐλπίς** ➤ 1:296

ἡ δὲ **ἐλπὶς** οὐ καταισχύνει. ὅτι ἡ ἀγάπη τοῦ θεοῦ **ἐκκέχυται** ἐν ταῖς καρδίαις ἡμῶν διὰ πνεύματος ἁγίου τοῦ **δοθέντος** ἡμῖν·

And **hope** does not disappoint	ἡ δὲ **ἐλπὶς** οὐ καταισχύνει
because the love of God	ὅτι ἡ ἀγάπη τοῦ θεοῦ
has been poured out	**ἐκκέχυται**
within our hearts	ἐν ταῖς καρδίαις ἡμῶν
through the Holy Spirit	διὰ πνεύματος ἁγίου
who **was given** to us	τοῦ **δοθέντος** ἡμῖν

Grace, **mercy (ἔλεος)**, and peace will be **with (μεθ᾽)** us from God the Father and from Jesus Christ, the Father's Son, in **truth (ἀληθείᾳ)** and love. (NRSV)

ἔλεος	mercy, pity	27x
eleos		S1656

μετά ➤ 1:41　　　　**ἀλήθεια** ➤ 1:154

ἔσται **μεθ**᾽ ἡμῶν χάρις **ἔλεος** εἰρήνη παρὰ θεοῦ πατρός, καὶ παρὰ Ἰησοῦ Χριστοῦ τοῦ υἱοῦ τοῦ πατρός, ἐν **ἀληθείᾳ** καὶ ἀγάπῃ.

Grace, **mercy**, and peace	χάρις **ἔλεος** εἰρήνη
will be **with** us	ἔσται **μεθ**᾽ ἡμῶν
from God the Father	παρὰ θεοῦ πατρός
and from Jesus Christ	καὶ παρὰ Ἰησοῦ Χριστοῦ
the Father's Son	τοῦ υἱοῦ τοῦ πατρός
in **truth** and love	ἐν **ἀληθείᾳ** καὶ ἀγάπῃ

The **night (νὺξ)** is well advanced and the day approaches; so let us put off the works of **darkness (σκότους)** and **let us put on (ἐνδυσώμεθα)** the armor of light. (MLB)

ἐνδύω *enduō*	to clothe, dress, put on	27x S1746

νύξ ➤ 1:266   **σκότος** ➤ DAY 99

ἡ **νὺξ** προέκοψεν, ἡ δὲ ἡμέρα ἤγγικεν. ἀποθώμεθα οὖν τὰ ἔργα τοῦ **σκότους**, **ἐνδυσώμεθα** [δὲ] τὰ ὅπλα τοῦ φωτός.

The **night** is well advanced	ἡ **νὺξ** προέκοψεν
and the day approaches	ἡ δὲ ἡμέρα ἤγγικεν
so let us put off	ἀποθώμεθα οὖν
the works of **darkness**	τὰ ἔργα τοῦ **σκότους**
and **let us put on**	**ἐνδυσώμεθα** [δὲ]
the armor of light	τὰ ὅπλα τοῦ φωτός

By faith **Jacob** (Ἰακὼβ), at the point of death, **blessed**
(εὐλόγησεν) each of Joseph's sons and **bowed in worship**
(προσεκύνησεν) on the top of his staff. (MLB)

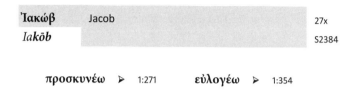

| Ἰακὼβ | Jacob | 27x |
| *Iakōb* | | S2384 |

προσκυνέω ➢ 1:271   εὐλογέω ➢ 1:354

Πίστει **Ἰακὼβ** ἀποθνήσκων ἕκαστον τῶν υἱῶν Ἰωσὴφ **εὐλόγησεν**,
καὶ **προσεκύνησεν** ἐπὶ τὸ ἄκρον τῆς ῥάβδου αὐτοῦ.

By faith **Jacob**	Πίστει **Ἰακὼβ**
at the point of death	ἀποθνήσκων
blessed	**εὐλόγησεν**
each of Joseph's sons	ἕκαστον τῶν υἱῶν Ἰωσὴφ
and **bowed in worship**	καὶ **προσεκύνησεν**
on the top	ἐπὶ τὸ ἄκρον
of his staff	τῆς ῥάβδου αὐτοῦ

Do we, then, **abrogate (καταργοῦμεν)** the Law through faith?
Not at all [lit., **may it** not **be (γένοιτο)**]; instead, **we uphold
(ἱστάνομεν)** the Law. (MLB)

| καταργέω | to annul, abolish, bring to naught | 27x |
| *katargeō* | | S2673 |

γίνομαι ➤ 1:27   ἵστημι ➤ 1:109

νόμον οὖν **καταργοῦμεν** διὰ τῆς πίστεως; μὴ **γένοιτο**, ἀλλὰ
νόμον **ἱστάνομεν**.

Do we, then, **abrogate** the Law	νόμον οὖν **καταργοῦμεν**
through faith?	διὰ τῆς πίστεως;
Not at all [lit., **may it** not **be**]	μὴ **γένοιτο**
instead	ἀλλὰ
we uphold the Law	νόμον **ἱστάνομεν**

Not many should become teachers, my brothers, because **you know (εἰδότες)** that **we will receive (λημψόμεθα)** a stricter **judgment (κρίμα)**. (CSB)

κρίμα *krima*	judgment, verdict, condemnation, lawsuit	27x S2917

     οἶδα ▷ 1:56   λαμβάνω ▷ 1:60

Μὴ πολλοὶ διδάσκαλοι γίνεσθε, ἀδελφοί μου, **εἰδότες** ὅτι μεῖζον **κρίμα λημψόμεθα·**

Not many should become teachers	Μὴ πολλοὶ διδάσκαλοι γίνεσθε
my brothers	ἀδελφοί μου
because **you know** that	**εἰδότες** ὅτι
we will receive	**λημψόμεθα**
a stricter **judgment**	μεῖζον **κρίμα**

Has not the Scripture said that the Christ comes from the **descendants (σπέρματος)** of David, and from Bethlehem, the **village (κώμης) where (ὅπου)** David was? (NASB)

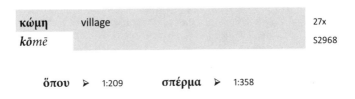

κώμη	village	27x
kōmē		S2968

ὅπου ➤ 1:209   σπέρμα ➤ 1:358

οὐχ ἡ γραφὴ εἶπεν ὅτι ἐκ τοῦ **σπέρματος** Δαυείδ, καὶ ἀπὸ Βηθλεὲμ τῆς **κώμης ὅπου** ἦν Δαυείδ, ἔρχεται ὁ χριστός;

Has not the Scripture said that	οὐχ ἡ γραφὴ εἶπεν ὅτι
the Christ comes	ἔρχεται ὁ χριστός;
from the **descendants** of David	ἐκ τοῦ **σπέρματος** Δαυείδ
and from Bethlehem	καὶ ἀπὸ Βηθλεὲμ
the **village**	τῆς **κώμης**
where David was?	**ὅπου** ἦν Δαυείδ

And Jesus said to his disciples, "**Truly (Ἀμὴν)**, I say to you, only with difficulty **will** a **rich person enter (πλούσιος . . . εἰσελεύσεται)** the kingdom of heaven." (ESV)

πλούσιος	rich, wealthy	27x
plousios		S4145

εἰσέρχομαι　➤　1:82　　　　ἀμήν　➤　1:132

Ὁ δὲ Ἰησοῦς εἶπεν τοῖς μαθηταῖς αὐτοῦ **Ἀμὴν** λέγω ὑμῖν ὅτι **πλούσιος** δυσκόλως **εἰσελεύσεται** εἰς τὴν βασιλείαν τῶν οὐρανῶν·

And Jesus said to his disciples	Ὁ δὲ Ἰησοῦς εἶπεν τοῖς μαθηταῖς αὐτοῦ
Truly	**Ἀμὴν**
I say to you	λέγω ὑμῖν ὅτι
only with difficulty	δυσκόλως
will a **rich person enter**	**πλούσιος . . . εἰσελεύσεται** εἰς
the kingdom of heaven	τὴν βασιλείαν τῶν οὐρανῶν

When they heard it, they praised God. Then they said to him, "**You see (Θεωρεῖς)**, brother, **how many (πόσαι)** thousands of believers there are among the Jews, and **they are (ὑπάρχουσιν)** all zealous for the law." (NRSV)

πόσος	how much, how many, how great;	27x
posos	how much? how many? how great?	S4214

ὑπάρχω ▷ 1:274   **θεωρέω** ▷ 1:297

οἱ δὲ ἀκούσαντες ἐδόξαζον τὸν θεόν, εἶπάν τε αὐτῷ **Θεωρεῖς**, ἀδελφέ, **πόσαι** μυριάδες εἰσὶν ἐν τοῖς Ἰουδαίοις τῶν πεπιστευκότων, καὶ πάντες ζηλωταὶ τοῦ νόμου **ὑπάρχουσιν**·

When they heard it	οἱ δὲ ἀκούσαντες
they praised God	ἐδόξαζον τὸν θεόν
Then they said to him	εἶπάν τε αὐτῷ
You see, brother	**Θεωρεῖς**, ἀδελφέ
how many thousands of believers	**πόσαι** μυριάδες . . . τῶν πεπιστευκότων
there are among the Jews	εἰσὶν ἐν τοῖς Ἰουδαίοις
and **they are** all zealous for the law	καὶ πάντες ζηλωταὶ τοῦ νόμου **ὑπάρχουσιν**

Then Jesus summoned [lit., **he summoned (προσκαλεσάμενος)**] his twelve disciples and gave them authority over **unclean (ἀκαθάρτων)** spirits, to cast them out, and **to cure (θεραπεύειν)** every disease and every sickness. (NRSV)

προσκαλέομαι	to summon, invite, call to	27x
proskaleomai		S4341

θεραπεύω ▷ 1:349   **ἀκάθαρτος** ▷ DAY 89

Καὶ **προσκαλεσάμενος** τοὺς δώδεκα μαθητὰς αὐτοῦ ἔδωκεν αὐτοῖς ἐξουσίαν πνευμάτων **ἀκαθάρτων** ὥστε ἐκβάλλειν αὐτὰ καὶ **θεραπεύειν** πᾶσαν νόσον καὶ πᾶσαν μαλακίαν.

Then Jesus summoned [lit., **he summoned**] his twelve disciples	Καὶ **προσκαλεσάμενος** τοὺς δώδεκα μαθητὰς αὐτοῦ
and gave them authority	ἔδωκεν αὐτοῖς ἐξουσίαν
over **unclean** spirits	πνευμάτων **ἀκαθάρτων**
to cast them out	ὥστε ἐκβάλλειν αὐτὰ
and **to cure** every disease	καὶ **θεραπεύειν** πᾶσαν νόσον
and every sickness	καὶ πᾶσαν μαλακίαν

Why **do you see** (βλέπεις) the speck that is in your brother's **eye** (ὀφθαλμῷ), but do not notice the log that is in **your own** (σῷ) **eye** (ὀφθαλμῷ)? (ESV)

σός, σή, σόν	your	27x
sos, sē, son		S4674

βλέπω ➤ 1:128   ὀφθαλμός ➤ 1:169

τί δὲ **βλέπεις** τὸ κάρφος τὸ ἐν τῷ **ὀφθαλμῷ** τοῦ ἀδελφοῦ σου, τὴν δὲ ἐν τῷ **σῷ ὀφθαλμῷ** δοκὸν οὐ κατανοεῖς;

Why **do you see**	τί δὲ **βλέπεις**
the speck	τὸ κάρφος
that is in your brother's **eye**	τὸ ἐν τῷ **ὀφθαλμῷ** τοῦ ἀδελφοῦ σου
but do not notice	δὲ . . . οὐ κατανοεῖς;
the log	τὴν . . . δοκὸν
that is in **your own eye**?	ἐν τῷ **σῷ ὀφθαλμῷ**

But far be it from me [lit., may it not be for me] **to boast
(καυχᾶσθαι)** except in the **cross (σταυρῷ)** of our Lord Jesus
Christ, by which the world has been crucified to me, **and I (κἀγὼ)**
to the world. (ESV)

σταυρός	cross, crucifixion	27x
stauros		S4716

κἀγώ ➤ 1:204   καυχάομαι ➤ DAY 32

ἐμοὶ δὲ μὴ γένοιτο **καυχᾶσθαι** εἰ μὴ ἐν τῷ **σταυρῷ** τοῦ κυρίου
ἡμῶν Ἰησοῦ Χριστοῦ, δι᾽ οὗ ἐμοὶ κόσμος ἐσταύρωται **κἀγὼ**
κόσμῳ.

But far be it from me [lit., may it not be for me]	ἐμοὶ δὲ μὴ γένοιτο
to boast	**καυχᾶσθαι**
except in the **cross**	εἰ μὴ ἐν τῷ **σταυρῷ**
of our Lord Jesus Christ	τοῦ κυρίου ἡμῶν Ἰησοῦ Χριστοῦ
by which the world has been crucified to me	δι᾽ οὗ ἐμοὶ κόσμος ἐσταύρωται
and I to the world	**κἀγὼ** κόσμῳ

On the other hand, I am writing a **new (καινὴν)** commandment to you, which is **true (ἀληθὲς)** in Him and in you, because the darkness is passing away and the true light **is** already **shining (φαίνει).** (NASB)

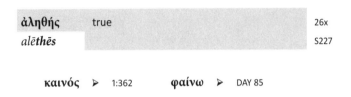

| ἀληθής | true | 26x |
| *alēthēs* | | S227 |

καινός ▷ 1:362   **φαίνω** ▷ DAY 85

πάλιν ἐντολὴν **καινὴν** γράφω ὑμῖν, ὅ ἐστιν **ἀληθὲς** ἐν αὐτῷ καὶ ἐν ὑμῖν, ὅτι ἡ σκοτία παράγεται καὶ τὸ φῶς τὸ ἀληθινὸν ἤδη **φαίνει.**

On the other hand	πάλιν
I am writing . . . to you	γράφω ὑμῖν
a **new** commandment	ἐντολὴν **καινὴν**
which is **true**	ὅ ἐστιν **ἀληθὲς**
in Him and in you	ἐν αὐτῷ καὶ ἐν ὑμῖν
because the darkness	ὅτι ἡ σκοτία
is passing away	παράγεται
and the true light	καὶ τὸ φῶς τὸ ἀληθινὸν
is already **shining**	ἤδη **φαίνει**

He made known (**γνωρίσας**) to us the mystery of His **will** (**θελήματος**), **according to** (**κατὰ**) His kind intention which He purposed in Him. (NASB)

| **γνωρίζω** | to make known | 26x |
| *gnōrizo* | | S1107 |

κατά ➤ 1:39   **θέλημα** ➤ 1:287

γνωρίσας ἡμῖν τὸ μυστήριον τοῦ **θελήματος** αὐτοῦ, **κατὰ** τὴν εὐδοκίαν αὐτοῦ ἣν προέθετο ἐν αὐτῷ

He made known to us	**γνωρίσας** ἡμῖν
the mystery	τὸ μυστήριον
of His **will**	τοῦ **θελήματος** αὐτοῦ
according to His kind intention	**κατὰ** τὴν εὐδοκίαν αὐτοῦ
which He purposed	ἣν προέθετο
in Him	ἐν αὐτῷ

Meanwhile, some **were shouting (ἔκραζον)** one thing, some another; for the assembly was in confusion, and most of them did not know why [lit., **on account of (ἕνεκα)** what] **they had come together (συνεληλύθεισαν)**. (NRSV)

| ἕνεκα | on account of, for the sake of, because of | 26x |
| *heneka* | | S1752 |

κράζω ➤ 1:282   συνέρχομαι ➤ DAY 100

ἄλλοι μὲν οὖν ἄλλο τι **ἔκραζον**, ἦν γὰρ ἡ ἐκκλησία συνκεχυμένη, καὶ οἱ πλείους οὐκ ᾔδεισαν τίνος **ἕνεκα συνεληλύθεισαν**.

Meanwhile, some **were shouting** one thing, some another	ἄλλοι μὲν οὖν ἄλλο τι **ἔκραζον**
for the assembly was in confusion	ἦν γὰρ ἡ ἐκκλησία συνκεχυμένη
and most of them did not know	καὶ οἱ πλείους οὐκ ᾔδεισαν
why [lit., **on account of** what] **they had come together**	τίνος **ἕνεκα συνεληλύθεισαν**

For a **will (διαθήκη)** takes effect only at death, **since (ἐπεὶ) it is**
not **in force (ἰσχύει)** as long as the one who made it is alive. (ESV)

| ἐπεί | after, for, since, otherwise | 26x |
| *epei* | | S1893 |

    διαθήκη ➤ DAY 64   **ἰσχύω** ➤ DAY 122

διαθήκη γὰρ ἐπὶ νεκροῖς βεβαία, **ἐπεὶ** μὴ τότε **ἰσχύει** ὅτε ζῇ ὁ
διαθέμενος.

For a **will**	**διαθήκη** γὰρ
takes effect only at death	ἐπὶ νεκροῖς βεβαία
since it is not **in force**	**ἐπεὶ** μὴ . . . **ἰσχύει**
as long as	τότε . . . ὅτε
the one who made it is alive	ζῇ ὁ διαθέμενος

One of them, when he saw **he was healed (ἰάθη)**, **came back (ὑπέστρεψεν)**, **praising (δοξάζων)** God in a loud voice. (NIV)

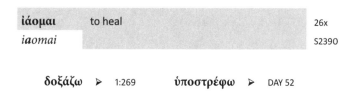

ἰάομαι	to heal	26x
iaomai		S2390

δοξάζω ➤ 1:269   **ὑποστρέφω** ➤ DAY 52

εἷς δὲ ἐξ αὐτῶν, ἰδὼν ὅτι **ἰάθη**, **ὑπέστρεψεν** μετὰ φωνῆς μεγάλης **δοξάζων** τὸν θεόν,

One of them	εἷς δὲ ἐξ αὐτῶν
when he saw **he was healed**	ἰδὼν ὅτι **ἰάθη**
came back	**ὑπέστρεψεν**
praising God	**δοξάζων** τὸν θεόν
in a loud voice	μετὰ φωνῆς μεγάλης

But the **goal (τέλος)** of our instruction is love from a **pure (καθαρᾶς)** heart and a good **conscience (συνειδήσεως)** and a sincere faith. (NASB)

καθαρός	clean, pure	26x
katharos		S2513

τέλος ➤ DAY 2   **συνείδησις** ➤ DAY 111

τὸ δὲ **τέλος** τῆς παραγγελίας ἐστὶν ἀγάπη ἐκ **καθαρᾶς** καρδίας καὶ **συνειδήσεως** ἀγαθῆς καὶ πίστεως ἀνυποκρίτου,

But the **goal** of our instruction	τὸ δὲ **τέλος** τῆς παραγγελίας
is love	ἐστὶν ἀγάπη
from a **pure** heart	ἐκ **καθαρᾶς** καρδίας
and a good **conscience**	καὶ **συνειδήσεως** ἀγαθῆς
and a sincere faith	καὶ πίστεως ἀνυποκρίτου

Tell us then, what is your opinion [lit., how **does it seem (δοκεῖ)** to you]? **Is it right (ἔξεστιν)** to pay the imperial tax to **Caesar (Καίσαρι)** or not? (NIV)

| Καῖσαρ | Caesar, Emperor | 26x |
| *Kaisar* | | S2541 |

δοκέω ➤ 1:256   **ἔξεστι** ➤ DAY 94

εἰπὸν οὖν ἡμῖν τί σοι **δοκεῖ· ἔξεστιν** δοῦναι κῆνσον **Καίσαρι** ἢ οὔ;

Tell us then	εἰπὸν οὖν ἡμῖν
what is your opinion [lit., how **does it seem** to you]?	τί σοι **δοκεῖ**
Is it right	**ἔξεστιν**
to pay the imperial tax	δοῦναι κῆνσον
to **Caesar**	**Καίσαρι**
or not?	ἢ οὔ;

Very truly I tell you, you **will weep (κλαύσετε)** and mourn while the world **rejoices (χαρήσεται)**. You **will grieve (λυπηθήσεσθε)**, but your grief will turn to joy. (NIV)

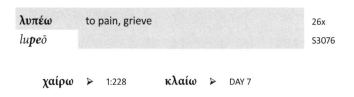

| λυπέω | to pain, grieve | 26x |
| *lupeō* | | S3076 |

χαίρω ➤ 1:228　　κλαίω ➤ DAY 7

ἀμὴν ἀμὴν λέγω ὑμῖν ὅτι **κλαύσετε** καὶ θρηνήσετε ὑμεῖς, ὁ δὲ κόσμος **χαρήσεται**· ὑμεῖς **λυπηθήσεσθε**, ἀλλ᾽ ἡ λύπη ὑμῶν εἰς χαρὰν γενήσεται.

Very truly I tell you	ἀμὴν ἀμὴν λέγω ὑμῖν ὅτι
you **will weep** and mourn	**κλαύσετε** καὶ θρηνήσετε ὑμεῖς
while the world **rejoices**	ὁ δὲ κόσμος **χαρήσεται**
You **will grieve**	ὑμεῖς **λυπηθήσεσθε**
but your grief	ἀλλ᾽ ἡ λύπη ὑμῶν
will turn to joy	εἰς χαρὰν γενήσεται

But I say to you, Do not **swear (ὀμόσαι)** at all, **either (μήτε)** by heaven, for it is the **throne (θρόνος)** of God, . . . (NRSV)

ὀμνύω	to swear, take an oath	26x
omnuō		S3660

θρόνος ▷ 1:259   **μήτε** ▷ DAY 58

Ἐγὼ δὲ λέγω ὑμῖν μὴ **ὀμόσαι** ὅλως· **μήτε** ἐν τῷ οὐρανῷ, ὅτι **θρόνος** ἐστὶν τοῦ θεοῦ·

But I say to you	Ἐγὼ δὲ λέγω ὑμῖν
Do not **swear** at all	μὴ **ὀμόσαι** ὅλως
either by heaven	**μήτε** ἐν τῷ οὐρανῷ
for it is the **throne** of God	ὅτι **θρόνος** ἐστὶν τοῦ θεοῦ

For the Sadducees say that there is no **resurrection (ἀνάστασιν)**,
nor angel, nor spirit, but the **Pharisees (Φαρισαῖοι) acknowledge
(ὁμολογοῦσιν)** them all. (ESV)

| ὁμολογέω | to promise, confess, acknowledge | 26x |
| *homologeō* | | S3670 |

Φαρισαῖος ➤ 1:176   **ἀνάστασις** ➤ 1:351

Σαδδουκαῖοι γὰρ λέγουσιν μὴ εἶναι **ἀνάστασιν** μήτε ἄγγελον
μήτε πνεῦμα, **Φαρισαῖοι** δὲ **ὁμολογοῦσιν** τὰ ἀμφότερα.

For the Sadducees say that	Σαδδουκαῖοι γὰρ λέγουσιν
there is no **resurrection**	μὴ εἶναι **ἀνάστασιν**
nor angel	μήτε ἄγγελον
nor spirit	μήτε πνεῦμα
but the **Pharisees acknowledge**	**Φαρισαῖοι** δὲ **ὁμολογοῦσιν**
them all	τὰ ἀμφότερα

If anyone thinks he is a prophet or **spiritual (πνευματικός), he should recognize (ἐπιγινωσκέτω)** that what I write to you is the Lord's **command (ἐντολή).** (CSB)

| πνευματικός | spiritual | 26x |
| *pneumatikos* | | S4152 |

ἐντολή ➤ 1:239   **ἐπιγινώσκω** ➤ 1:353

Εἴ τις δοκεῖ προφήτης εἶναι ἢ **πνευματικός, ἐπιγινωσκέτω** ἃ γράφω ὑμῖν ὅτι κυρίου ἐστὶν **ἐντολή·**

If anyone thinks he is a prophet	Εἴ τις δοκεῖ προφήτης εἶναι
or **spiritual**	ἢ **πνευματικός**
he should recognize that	**ἐπιγινωσκέτω** . . . ὅτι
what I write to you	ἃ γράφω ὑμῖν
is the Lord's **command**	κυρίου ἐστὶν **ἐντολή**

And when **they had assembled (συναχθέντες)** with the elders and taken counsel, they gave a **sufficient (ἱκανὰ)** sum of money to the **soldiers (στρατιῶται)**. (ESV)

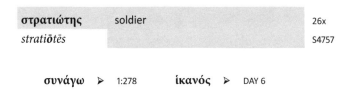

| στρατιώτης | soldier | 26x |
| *stratiōtēs* | | S4757 |

συνάγω　➤　1:278　　　**ἱκανός**　➤　DAY 6

καὶ **συναχθέντες** μετὰ τῶν πρεσβυτέρων συμβούλιόν τε λαβόντες ἀργύρια **ἱκανὰ** ἔδωκαν τοῖς **στρατιώταις**

And when **they had assembled**	καὶ **συναχθέντες**
with the elders	μετὰ τῶν πρεσβυτέρων
and taken counsel	συμβούλιόν τε λαβόντες
they gave	ἔδωκαν
a **sufficient** sum of money	ἀργύρια **ἱκανὰ**
to the **soldiers**	τοῖς **στρατιώταις**

He supposed that his brothers **would understand (συνιέναι)** that God was giving them **salvation (σωτηρίαν)** by his **hand (χειρὸς)**, but they **did** not **understand (συνῆκαν)**. (ESV)

συνίημι	to understand	26x
suniēmi		S4920

χείρ ➤ 1:88   **σωτηρία** ➤ 1:331

ἐνόμιζεν δὲ **συνιέναι** τοὺς ἀδελφοὺς ὅτι ὁ θεὸς διὰ **χειρὸς** αὐτοῦ δίδωσιν **σωτηρίαν** αὐτοῖς, οἱ δὲ οὐ **συνῆκαν**.

He supposed that	ἐνόμιζεν δὲ
his brothers **would understand** that	**συνιέναι** τοὺς ἀδελφοὺς ὅτι
God was giving them **salvation**	ὁ θεὸς . . . δίδωσιν **σωτηρίαν** αὐτοῖς
by his **hand**	διὰ **χειρὸς** αὐτοῦ
but they **did** not **understand**	οἱ δὲ οὐ **συνῆκαν**

True enough (καλῶς); they were broken off because of unbelief, but you stand by faith. Do not be arrogant [lit., do not **think (φρόνει)** of yourselves highly], but **beware (φοβοῦ)**. (CSB)

φρονέω	to think (of), set one's mind upon	26x
phroneō		S5426

φοβέομαι ➤ 1:183   καλῶς ➤ DAY 39

καλῶς· τῇ ἀπιστίᾳ ἐξεκλάσθησαν, σὺ δὲ τῇ πίστει ἔστηκας. μὴ ὑψηλὰ **φρόνει**, ἀλλὰ **φοβοῦ**·

True enough	καλῶς
they were broken off	ἐξεκλάσθησαν
because of unbelief	τῇ ἀπιστίᾳ
but you stand	σὺ δὲ . . . ἔστηκας
by faith	τῇ πίστει
Do not be arrogant [lit., do not **think** of yourselves highly]	μὴ ὑψηλὰ **φρόνει**
but **beware**	ἀλλὰ **φοβοῦ**

They devour **widows' (χηρῶν)** houses and for the sake of appearance **say** long **prayers (προσευχόμενοι)**. They will receive the greater **condemnation (κρίμα)**. (NRSV)

χήρα	widow	26x
chēra		S5503

προσεύχομαι ➢ 1:198   **κρίμα** ➢ DAY 137

οἱ κατέσθοντες τὰς οἰκίας τῶν **χηρῶν** καὶ προφάσει μακρὰ **προσευχόμενοι·** οὗτοι λήμψονται περισσότερον **κρίμα.**

They devour	οἱ κατέσθοντες
widows' houses	τὰς οἰκίας τῶν **χηρῶν**
and for the sake of appearance	καὶ προφάσει
say long **prayers**	μακρὰ **προσευχόμενοι**
They will receive	οὗτοι λήμψονται
the greater **condemnation**	περισσότερον **κρίμα**

Now the son of Paul's **sister (ἀδελφῆς)** heard of their ambush,
so **he went (παραγενόμενος)** and entered the barracks and **told
(ἀπήγγειλεν)** Paul. (ESV)

| ἀδελφή | sister | 25x |
| *adelphē* | | S79 |

ἀπαγγέλλω ➤ 1:343   παραγίνομαι ➤ DAY 41

Ἀκούσας δὲ ὁ υἱὸς τῆς **ἀδελφῆς** Παύλου τὴν ἐνέδραν
παραγενόμενος καὶ εἰσελθὼν εἰς τὴν παρεμβολὴν **ἀπήγγειλεν** τῷ
Παύλῳ.

Now the son of Paul's **sister** heard of	Ἀκούσας δὲ ὁ υἱὸς τῆς **ἀδελφῆς** Παύλου
their ambush	τὴν ἐνέδραν
so **he went**	**παραγενόμενος**
and entered the barracks	καὶ εἰσελθὼν εἰς τὴν παρεμβολὴν
and **told** Paul	**ἀπήγγειλεν** τῷ Παύλῳ

But he will say, "I tell you, **I do** not **know (οἶδα) where** you come [lit., are] **from (πόθεν)**. Depart from me, all you workers of **evil (ἀδικίας)**!" (ESV)

ἀδικία	injustice, unrighteousness	25x
adikia		S93

    οἶδα ➤ 1:56   **πόθεν** ➤ DAY 108

καὶ ἐρεῖ λέγων ὑμῖν Οὐκ **οἶδα πόθεν** ἐστέ· ἀπόστητε ἀπ᾽ ἐμοῦ, πάντες ἐργάται **ἀδικίας**.

But he will say	καὶ ἐρεῖ
I tell you	λέγων ὑμῖν
I do not **know**	Οὐκ **οἶδα**
where you come [lit., are] **from**	**πόθεν** ἐστέ
Depart from me	ἀπόστητε ἀπ᾽ ἐμοῦ
all you workers of **evil**!	πάντες ἐργάται **ἀδικίας**

For **who (τίνες)** were those who heard and yet rebelled? Was it
not all those **who left (ἐξελθόντες) Egypt (Αἰγύπτου)** led by
Moses? (ESV)

Αἴγυπτος	Egypt	25x
Aiguptos		S125

τίς, τί ▷ 1:32   ἐξέρχομαι ▷ 1:71

τίνες γὰρ ἀκούσαντες παρεπίκραναν; ἀλλ᾿ οὐ πάντες οἱ
ἐξελθόντες ἐξ **Αἰγύπτου** διὰ Μωυσέως;

For **who** were those	**τίνες** γὰρ
who heard	ἀκούσαντες
and yet rebelled?	παρεπίκραναν;
Was it not all	ἀλλ᾿ οὐ πάντες
those **who left Egypt**	οἱ **ἐξελθόντες** ἐξ **Αἰγύπτου**
led by Moses?	διὰ Μωυσέως;

For **I consider (Λογίζομαι)** that the sufferings of this present time are not worthy to be compared with the glory **that is (μέλλουσαν) to be revealed (ἀποκαλυφθῆναι)** to us. (NASB)

ἀποκαλύπτω	to reveal, unveil	25x
apokaluptō		S601

μέλλω ➤ 1:152   λογίζομαι ➤ DAY 8

Λογίζομαι γὰρ ὅτι οὐκ ἄξια τὰ παθήματα τοῦ νῦν καιροῦ πρὸς τὴν **μέλλουσαν** δόξαν **ἀποκαλυφθῆναι** εἰς ἡμᾶς.

For **I consider** that	**Λογίζομαι** γὰρ ὅτι
the sufferings of this present time	τὰ παθήματα τοῦ νῦν καιροῦ
are not worthy	οὐκ ἄξια
to be compared with	πρὸς
the glory **that is**	τὴν **μέλλουσαν** δόξαν
to be revealed to us	**ἀποκαλυφθῆναι** εἰς ἡμᾶς

And **we urge (Παρακαλοῦμεν)** you, **brothers (ἀδελφοί)**,
admonish the idle, encourage the fainthearted, help the **weak
(ἀσθενῶν)**, be patient with them all. (ESV)

ἀσθενής	weak, ill	25x
asthenēs		S772

ἀδελφός ▷ 1:51　　παρακαλέω ▷ 1:157

Παρακαλοῦμεν δὲ ὑμᾶς, **ἀδελφοί**, νουθετεῖτε τοὺς ἀτάκτους,
παραμυθεῖσθε τοὺς ὀλιγοψύχους, ἀντέχεσθε τῶν **ἀσθενῶν**,
μακροθυμεῖτε πρὸς πάντας.

And **we urge** you	**Παρακαλοῦμεν** δὲ ὑμᾶς
brothers	ἀδελφοί
admonish the idle	νουθετεῖτε τοὺς ἀτάκτους
encourage the fainthearted	παραμυθεῖσθε τοὺς ὀλιγοψύχους
help the **weak**	ἀντέχεσθε τῶν **ἀσθενῶν**
be patient with them all	μακροθυμεῖτε πρὸς πάντας

Do not **harm (ἀδικήσητε)** the earth or the sea or the **trees (δένδρα)**, **until (ἄχρι)** we have sealed the servants of our God on their foreheads. (ESV)

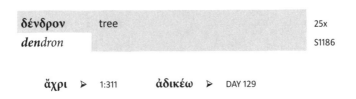

| **δένδρον** | tree | 25x |
| *dendron* | | S1186 |

   ἄχρι   ▷   1:311   **ἀδικέω**   ▷   DAY 129

Μὴ **ἀδικήσητε** τὴν γῆν μήτε τὴν θάλασσαν μήτε τὰ **δένδρα**, **ἄχρι** σφραγίσωμεν τοὺς δούλους τοῦ θεοῦ ἡμῶν ἐπὶ τῶν μετώπων αὐτῶν.

Do not **harm** the earth	Μὴ **ἀδικήσητε** τὴν γῆν
or the sea	μήτε τὴν θάλασσαν
or the **trees**	μήτε τὰ **δένδρα**
until we have sealed	**ἄχρι** σφραγίσωμεν
the servants of our God	τοὺς δούλους τοῦ θεοῦ ἡμῶν
on their foreheads	ἐπὶ τῶν μετώπων αὐτῶν

No one **can (δύναται) serve (δουλεύειν) two (δυσὶ)** masters,
for either he will hate the one and love the other, or he will be
devoted to the one and despise the other. **You can**not **(δύνασθε)
serve (δουλεύειν)** God and money. (ESV)

| δουλεύω | to serve (as a slave) | 25x |
| *douleuō* | | S1398 |

δύναμαι ➤ 1:75   **δύο** ➤ 1:124

Οὐδεὶς **δύναται δυσὶ** κυρίοις **δουλεύειν**· ἢ γὰρ τὸν ἕνα μισήσει
καὶ τὸν ἕτερον ἀγαπήσει, ἢ ἑνὸς ἀνθέξεται καὶ τοῦ ἑτέρου
καταφρονήσει· οὐ **δύνασθε** θεῷ **δουλεύειν** καὶ μαμωνᾷ.

No one **can serve**	Οὐδεὶς **δύναται** . . . **δουλεύειν**
two masters	**δυσὶ** κυρίοις
for either he will hate the one	ἢ γὰρ τὸν ἕνα μισήσει
and love the other	καὶ τὸν ἕτερον ἀγαπήσει
or he will be devoted to the one	ἢ ἑνὸς ἀνθέξεται
and despise the other	καὶ τοῦ ἑτέρου καταφρονήσει
You cannot **serve** God	οὐ **δύνασθε** θεῷ **δουλεύειν**
and money	καὶ μαμωνᾷ

Therefore, don't **let** anyone **judge (κρινέτω)** you in regard to food and drink or in the **matter (μέρει)** of a **festival (ἑορτῆς)** or a new moon or a Sabbath day. (CSB)

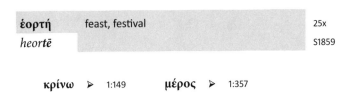

| ἑορτή | feast, festival | 25x |
| *heortē* | | S1859 |

κρίνω ➤ 1:149   μέρος ➤ 1:357

Μὴ οὖν τις ὑμᾶς **κρινέτω** ἐν βρώσει καὶ ἐν πόσει ἢ ἐν **μέρει**
ἑορτῆς ἢ νεομηνίας ἢ σαββάτων,

Therefore	οὖν
don't **let** anyone **judge** you	Μὴ . . . τις ὑμᾶς **κρινέτω**
in regard to food	ἐν βρώσει
and drink	καὶ ἐν πόσει
or in the **matter** of a **festival**	ἢ ἐν **μέρει ἑορτῆς**
or a new moon	ἢ νεομηνίας
or a Sabbath day	ἢ σαββάτων

And I saw a **mighty (ἰσχυρὸν)** angel proclaiming with a loud voice, "Who is **worthy (ἄξιος)** to open the **scroll (βιβλίον)** and break its seals?" (ESV)

ἰσχυρός	strong, powerful	25x
ischuros		S2478

    ἄξιος ➤ 1:359   **βιβλίον** ➤ DAY 53

καὶ εἶδον ἄγγελον **ἰσχυρὸν** κηρύσσοντα ἐν φωνῇ μεγάλῃ Τίς **ἄξιος** ἀνοῖξαι τὸ **βιβλίον** καὶ λῦσαι τὰς σφραγῖδας αὐτοῦ;

And I saw	καὶ εἶδον
a **mighty** angel	ἄγγελον **ἰσχυρὸν**
proclaiming with a loud voice	κηρύσσοντα ἐν φωνῇ μεγάλῃ
Who is **worthy**	Τίς **ἄξιος**
to open the **scroll**	ἀνοῖξαι τὸ **βιβλίον**
and break its seals?	καὶ λῦσαι τὰς σφραγῖδας αὐτοῦ;

They entered the **tomb (μνημεῖον)** and saw a young man sitting to the **right (δεξιοῖς)**, dressed in a **white (λευκήν)** robe, and they were struck with terror. (MLB)

λευκός	white	25x
leukos		S3022

δεξιός ➤ 1:290   **μνημεῖον** ➤ DAY 17

καὶ εἰσελθοῦσαι εἰς τὸ **μνημεῖον** εἶδον νεανίσκον καθήμενον ἐν τοῖς **δεξιοῖς** περιβεβλημένον στολὴν **λευκήν**, καὶ ἐξεθαμβήθησαν.

They entered the **tomb**	καὶ εἰσελθοῦσαι εἰς τὸ **μνημεῖον**
and saw a young man	εἶδον νεανίσκον
sitting	καθήμενον
to the **right**	ἐν τοῖς **δεξιοῖς**
dressed in	περιβεβλημένον
a **white** robe	στολὴν **λευκήν**
and they were struck with terror	καὶ ἐξεθαμβήθησαν

But go and **learn (μάθετε)** what this means: "I desire **mercy** (Ἔλεος), not **sacrifice (θυσίαν)**." For I have not come to call the righteous, but sinners. (NIV)

μανθάνω	to learn, ascertain	25x
manthanō		S3129

θυσία ➤ DAY 121　　　　**ἔλεος** ➤ DAY 133

πορευθέντες δὲ **μάθετε** τί ἐστιν Ἔλεος θέλω καὶ οὐ **θυσίαν·** οὐ γὰρ ἦλθον καλέσαι δικαίους ἀλλὰ ἁμαρτωλούς.

But go	πορευθέντες δὲ
and **learn**	**μάθετε**
what this means	τί ἐστιν
I desire **mercy**	Ἔλεος θέλω
not **sacrifice**	καὶ οὐ **θυσίαν**
For I have not come	οὐ γὰρ ἦλθον
to call the righteous	καλέσαι δικαίους
but sinners	ἀλλὰ ἁμαρτωλούς

These are hidden reefs at your love feasts, as they feast with you without fear, shepherds feeding themselves; waterless **clouds** (**νεφέλαι**), swept along by **winds (ἀνέμων)**; fruitless **trees** (**δένδρα**) in late autumn, twice dead, uprooted; . . . (ESV)

| **νεφέλη** | cloud | 25x |
| *nephelē* | | S3507 |

     ἄνεμος ➤ DAY 77   **δένδρον** ➤ DAY 164

οὗτοί εἰσιν οἱ ἐν ταῖς ἀγάπαις ὑμῶν σπιλάδες συνευωχούμενοι, ἀφόβως ἑαυτοὺς ποιμαίνοντες, **νεφέλαι** ἄνυδροι ὑπὸ **ἀνέμων** παραφερόμεναι, **δένδρα** φθινοπωρινὰ ἄκαρπα δὶς ἀποθανόντα ἐκριζωθέντα,

These are hidden reefs at your love feasts	οὗτοί εἰσιν οἱ ἐν ταῖς ἀγάπαις ὑμῶν σπιλάδες
as they feast with you without fear	συνευωχούμενοι, ἀφόβως
shepherds feeding themselves	ἑαυτοὺς ποιμαίνοντες
waterless **clouds**	**νεφέλαι** ἄνυδροι
swept along by **winds**	ὑπὸ **ἀνέμων** παραφερόμεναι
fruitless **trees** in late autumn	**δένδρα** φθινοπωρινὰ ἄκαρπα
twice dead	δὶς ἀποθανόντα
uprooted	ἐκριζωθέντα

The kings of the earth committed sexual immorality with her, and those **who live (κατοικοῦντες)** on the earth became drunk on the **wine (οἴνου)** of her **sexual immorality (πορνείας)**. (CSB)

πορνεία	sexual immorality	25x
porneia		S4202

κατοικέω ➤ 1:341   **οἶνος** ➤ DAY 60

μεθ᾽ ἧς ἐπόρνευσαν οἱ βασιλεῖς τῆς γῆς, καὶ ἐμεθύσθησαν οἱ **κατοικοῦντες** τὴν γῆν ἐκ τοῦ **οἴνου** τῆς **πορνείας** αὐτῆς.

The kings of the earth	οἱ βασιλεῖς τῆς γῆς
committed sexual immorality	ἐπόρνευσαν
with her	μεθ᾽ ἧς
and those **who live** on the earth	καὶ . . . οἱ **κατοικοῦντες** τὴν γῆν
became drunk	ἐμεθύσθησαν
on the **wine**	ἐκ τοῦ **οἴνου**
of her **sexual immorality**	τῆς **πορνείας** αὐτῆς

When they had eaten breakfast, Jesus said to Simon Peter, "Simon, son of John, do you love Me more than these do?" He said to Him, "Yes, Lord, You **know (οἶδας)** that **I love (φιλῶ)** You as a dear friend." He told him, "Feed My **lambs (ἀρνία)**." (MLB)

| φιλέω | to love, kiss | 25x |
| *phileō* | | S5368 |

οἶδα ➤ 1:56   ἀρνίον ➤ DAY 90

Ὅτε οὖν ἠρίστησαν λέγει τῷ Σίμωνι Πέτρῳ ὁ Ἰησοῦς Σίμων Ἰωάνου, ἀγαπᾷς με πλέον τούτων; λέγει αὐτῷ Ναί, κύριε, σὺ **οἶδας** ὅτι **φιλῶ** σε. λέγει αὐτῷ Βόσκε τὰ **ἀρνία** μου.

When they had eaten breakfast	Ὅτε οὖν ἠρίστησαν
Jesus said to Simon Peter	λέγει τῷ Σίμωνι Πέτρῳ ὁ Ἰησοῦς
Simon, son of John	Σίμων Ἰωάνου
do you love Me more than these do?	ἀγαπᾷς με πλέον τούτων;
He said to Him	λέγει αὐτῷ
Yes, Lord	Ναί, κύριε
You **know** that **I love** You as a dear friend	σὺ **οἶδας** ὅτι **φιλῶ** σε
He told him	λέγει αὐτῷ
Feed My **lambs**	Βόσκε τὰ **ἀρνία** μου

I **only (μόνον)** want **to learn (μαθεῖν)** this from you: Did you receive the Spirit by the works of the law or by **hearing (ἀκοῆς)** with faith? (HCSB)

ἀκοή	hearing, report, rumor	24x
akoē		S189

μόνον ➢ 1:244   **μανθάνω** ➢ DAY 169

τοῦτο **μόνον** θέλω **μαθεῖν** ἀφ᾽ ὑμῶν, ἐξ ἔργων νόμου τὸ πνεῦμα ἐλάβετε ἢ ἐξ **ἀκοῆς** πίστεως;

I . . . want **to learn**	θέλω **μαθεῖν**
only . . . this	τοῦτο **μόνον**
from you	ἀφ᾽ ὑμῶν
Did you receive the Spirit	τὸ πνεῦμα ἐλάβετε
by the works of the law	ἐξ ἔργων νόμου
or by **hearing** with faith?	ἢ ἐξ **ἀκοῆς** πίστεως;

At once (εὐθέως) something like scales fell from his eyes, and
he regained his sight (ἀνέβλεψέν). Then he got up and **was
baptized (ἐβαπτίσθη).** (CSB)

| ἀναβλέπω | to look up, recover one's sight | 24x |
| *anablepō* | | S308 |

βαπτίζω ➤ 1:219   **εὐθέως** ➤ DAY 65

καὶ **εὐθέως** ἀπέπεσαν αὐτοῦ ἀπὸ τῶν ὀφθαλμῶν ὡς λεπίδες,
ἀνέβλεψέν τε, καὶ ἀναστὰς **ἐβαπτίσθη,**

At once	καὶ **εὐθέως**
something like scales fell	ἀπέπεσαν . . . ὡς λεπίδες
from his eyes	αὐτοῦ ἀπὸ τῶν ὀφθαλμῶν
and **he regained his sight**	**ἀνέβλεψέν** τε
Then he got up	καὶ ἀναστὰς
and **was baptized**	**ἐβαπτίσθη**

Two **others (ἕτεροι)** also, who were criminals, **were being led away (Ἤγοντο) to be put to death (ἀναιρεθῆναι)** with Him.
(NASB)

| ἀναιρέω | to murder, take up | 24x |
| *anaireō* | | S337 |

ἕτερος　▷　1:171　　　ἄγω　▷　1:238

Ἤγοντο δὲ καὶ ἕτεροι κακοῦργοι δύο σὺν αὐτῷ ἀναιρεθῆναι.

Two **others** also	δὲ καὶ ἕτεροι . . . δύο
who were criminals	κακοῦργοι
were being led away	Ἤγοντο
to be put to death	ἀναιρεθῆναι
with Him	σὺν αὐτῷ

But word about Him spread even more, and large crowds
gathered (συνήρχοντο) to listen and **to be healed
(θεραπεύεσθαι)** of their **diseases (ἀσθενειῶν)**. (MLB)

ἀσθένεια	weakness, illness	24x
astheneia		S769

θεραπεύω ▷ 1:349   **συνέρχομαι** ▷ DAY 100

διήρχετο δὲ μᾶλλον ὁ λόγος περὶ αὐτοῦ, καὶ **συνήρχοντο** ὄχλοι
πολλοὶ ἀκούειν καὶ **θεραπεύεσθαι** ἀπὸ τῶν **ἀσθενειῶν** αὐτῶν·

But word about Him	δὲ . . . ὁ λόγος περὶ αὐτοῦ
spread even more	διήρχετο . . . μᾶλλον
and large crowds **gathered**	καὶ **συνήρχοντο** ὄχλοι πολλοὶ
to listen	ἀκούειν
and **to be healed**	καὶ **θεραπεύεσθαι**
of their **diseases**	ἀπὸ τῶν **ἀσθενειῶν** αὐτῶν

Where (Ποῦ) is the newborn king of the Jews? For we saw His **star (ἀστέρα)** in the east and we have come **to worship (προσκυνῆσαι)** Him. (MLB)

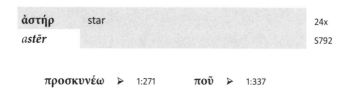

| ἀστήρ | star | 24x |
| astēr | | S792 |

    προσκυνέω ➤ 1:271   **ποῦ** ➤ 1:337

Ποῦ ἐστὶν ὁ τεχθεὶς βασιλεὺς τῶν Ἰουδαίων; εἴδομεν γὰρ αὐτοῦ τὸν **ἀστέρα** ἐν τῇ ἀνατολῇ καὶ ἤλθομεν **προσκυνῆσαι** αὐτῷ.

Where is	**Ποῦ** ἐστὶν
the newborn king	ὁ τεχθεὶς βασιλεὺς
of the Jews?	τῶν Ἰουδαίων;
For we saw His **star**	εἴδομεν γὰρ αὐτοῦ τὸν **ἀστέρα**
in the east	ἐν τῇ ἀνατολῇ
and we have come	καὶ ἤλθομεν
to worship Him	**προσκυνῆσαι** αὐτῷ

So then, brethren, stand firm and hold to the traditions which **you were taught (ἐδιδάχθητε)**, **whether (εἴτε)** by word of mouth **or (εἴτε)** by **letter (ἐπιστολῆς)** from us. (NASB)

ἐπιστολή	letter	24x
epistolē		S1992

διδάσκω ➤ 1:177   **εἴτε** ➤ 1:251

Ἄρα οὖν, ἀδελφοί, στήκετε, καὶ κρατεῖτε τὰς παραδόσεις ἃς **ἐδιδάχθητε εἴτε** διὰ λόγου **εἴτε** δι᾽ **ἐπιστολῆς** ἡμῶν.

So then	Ἄρα οὖν
brethren	ἀδελφοί
stand firm	στήκετε
and hold to the traditions	καὶ κρατεῖτε τὰς παραδόσεις
which **you were taught**	ἃς **ἐδιδάχθητε**
whether by word of mouth	**εἴτε** διὰ λόγου
or by **letter** from us	**εἴτε** δι᾽ **ἐπιστολῆς** ἡμῶν

Then he added, "See, **I have come (ἥκω)** to do your will." **He abolishes (ἀναιρεῖ)** the first in order **to establish (στήσῃ)** the second. (NRSV)

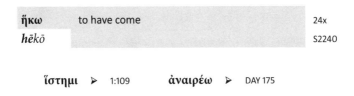

| **ἥκω** | to have come | 24x |
| *hēkō* | | S2240 |

ἵστημι ➤ 1:109   **ἀναιρέω** ➤ DAY 175

τότε εἴρηκεν Ἰδοὺ **ἥκω** τοῦ ποιῆσαι τὸ θέλημά σου· **ἀναιρεῖ** τὸ πρῶτον ἵνα τὸ δεύτερον **στήσῃ**.

Then he added	τότε εἴρηκεν
See	Ἰδοὺ
I have come	**ἥκω**
to do your will	τοῦ ποιῆσαι τὸ θέλημά σου
He abolishes the first	**ἀναιρεῖ** τὸ πρῶτον
in order **to establish** the second	ἵνα τὸ δεύτερον **στήσῃ**

And the twelve **called together (προσκαλεσάμενοι)** the **whole community (πλῆθος)** of the disciples and said, "It is not right that we **should neglect (καταλείψαντας)** the word of God in order to wait on tables." (NRSV)

καταλείπω	to leave behind, desert, abandon	24x
kataleipō		S2641

  πλῆθος ➤ DAY 83   **προσκαλέομαι** ➤ DAY 141

προσκαλεσάμενοι δὲ οἱ δώδεκα τὸ **πλῆθος** τῶν μαθητῶν εἶπαν Οὐκ ἀρεστόν ἐστιν ἡμᾶς **καταλείψαντας** τὸν λόγον τοῦ θεοῦ διακονεῖν τραπέζαις·

And the twelve **called together**	**προσκαλεσάμενοι** δὲ οἱ δώδεκα
the **whole community** of the disciples	τὸ **πλῆθος** τῶν μαθητῶν
and said	εἶπαν
It is not right that we	Οὐκ ἀρεστόν ἐστιν ἡμᾶς
should neglect the word of God	**καταλείψαντας** τὸν λόγον τοῦ θεοῦ
in order to wait on tables	διακονεῖν τραπέζαις

Even **now (ἤδη)** the ax **is lying (κεῖται)** at the root of the **trees
(δένδρων)**; every **tree (δένδρον)** therefore that does not bear
good fruit is cut down and thrown into the fire. (NRSV)

| κεῖμαι | to lie, be placed | 24x |
| *keimai* | | S2749 |

ἤδη ➢ 1:258   **δένδρον** ➢ DAY 164

ἤδη δὲ ἡ ἀξίνη πρὸς τὴν ῥίζαν τῶν **δένδρων κεῖται**· πᾶν οὖν
δένδρον μὴ ποιοῦν καρπὸν καλὸν ἐκκόπτεται καὶ εἰς πῦρ
βάλλεται.

Even **now**	**ἤδη** δὲ
the ax **is lying**	ἡ ἀξίνη . . . **κεῖται**
at the root of the **trees**	πρὸς τὴν ῥίζαν τῶν **δένδρων**
every **tree** therefore	πᾶν οὖν **δένδρον**
that does not bear good fruit	μὴ ποιοῦν καρπὸν καλὸν
is cut down	ἐκκόπτεται
and thrown into the fire	καὶ εἰς πῦρ βάλλεται

Take care (**βλέπετε**), brothers, **lest (μήποτε)** there be in any of you an evil, unbelieving heart, leading you to fall away from the **living (ζῶντος)** God. (ESV)

μήποτε	lest (at any time), whether perhaps	24x
mēpote		S3379

ζάω ➤ 1:121   βλέπω ➤ 1:128

βλέπετε, ἀδελφοί, **μήποτε** ἔσται ἔν τινι ὑμῶν καρδία πονηρὰ ἀπιστίας ἐν τῷ ἀποστῆναι ἀπὸ θεοῦ **ζῶντος**,

Take care	βλέπετε
brothers	ἀδελφοί
lest there be	**μήποτε** ἔσται
in any of you	ἔν τινι ὑμῶν
an evil, unbelieving heart	καρδία πονηρὰ ἀπιστίας
leading you to fall away	ἐν τῷ ἀποστῆναι
from the **living** God	ἀπὸ θεοῦ **ζῶντος**

Don't rebuke an **older man (Πρεσβυτέρῳ)**, but **exhort (παρακάλει)** him as a father, **younger men (νεωτέρους)** as brothers, . . . (CSB)

νέος	young, new	24x
neos		S3501

παρακαλέω   ➤   1:157   πρεσβύτερος   ➤   1:248

Πρεσβυτέρῳ μὴ ἐπιπλήξῃς, ἀλλὰ **παρακάλει** ὡς πατέρα, **νεωτέρους** ὡς ἀδελφούς,

Don't rebuke	μὴ ἐπιπλήξῃς
an **older man**	**Πρεσβυτέρῳ**
but **exhort** him	ἀλλὰ **παρακάλει**
as a father	ὡς πατέρα
younger men	**νεωτέρους**
as brothers	ὡς ἀδελφούς

Then He opened their **minds (νοῦν) to understand (συνιέναι)** the **Scriptures (γραφάς).** (MLB)

νοῦς	mind, reason	24x
nous		S3563

γραφή ➤ 1:306   **συνίημι** ➤ DAY 156

τότε διήνοιξεν αὐτῶν τὸν **νοῦν** τοῦ **συνιέναι** τὰς **γραφάς**.

Then	τότε
He opened	διήνοιξεν
their **minds**	αὐτῶν τὸν **νοῦν**
to understand	τοῦ **συνιέναι**
the **Scriptures**	τὰς **γραφάς**

For **as (ὥσπερ)** were the days of Noah, **so (οὕτως)** will be the **coming (παρουσία)** of the Son of Man. (ESV)

παρουσία	presence, coming, arrival, advent	24x
parousia		S3952

οὕτως   ➤   1:77   ὥσπερ   ➤   DAY 47

ὥσπερ γὰρ αἱ ἡμέραι τοῦ Νῶε, **οὕτως** ἔσται ἡ **παρουσία** τοῦ υἱοῦ τοῦ ἀνθρώπου·

For **as** were	**ὥσπερ** γὰρ
the days of Noah	αἱ ἡμέραι τοῦ Νῶε
so will be	**οὕτως** ἔσται
the **coming**	ἡ **παρουσία**
of the Son of Man	τοῦ υἱοῦ τοῦ ἀνθρώπου

But when the Jews saw the **crowds (ὄχλους)**, **they were filled
(ἐπλήσθησαν)** with jealousy and began to contradict what was
spoken by Paul, **reviling (βλασφημοῦντες)** him. (ESV)

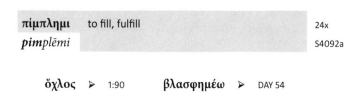

| πίμπλημι | to fill, fulfill | 24x |
| *pimplēmi* | | S4092a |

    ὄχλος   ➤   1:90   βλασφημέω   ➤   DAY 54

ἰδόντες δὲ οἱ Ἰουδαῖοι τοὺς **ὄχλους ἐπλήσθησαν** ζήλου καὶ
ἀντέλεγον τοῖς ὑπὸ Παύλου λαλουμένοις **βλασφημοῦντες**.

But when the Jews saw the **crowds**	ἰδόντες δὲ οἱ Ἰουδαῖοι τοὺς **ὄχλους**
they were filled with jealousy	**ἐπλήσθησαν** ζήλου
and began to contradict	καὶ ἀντέλεγον
what was spoken by Paul	τοῖς ὑπὸ Παύλου λαλουμένοις
reviling him	**βλασφημοῦντες**

For this reason we must [lit., **it is necessary (δεῖ)** for us to] **pay** much closer **attention (προσέχειν)** to what we have heard, **so that** we do **not (μήποτε)** drift away from it. (NASB)

| προσέχω | to beware, be cautious, pay attention to, devote oneself to | 24x |
| *prosechō* | | S4337 |

    δεῖ ➤ 1:161   **μήποτε** ➤ DAY 182

Διὰ τοῦτο **δεῖ** περισσοτέρως **προσέχειν** ἡμᾶς τοῖς ἀκουσθεῖσιν, **μήποτε** παραρυῶμεν.

For this reason	Διὰ τοῦτο
we must [lit., **it is necessary** for us to]	**δεῖ** . . . ἡμᾶς
pay much closer **attention**	περισσοτέρως **προσέχειν**
to what we have heard	τοῖς ἀκουσθεῖσιν
so that we do **not** drift away from it	**μήποτε** παραρυῶμεν

Paul [lit., he] came also to Derbe and to Lystra. And a disciple
was **there (ἐκεῖ)**, named **Timothy (Τιμόθεος)**, the son of a Jewish
woman who was a **believer (πιστῆς)**, but his father was a Greek.
(NASB)

Τιμόθεος	Timothy	24x
Timotheos		S5095

   ἐκεῖ   ➤   1:158   **πιστός**   ➤   1:245

Κατήντησεν δὲ καὶ εἰς Δέρβην καὶ εἰς Λύστραν. καὶ ἰδοὺ μαθητής
τις ἦν **ἐκεῖ** ὀνόματι **Τιμόθεος**, υἱὸς γυναικὸς Ἰουδαίας **πιστῆς**
πατρὸς δὲ Ἕλληνος,

Paul [lit., he] came also	Κατήντησεν δὲ καὶ
to Derbe and to Lystra	εἰς Δέρβην καὶ εἰς Λύστραν
And a disciple was **there**	καὶ ἰδοὺ μαθητής τις ἦν **ἐκεῖ**
named **Timothy**	ὀνόματι **Τιμόθεος**
the son of a Jewish woman who was a **believer**	υἱὸς γυναικὸς Ἰουδαίας **πιστῆς**
but his father was a Greek	πατρὸς δὲ Ἕλληνος

For the kingdom of heaven is **like (Ὁμοία)** a landowner **who (ὅστις)** went out early in the morning to hire workers for his **vineyard (ἀμπελῶνα)**. (NIV)

| **ἀμπελών** | vineyard | 23x |
| *ampelōn* | | S290 |

ὅστις, ἥτις, ὅ τι ▷ 1:127   **ὅμοιος** ▷ 1:364

Ὁμοία γάρ ἐστιν ἡ βασιλεία τῶν οὐρανῶν ἀνθρώπῳ οἰκοδεσπότῃ **ὅστις** ἐξῆλθεν ἅμα πρωὶ μισθώσασθαι ἐργάτας εἰς τὸν **ἀμπελῶνα** αὐτοῦ·

For the kingdom of heaven	γάρ . . . ἡ βασιλεία τῶν οὐρανῶν
is **like**	**Ὁμοία** . . . ἐστιν
a landowner	ἀνθρώπῳ οἰκοδεσπότῃ
who went out	**ὅστις** ἐξῆλθεν
early in the morning	ἅμα πρωὶ
to hire workers	μισθώσασθαι ἐργάτας
for his **vineyard**	εἰς τὸν **ἀμπελῶνα** αὐτοῦ

They honored us in many ways [lit., with many **honors (τιμαῖς)**]; and when **we were ready to sail (ἀναγομένοις)**, they furnished us with the supplies we needed [lit., as far as the **necessities (χρείας)** were concerned]. (NIV)

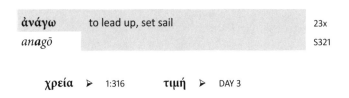

οἳ καὶ πολλαῖς **τιμαῖς** ἐτίμησαν ἡμᾶς καὶ **ἀναγομένοις** ἐπέθεντο τὰ πρὸς τὰς **χρείας**.

They honored us	οἳ καὶ . . . ἐτίμησαν ἡμᾶς
in many ways [lit., with many **honors**]	πολλαῖς **τιμαῖς**
and when **we were ready to sail**	καὶ **ἀναγομένοις**
they furnished us	ἐπέθεντο
with the supplies we needed [lit., as far as the **necessities** were concerned]	τὰ πρὸς τὰς **χρείας**

To the pure, all things are pure; but to those who are defiled and
unbelieving (ἀπίστοις), nothing is pure, but both their **mind
(νοῦς)** and their **conscience (συνείδησις)** are defiled. (NASB)

ἄπιστος	unbelieving, unbeliever	23x
apistos		S571

συνείδησις	➤ DAY 111	**νοῦς** ➤ DAY 184

πάντα καθαρὰ τοῖς καθαροῖς· τοῖς δὲ μεμιαμμένοις καὶ **ἀπίστοις**
οὐδὲν καθαρόν, ἀλλὰ μεμίανται αὐτῶν καὶ ὁ **νοῦς** καὶ ἡ
συνείδησις.

To the pure	τοῖς καθαροῖς
all things are pure	πάντα καθαρὰ
but to those who are defiled	τοῖς δὲ μεμιαμμένοις
and **unbelieving**	καὶ **ἀπίστοις**
nothing is pure	οὐδὲν καθαρόν
but both their **mind**	ἀλλὰ . . . αὐτῶν καὶ ὁ **νοῦς**
and their **conscience**	καὶ ἡ **συνείδησις**
are defiled	μεμίανται

The child **grew (ηὔξανεν)** and became strong, **filled
(πληρούμενον)** with **wisdom (σοφίᾳ)**; and the favor of God was
upon him. (NRSV)

αὐξάνω	to grow, increase, cause to grow	23x
auxanō		S837

    πληρόω ➤ 1:200   **σοφία** ➤ 1:305

Τὸ δὲ παιδίον **ηὔξανεν** καὶ ἐκραταιοῦτο **πληρούμενον σοφίᾳ**, καὶ
χάρις θεοῦ ἦν ἐπ᾽ αὐτό.

The child **grew**	Τὸ δὲ παιδίον **ηὔξανεν**
and became strong	καὶ ἐκραταιοῦτο
filled with **wisdom**	**πληρούμενον σοφίᾳ**
and the favor of God	καὶ χάρις θεοῦ
was upon him	ἦν ἐπ᾽ αὐτό

Keep watch (γρηγορεῖτε), therefore, because you do not **know (οἴδατε)** on **what (ποίᾳ)** day your Lord is coming. (MLB)

γρηγορέω	to watch, be on the alert	23x
grēgoreō		S1127

οἶδα ➤ 1:56   ποῖος ➤ DAY 66

γρηγορεῖτε οὖν, ὅτι οὐκ **οἴδατε ποίᾳ** ἡμέρᾳ ὁ κύριος ὑμῶν ἔρχεται.

Keep watch	γρηγορεῖτε
therefore	οὖν
because **you do** not **know**	ὅτι οὐκ **οἴδατε**
on **what** day	**ποίᾳ** ἡμέρᾳ
your Lord	ὁ κύριος ὑμῶν
is coming	ἔρχεται

For (διότι) I am with you, and no one **will lay a hand on (ἐπιθήσεταί)** you to harm you, **for (διότι)** there are many in this city who are my **people (λαός)**. (NRSV)

διότι	therefore, because	23x
dioti		S1360

λαός ➤ 1:116   **ἐπιτίθημι** ➤ DAY 23

διότι ἐγώ εἰμι μετὰ σοῦ καὶ οὐδεὶς **ἐπιθήσεταί** σοι τοῦ κακῶσαί σε, **διότι λαός** ἐστί μοι πολὺς ἐν τῇ πόλει ταύτῃ.

For I am with you	**διότι** ἐγώ εἰμι μετὰ σοῦ
and no one **will lay a hand on** you	καὶ οὐδεὶς **ἐπιθήσεταί** σοι
to harm you	τοῦ κακῶσαί σε
for there are many . . . who are my **people**	**διότι λαός** ἐστί μοι πολὺς
in this city	ἐν τῇ πόλει ταύτῃ

. . . and **have put on** (**ἐνδυσάμενοι**) the **new** (**νέον**) self, which is being renewed in knowledge in the **image** (**εἰκόνα**) of its Creator.
(NIV)

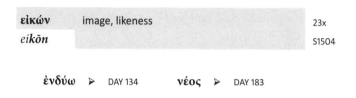

| **εἰκών** | image, likeness | 23x |
| *eikōn* | | S1504 |

ἐνδύω ➤ DAY 134   **νέος** ➤ DAY 183

καὶ **ἐνδυσάμενοι** τὸν **νέον** τὸν ἀνακαινούμενον εἰς ἐπίγνωσιν κατ᾽ **εἰκόνα** τοῦ κτίσαντος αὐτόν,

and **have put on**	καὶ **ἐνδυσάμενοι**
the **new** self	τὸν **νέον**
which is being renewed	τὸν ἀνακαινούμενον
in knowledge	εἰς ἐπίγνωσιν
in the **image**	κατ᾽ **εἰκόνα**
of its Creator	τοῦ κτίσαντος αὐτόν

Now there were some **Greeks** (Ἕλληνές) among those who went up to **worship** (προσκυνήσωσιν) at the **festival** (ἑορτῇ). (NIV)

Ἕλλην	Greek	23x
Hellēn		S1672

προσκυνέω ➤ 1:271   ἑορτή ➤ DAY 166

Ἦσαν δὲ Ἕλληνές τινες ἐκ τῶν ἀναβαινόντων ἵνα **προσκυνήσωσιν** ἐν τῇ **ἑορτῇ**·

Now there were some **Greeks**	Ἦσαν δὲ Ἕλληνές τινες
among those who went up	ἐκ τῶν ἀναβαινόντων
to **worship**	ἵνα **προσκυνήσωσιν**
at the **festival**	ἐν τῇ **ἑορτῇ**

The first **living creature (ζῷον)** was **like (ὅμοιον)** a lion; the second **living creature (ζῷον)** was **like (ὅμοιον)** an ox; the third **living creature (ζῷον)** had a **face (πρόσωπον)** like a man; and the fourth **living creature (ζῷον)** was **like (ὅμοιον)** a flying eagle.
(CSB)

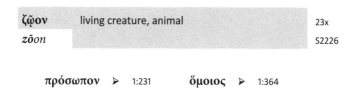

| **ζῷον** | living creature, animal | 23x |
| *zōon* | | S2226 |

πρόσωπον ➤ 1:231   **ὅμοιος** ➤ 1:364

καὶ τὸ **ζῷον** τὸ πρῶτον **ὅμοιον** λέοντι, καὶ τὸ δεύτερον **ζῷον ὅμοιον** μόσχῳ, καὶ τὸ τρίτον **ζῷον** ἔχων τὸ **πρόσωπον** ὡς ἀνθρώπου, καὶ τὸ τέταρτον **ζῷον ὅμοιον** ἀετῷ πετομένῳ·

The first **living creature**	καὶ τὸ **ζῷον** τὸ πρῶτον
was **like** a lion	**ὅμοιον** λέοντι
the second **living creature**	καὶ τὸ δεύτερον **ζῷον**
was **like** an ox	**ὅμοιον** μόσχῳ
the third **living creature**	καὶ τὸ τρίτον **ζῷον**
had a **face** like a man	ἔχων τὸ **πρόσωπον** ὡς ἀνθρώπου
and the fourth **living creature**	καὶ τὸ τέταρτον **ζῷον**
was **like** a flying eagle	**ὅμοιον** ἀετῷ πετομένῳ

But an angel of the Lord **appeared (ὤφθη)** to him, **standing (ἑστὼς)** to the right of the **altar (θυσιαστηρίου)** of incense. (MLB)

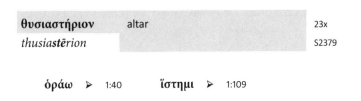

| θυσιαστήριον | altar | 23x |
| *thusiastērion* | | S2379 |

| ὁράω ▸ 1:40 | ἵστημι ▸ 1:109 |

ὤφθη δὲ αὐτῷ ἄγγελος Κυρίου ἑστὼς ἐκ δεξιῶν τοῦ θυσιαστηρίου τοῦ θυμιάματος.

But an angel of the Lord	δὲ . . . ἄγγελος Κυρίου
appeared to him	ὤφθη . . . αὐτῷ
standing	ἑστὼς
to the right	ἐκ δεξιῶν
of the **altar**	τοῦ **θυσιαστηρίου**
of incense	τοῦ θυμιάματος

He said, "I will give you a hearing when your accusers **arrive (παραγένωνται).**" Then **he ordered (κελεύσας)** that he **be kept under guard (φυλάσσεσθαι)** in Herod's headquarters. (NRSV)

| **κελεύω** | to order, command | 23x |
| *keleuō* | | S2753 |

παραγίνομαι ▷ DAY 41　　　　**φυλάσσω** ▷ DAY 86

Διακούσομαί σου, ἔφη, ὅταν καὶ οἱ κατήγοροί σου **παραγένωνται·** **κελεύσας** ἐν τῷ πραιτωρίῳ τοῦ Ἡρῴδου **φυλάσσεσθαι** αὐτόν.

He said	ἔφη
I will give you a hearing	Διακούσομαί σου
when your accusers **arrive**	ὅταν καὶ οἱ κατήγοροί σου **παραγένωνται**
Then **he ordered** that	**κελεύσας**
he **be kept under guard**	**φυλάσσεσθαι** αὐτόν
in Herod's headquarters	ἐν τῷ πραιτωρίῳ τοῦ Ἡρῴδου

He who steals must steal no longer; but **rather (μᾶλλον) he must labor (κοπιάτω)**, performing with his own hands what is good, so that he will have something to share with one who has **need (χρείαν)**. (NASB)

κοπιάω	to toil, grow weary	23x
kopiaō		S2872

      μᾶλλον ➤ 1:211   **χρεία** ➤ 1:316

ὁ κλέπτων μηκέτι κλεπτέτω, **μᾶλλον** δὲ **κοπιάτω** ἐργαζόμενος ταῖς χερσὶν τὸ ἀγαθόν, ἵνα ἔχῃ μεταδιδόναι τῷ **χρείαν** ἔχοντι.

He who steals must steal no longer	ὁ κλέπτων μηκέτι κλεπτέτω
but **rather**	**μᾶλλον** δὲ
he must labor	**κοπιάτω**
performing with his own hands	ἐργαζόμενος ταῖς χερσὶν
what is good	τὸ ἀγαθόν
so that he will have something to share	ἵνα ἔχῃ μεταδιδόναι
with one who has **need**	τῷ **χρείαν** ἔχοντι

"Lord," he said, "my **servant (παῖς) lies (βέβληται)** at **home (οἰκίᾳ)** paralyzed, suffering terribly." (NIV)

| **παῖς** | boy, child, girl; slave, servant | 23x |
| *pais* | | S3816 |

βάλλω ➤ 1:134   **οἰκία** ➤ 1:178

καὶ λέγων Κύριε, ὁ **παῖς** μου **βέβληται** ἐν τῇ **οἰκίᾳ** παραλυτικός, δεινῶς βασανιζόμενος.

Lord	Κύριε
he said	καὶ λέγων
my **servant**	ὁ **παῖς** μου
lies	**βέβληται**
at **home**	ἐν τῇ **οἰκίᾳ**
paralyzed	παραλυτικός
suffering terribly	δεινῶς βασανιζόμενος

There **were** some **present (Παρῆσαν)** at that very time **who told (ἀπαγγέλλοντες)** him about the Galileans whose blood Pilate had mingled with their **sacrifices (θυσιῶν)**. (ESV)

πάρειμι	to be present, come, arrive	23x
pareimi		S3918

ἀπαγγέλλω ➤ 1:343   θυσία ➤ DAY 121

Παρῆσαν δέ τινες ἐν αὐτῷ τῷ καιρῷ **ἀπαγγέλλοντες** αὐτῷ περὶ τῶν Γαλιλαίων ὧν τὸ αἷμα Πειλᾶτος ἔμιξεν μετὰ τῶν **θυσιῶν** αὐτῶν.

There **were** some **present**	**Παρῆσαν** δέ τινες
at that very time	ἐν αὐτῷ τῷ καιρῷ
who told him	**ἀπαγγέλλοντες** αὐτῷ
about the Galileans	περὶ τῶν Γαλιλαίων
whose blood Pilate had mingled	ὧν τὸ αἷμα Πειλᾶτος ἔμιξεν
with their **sacrifices**	μετὰ τῶν **θυσιῶν** αὐτῶν

But He said to them, "**Have you** not **read (ἀνέγνωτε)** what David **did (ἐποίησεν)** when **he became hungry (ἐπείνασεν)**, he and his companions [lit., also those with him], . . . ?" (NASB)

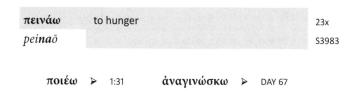

| πεινάω | to hunger | 23x |
| *peinaō* | | S3983 |

ποιέω ➤ 1:31   **ἀναγινώσκω** ➤ DAY 67

ὁ δὲ εἶπεν αὐτοῖς Οὐκ **ἀνέγνωτε** τί **ἐποίησεν** Δαυεὶδ ὅτε **ἐπείνασεν** καὶ οἱ μετ᾽ αὐτοῦ;

But He said to them	ὁ δὲ εἶπεν αὐτοῖς
Have you not **read**	Οὐκ **ἀνέγνωτε**
what David **did**	τί **ἐποίησεν** Δαυεὶδ
when **he became hungry**	ὅτε **ἐπείνασεν**
he and his companions [lit., also those with him]	καὶ οἱ μετ᾽ αὐτοῦ;

And they came to John and said to him, "Rabbi, he who was with you **across (πέραν)** the Jordan, to whom you **bore witness (μεμαρτύρηκας)**—look, he **is baptizing (βαπτίζει)**, and all are going to him." (ESV)

πέραν	beyond, across, on the other side of	23x
peran		S4008

βαπτίζω ➤ 1:219   **μαρτυρέω** ➤ 1:225

καὶ ἦλθαν πρὸς τὸν Ἰωάνην καὶ εἶπαν αὐτῷ Ῥαββεί, ὃς ἦν μετὰ σοῦ **πέραν** τοῦ Ἰορδάνου, ᾧ σὺ **μεμαρτύρηκας**, ἴδε οὗτος **βαπτίζει** καὶ πάντες ἔρχονται πρὸς αὐτόν.

And they came to John	καὶ ἦλθαν πρὸς τὸν Ἰωάνην
and said to him	καὶ εἶπαν αὐτῷ
Rabbi	Ῥαββεί
he who was with you	ὃς ἦν μετὰ σοῦ
across the Jordan	**πέραν** τοῦ Ἰορδάνου
to whom you **bore witness**	ᾧ σὺ **μεμαρτύρηκας**
look, he **is baptizing**	ἴδε οὗτος **βαπτίζει**
and all are going to him	καὶ πάντες ἔρχονται πρὸς αὐτόν

I was a stranger and you did not welcome me, naked and **you did** not **clothe (περιεβάλετέ)** me, **sick (ἀσθενὴς)** and in **prison (φυλακῇ)** and you did not visit me. (ESV)

| περιβάλλω | to clothe, put on, put around | 23x |
| *peri**ballō*** | | S4016 |

φυλακή ➢ 1:332	**ἀσθενής** ➢ DAY 163

ξένος ἤμην καὶ οὐ συνηγάγετέ με, γυμνὸς καὶ οὐ **περιεβάλετέ** με, **ἀσθενὴς** καὶ ἐν **φυλακῇ** καὶ οὐκ ἐπεσκέψασθέ με.

I was a stranger	ξένος ἤμην
and you did not welcome me	καὶ οὐ συνηγάγετέ με
naked	γυμνὸς
and **you did** not **clothe** me	καὶ οὐ **περιεβάλετέ** με
sick	**ἀσθενὴς**
and in **prison**	καὶ ἐν **φυλακῇ**
and you did not visit me	καὶ οὐκ ἐπεσκέψασθέ με

But **grow (αὐξάνετε)** in the grace and **knowledge (γνώσει)** of our Lord and **Savior (σωτῆρος)** Jesus Christ. To him be the glory both now and to the day of eternity. (CSB)

σωτήρ	savior, rescuer		23x
sōtēr			S4990

γνῶσις ▷ DAY 101   αὐξάνω ▷ DAY 192

αὐξάνετε δὲ ἐν χάριτι καὶ **γνώσει** τοῦ κυρίου ἡμῶν καὶ **σωτῆρος** Ἰησοῦ Χριστοῦ. αὐτῷ ἡ δόξα καὶ νῦν καὶ εἰς ἡμέραν αἰῶνος.

But **grow**	**αὐξάνετε** δὲ
in the grace and **knowledge**	ἐν χάριτι καὶ **γνώσει**
of our Lord	τοῦ κυρίου ἡμῶν
and **Savior**	καὶ **σωτῆρος**
Jesus Christ	Ἰησοῦ Χριστοῦ
To him be the glory	αὐτῷ ἡ δόξα
both now	καὶ νῦν
and to the day of eternity	καὶ εἰς ἡμέραν αἰῶνος

Not that I have **already (ἤδη)** obtained it or **have already become perfect (ἤδη τετελείωμαι)**, but **I press on (διώκω)** so that I may lay hold of that for which also I was laid hold of by Christ Jesus.
(NASB)

τελειόω	to complete, bring to completion, fulfill	23x
teleioō		S5048

ἤδη ➤ 1:258   **διώκω** ➤ 1:333

οὐχ ὅτι **ἤδη** ἔλαβον ἢ **ἤδη τετελείωμαι, διώκω** δὲ εἰ καὶ καταλάβω, ἐφ᾽ ᾧ καὶ κατελήμφθην ὑπὸ Χριστοῦ [Ἰησοῦ].

Not that I have **already** obtained it	οὐχ ὅτι **ἤδη** ἔλαβον
or **have already become perfect**	ἢ **ἤδη τετελείωμαι**
but **I press on**	**διώκω** δὲ
so that I may lay hold of that	εἰ καὶ καταλάβω
for which also I was laid hold of	ἐφ᾽ ᾧ καὶ κατελήμφθην
by Christ Jesus	ὑπὸ Χριστοῦ [Ἰησοῦ]

And at that hour there was a great earthquake, and a tenth of
the city fell. Seven **thousand (χιλιάδες)** people **were killed
(ἀπεκτάνθησαν)** in the earthquake, and the rest were terrified
and **gave (ἔδωκαν)** glory to the God of heaven. (ESV)

χιλιάς	thousand		23x
chilias			S5505

δίδωμι ➤ 1:43   **ἀποκτείνω** ➤ 1:226

Καὶ ἐν ἐκείνῃ τῇ ὥρᾳ ἐγένετο σεισμὸς μέγας, καὶ τὸ δέκατον
τῆς πόλεως ἔπεσεν, καὶ **ἀπεκτάνθησαν** ἐν τῷ σεισμῷ ὀνόματα
ἀνθρώπων **χιλιάδες** ἑπτά, καὶ οἱ λοιποὶ ἔμφοβοι ἐγένοντο καὶ
ἔδωκαν δόξαν τῷ θεῷ τοῦ οὐρανοῦ.

And at that hour	Καὶ ἐν ἐκείνῃ τῇ ὥρᾳ
there was a great earthquake	ἐγένετο σεισμὸς μέγας
and a tenth of the city fell	καὶ τὸ δέκατον τῆς πόλεως ἔπεσεν
Seven **thousand** people **were killed**	καὶ **ἀπεκτάνθησαν** . . . ὀνόματα ἀνθρώπων **χιλιάδες** ἑπτά
in the earthquake	ἐν τῷ σεισμῷ
and the rest were terrified	καὶ οἱ λοιποὶ ἔμφοβοι ἐγένοντο
and **gave** glory to the God of heaven	καὶ **ἔδωκαν** δόξαν τῷ θεῷ τοῦ οὐρανοῦ

I do not want you **to be unaware (ἀγνοεῖν)**, brothers and sisters, that our ancestors were all under the **cloud (νεφέλην)**, and all **passed through (διῆλθον)** the sea. (NRSV)

ἀγνοέω	to not know, be ignorant of	22x
agnoeō		S50

διέρχομαι ➤ 1:360   **νεφέλη** ➤ DAY 170

Οὐ θέλω γὰρ ὑμᾶς **ἀγνοεῖν**, ἀδελφοί, ὅτι οἱ πατέρες ἡμῶν πάντες ὑπὸ τὴν **νεφέλην** ἦσαν καὶ πάντες διὰ τῆς θαλάσσης **διῆλθον**,

I do not want	Οὐ θέλω γὰρ
you **to be unaware**	ὑμᾶς **ἀγνοεῖν**
brothers and sisters	ἀδελφοί
that our ancestors	ὅτι οἱ πατέρες ἡμῶν
were all under the **cloud**	πάντες ὑπὸ τὴν **νεφέλην** ἦσαν
and all **passed through** the sea	καὶ πάντες διὰ τῆς θαλάσσης **διῆλθον**

Instead (ἀντὶ) you ought to say, "If the Lord wishes, **we will live (ζήσομεν)** and do this or **that (ἐκεῖνο)**." (NRSV)

ἀντί	instead of, in return for, in exchange for, on behalf of	22x
anti		S473

ἐκεῖνος ▷ 1:64   ζάω ▷ 1:121

ἀντὶ τοῦ λέγειν ὑμᾶς Ἐὰν ὁ κύριος θέλῃ, καὶ **ζήσομεν** καὶ ποιήσομεν τοῦτο ἢ **ἐκεῖνο**.

Instead	ἀντὶ
you ought to say	τοῦ λέγειν ὑμᾶς
If the Lord wishes	Ἐὰν ὁ κύριος θέλῃ
we will live	καὶ **ζήσομεν**
and do	καὶ ποιήσομεν
this or **that**	τοῦτο ἢ **ἐκεῖνο**

Therefore, we are ambassadors **for** (Ὑπὲρ) Christ, as though God **were making an appeal** (παρακαλοῦντος) through us; **we beg** (δεόμεθα) you **on behalf of** (ὑπὲρ) Christ, be reconciled to God.

(NASB)

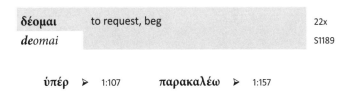

| δέομαι | to request, beg | 22x |
| *de*omai | | S1189 |

ὑπέρ ▷ 1:107   παρακαλέω ▷ 1:157

Ὑπὲρ Χριστοῦ οὖν πρεσβεύομεν ὡς τοῦ θεοῦ **παρακαλοῦντος** δι᾽ ἡμῶν· **δεόμεθα ὑπὲρ** Χριστοῦ, καταλλάγητε τῷ θεῷ.

Therefore, we are ambassadors	οὖν πρεσβεύομεν
for Christ	Ὑπὲρ Χριστοῦ
as though God **were making an appeal**	ὡς τοῦ θεοῦ **παρακαλοῦντος**
through us	δι᾽ ἡμῶν
we beg you	**δεόμεθα**
on behalf of Christ	ὑπὲρ Χριστοῦ
be reconciled to God	καταλλάγητε τῷ θεῷ

Beloved ones (Ἀγαπητοί), do not believe every spirit, but **put** the spirits **to the test (δοκιμάζετε)** whether they are from God; for many false prophets **have gone out (ἐξεληλύθασιν)** into the world. (MLB)

| δοκιμάζω | to prove, examine, put to the test | 22x |
| *dokimazō* | | S1381 |

ἐξέρχομαι ▷ 1:71   ἀγαπητός ▷ 1:261

Ἀγαπητοί, μὴ παντὶ πνεύματι πιστεύετε, ἀλλὰ **δοκιμάζετε** τὰ πνεύματα εἰ ἐκ τοῦ θεοῦ ἐστίν, ὅτι πολλοὶ ψευδοπροφῆται **ἐξεληλύθασιν** εἰς τὸν κόσμον.

Beloved ones	Ἀγαπητοί
do not believe every spirit	μὴ παντὶ πνεύματι πιστεύετε
but **put** the spirits **to the test**	ἀλλὰ **δοκιμάζετε** τὰ πνεύματα
whether they are from God	εἰ ἐκ τοῦ θεοῦ ἐστίν
for many false prophets	ὅτι πολλοὶ ψευδοπροφῆται
have gone out	**ἐξεληλύθασιν**
into the world	εἰς τὸν κόσμον

Listen, my dear brothers. **Has** not God **chosen (ἐξελέξατο)** the
poor (πτωχοὺς) in the world to be rich in faith and to be heirs
of the kingdom He has promised to those **who love (ἀγαπῶσιν)**
Him? (MLB)

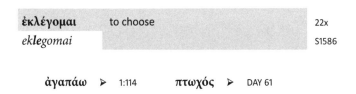

ἐκλέγομαι	to choose	22x
eklegomai		S1586

ἀγαπάω   ▷   1:114   πτωχός   ▷   DAY 61

Ἀκούσατε, ἀδελφοί μου ἀγαπητοί. οὐχ ὁ θεὸς **ἐξελέξατο** τοὺς
πτωχοὺς τῷ κόσμῳ πλουσίους ἐν πίστει καὶ κληρονόμους τῆς
βασιλείας ἧς ἐπηγγείλατο τοῖς **ἀγαπῶσιν** αὐτόν;

Listen	Ἀκούσατε
my dear brothers	ἀδελφοί μου ἀγαπητοί
Has not God **chosen**	οὐχ ὁ θεὸς **ἐξελέξατο**
the **poor** in the world	τοὺς **πτωχοὺς** τῷ κόσμῳ
to be rich in faith	πλουσίους ἐν πίστει
and to be heirs of the kingdom	καὶ κληρονόμους τῆς βασιλείας
He has promised	ἧς ἐπηγγείλατο
to those **who love** Him?	τοῖς **ἀγαπῶσιν** αὐτόν;

But you are a **chosen (ἐκλεκτόν)** race, a royal priesthood, a holy **nation (ἔθνος)**, a **people (λαὸς)** for his own possession, that you may proclaim the excellencies of him who called you out of darkness into his marvelous light. (ESV)

ἐκλεκτός	chosen, select	22x
eklektos		S1588

ἔθνος ➢ 1:98   **λαός** ➢ 1:116

ὑμεῖς δὲ γένος **ἐκλεκτόν**, βασίλειον ἱεράτευμα, **ἔθνος** ἅγιον, **λαὸς** εἰς περιποίησιν, ὅπως τὰς ἀρετὰς ἐξαγγείλητε τοῦ ἐκ σκότους ὑμᾶς καλέσαντος εἰς τὸ θαυμαστὸν αὐτοῦ φῶς·

But you are a **chosen** race	ὑμεῖς δὲ γένος **ἐκλεκτόν**
a royal priesthood	βασίλειον ἱεράτευμα
a holy **nation**	**ἔθνος** ἅγιον
a **people** for his own possession	**λαὸς** εἰς περιποίησιν
that you may proclaim the excellencies	ὅπως τὰς ἀρετὰς ἐξαγγείλητε
of him who called you	τοῦ . . . ὑμᾶς καλέσαντος
out of darkness	ἐκ σκότους
into his marvelous light	εἰς τὸ θαυμαστὸν αὐτοῦ φῶς

There is neither Jew nor **Greek** (Ἕλλην), there is neither slave nor **free** (ἐλεύθερος), there is no male and female, for **you** (ὑμεῖς) are all one in Christ Jesus. (ESV)

ἐλεύθερος	free	22x
eleutheros		S1658

σύ, (pl) **ὑμεῖς** ➤ 1:4   **Ἕλλην** ➤ DAY 196

οὐκ ἔνι Ἰουδαῖος οὐδὲ **Ἕλλην**, οὐκ ἔνι δοῦλος οὐδὲ **ἐλεύθερος**, οὐκ ἔνι ἄρσεν καὶ θῆλυ· πάντες γὰρ **ὑμεῖς** εἷς ἐστὲ ἐν Χριστῷ Ἰησοῦ.

There is neither Jew	οὐκ ἔνι Ἰουδαῖος
nor **Greek**	οὐδὲ **Ἕλλην**
there is neither slave	οὐκ ἔνι δοῦλος
nor **free**	οὐδὲ **ἐλεύθερος**
there is no male	οὐκ ἔνι ἄρσεν
and female	καὶ θῆλυ
for **you** are all one	πάντες γὰρ **ὑμεῖς** εἷς ἐστὲ
in Christ Jesus	ἐν Χριστῷ Ἰησοῦ

so that the word spoken through the Prophet **Isaiah ('Ησαίου)**
might be fulfilled, "He Himself took our **weaknesses (ἀσθενείας)**
and **carried away (ἐβάστασεν)** our diseases." (MLB)

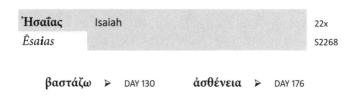

Ἠσαΐας	Isaiah	22x
Ēsaias		S2268

βαστάζω ➤ DAY 130   **ἀσθένεια** ➤ DAY 176

ὅπως πληρωθῇ τὸ ῥηθὲν διὰ **Ἠσαΐου** τοῦ προφήτου λέγοντος
Αὐτὸς τὰς **ἀσθενείας** ἡμῶν ἔλαβεν καὶ τὰς νόσους **ἐβάστασεν**.

so that the word spoken	ὅπως . . . τὸ ῥηθὲν . . . λέγοντος
through the Prophet **Isaiah**	διὰ **Ἠσαΐου** τοῦ προφήτου
might be fulfilled	πληρωθῇ
He Himself took	Αὐτὸς . . . ἔλαβεν
our **weaknesses**	τὰς **ἀσθενείας** ἡμῶν
and **carried away**	καὶ . . . **ἐβάστασεν**
our diseases	τὰς νόσους

No one **has** ever **seen (τεθέαται)** God. If we love one another,
God **remains (μένει)** in us and His love has been **perfected
(τετελειωμένη)** in us. (MLB)

θεάομαι	to behold, see, observe	22x
theaomai		S2300

    μένω ➤ 1:139   **τελειόω** ➤ DAY 207

θεὸν οὐδεὶς πώποτε **τεθέαται**· ἐὰν ἀγαπῶμεν ἀλλήλους, ὁ θεὸς ἐν
ἡμῖν **μένει** καὶ ἡ ἀγάπη αὐτοῦ **τετελειωμένη** ἐν ἡμῖν ἐστίν.

No one **has** ever **seen** God	θεὸν οὐδεὶς πώποτε **τεθέαται**
If we love one another	ἐὰν ἀγαπῶμεν ἀλλήλους
God **remains**	ὁ θεὸς . . . **μένει**
in us	ἐν ἡμῖν
and His love	καὶ ἡ ἀγάπη αὐτοῦ
has been **perfected**	**τετελειωμένη** . . . ἐστίν
in us	ἐν ἡμῖν

Suddenly, a violent storm arose on the **sea (θαλάσσῃ)**, so that the **boat (πλοῖον)** was being swamped by the waves—but Jesus [lit., he] **kept sleeping (ἐκάθευδεν)**. (CSB)

καθεύδω	to sleep	22x
katheudō		S2518

θάλασσα ➤ 1:188   **πλοῖον** ➤ 1:241

καὶ ἰδοὺ σεισμὸς μέγας ἐγένετο ἐν τῇ **θαλάσσῃ**, ὥστε τὸ **πλοῖον** καλύπτεσθαι ὑπὸ τῶν κυμάτων· αὐτὸς δὲ **ἐκάθευδεν**.

Suddenly	καὶ ἰδοὺ
a violent storm arose	σεισμὸς μέγας ἐγένετο
on the **sea**	ἐν τῇ **θαλάσσῃ**
so that the **boat** was being swamped	ὥστε τὸ **πλοῖον** καλύπτεσθαι
by the waves	ὑπὸ τῶν κυμάτων
but Jesus [lit., he]	αὐτὸς δὲ
kept sleeping	**ἐκάθευδεν**

And the Lord said, "Who **then (ἄρα)** is the faithful and prudent manager whom his master **will put in charge (καταστήσει)** of his slaves, **to give (διδόναι)** them their allowance of food at the proper time?" (NRSV)

καθίστημι *kathistēmi*	to bring, conduct, appoint, put in charge, make, be	22x S2525

     δίδωμι ➤ 1:43   **ἄρα / ἆρα** ➤ 1:310

καὶ εἶπεν ὁ κύριος Τίς **ἄρα** ἐστὶν ὁ πιστὸς οἰκονόμος, ὁ φρόνιμος, ὃν **καταστήσει** ὁ κύριος ἐπὶ τῆς θεραπείας αὐτοῦ τοῦ **διδόναι** ἐν καιρῷ [τὸ] σιτομέτριον;

And the Lord said	καὶ εἶπεν ὁ κύριος
Who **then** is	Τίς **ἄρα** ἐστὶν
the faithful . . . manager	ὁ πιστὸς οἰκονόμος
and prudent	ὁ φρόνιμος
whom his master **will put in charge**	ὃν **καταστήσει** ὁ κύριος
of his slaves	ἐπὶ τῆς θεραπείας αὐτοῦ
to give them	τοῦ **διδόναι**
their allowance of food	[τὸ] σιτομέτριον;
at the proper time?	ἐν καιρῷ

because **you know (γινώσκοντες)** that the testing of your faith
produces (κατεργάζεται) perseverance (ὑπομονήν). (NIV)

κατεργάζομαι	to produce, accomplish	22x
katergazomai		S2716

    γινώσκω ➤ 1:70   **ὑπομονή** ➤ DAY 76

γινώσκοντες ὅτι τὸ δοκίμιον ὑμῶν τῆς πίστεως **κατεργάζεται**
ὑπομονήν·

because **you know** that	**γινώσκοντες** ὅτι
the testing	τὸ δοκίμιον
of your faith	ὑμῶν τῆς πίστεως
produces	**κατεργάζεται**
perseverance	**ὑπομονήν**

whose **end (τέλος)** is destruction, whose god is their **appetite (κοιλία)**, and whose glory is in their shame, who **set their minds on (φρονοῦντες)** earthly things. (NASB)

κοιλία	stomach, belly, womb	22x
koilia		S2836

τέλος ▷ DAY 2   φρονέω ▷ DAY 157

ὧν τὸ **τέλος** ἀπώλεια, ὧν ὁ θεὸς ἡ **κοιλία** καὶ ἡ δόξα ἐν τῇ αἰσχύνῃ αὐτῶν, οἱ τὰ ἐπίγεια **φρονοῦντες**.

whose **end** is	ὧν τὸ **τέλος**
destruction	ἀπώλεια
whose god is	ὧν ὁ θεὸς
their **appetite**	ἡ **κοιλία**
and whose glory is	καὶ ἡ δόξα
in their shame	ἐν τῇ αἰσχύνῃ αὐτῶν
who **set their minds on**	οἱ . . . **φρονοῦντες**
earthly things	τὰ ἐπίγεια

But Jesus said, "**Let** the **children alone** (Ἄφετε . . . παιδία),
and do not **hinder** (κωλύετε) them from coming to Me; for the
kingdom of heaven belongs to such as these." (NASB)

| κωλύω | to prevent, hinder | 22x |
| *kōluō* | | S2967 |

| ἀφίημι | ➤ | 1:115 | παιδίον | ➤ | 1:302 |

ὁ δὲ Ἰησοῦς εἶπεν Ἄφετε τὰ παιδία καὶ μὴ κωλύετε αὐτὰ ἐλθεῖν
πρός με, τῶν γὰρ τοιούτων ἐστὶν ἡ βασιλεία τῶν οὐρανῶν.

But Jesus said	ὁ δὲ Ἰησοῦς εἶπεν
Let the **children alone**	Ἄφετε τὰ παιδία
and do not **hinder** them	καὶ μὴ κωλύετε αὐτὰ
from coming to Me	ἐλθεῖν πρός με
for the kingdom of heaven belongs	γὰρ . . . ἐστὶν ἡ βασιλεία τῶν οὐρανῶν
to such as these	τῶν . . . τοιούτων

A vision appeared to Paul in the **night (νυκτὸς)**: a man of
Macedonia was standing and **appealing to (παρακαλῶν)** him,
and saying, "Come over to **Macedonia (Μακεδονίαν)** and help
us." (NASB)

Μακεδονία	Macedonia	22x
Makedonia		S3109

   παρακαλέω ➤ 1:157   **νύξ** ➤ 1:266

καὶ ὅραμα διὰ **νυκτὸς** τῷ Παύλῳ ὤφθη, ἀνὴρ Μακεδών τις ἦν
ἑστὼς καὶ **παρακαλῶν** αὐτὸν καὶ λέγων Διαβὰς εἰς **Μακεδονίαν**
βοήθησον ἡμῖν.

A vision appeared to Paul	καὶ ὅραμα . . . τῷ Παύλῳ ὤφθη
in the **night**	διὰ **νυκτὸς**
a man of Macedonia	ἀνὴρ Μακεδών τις
was standing	ἦν ἑστὼς
and **appealing to** him	καὶ **παρακαλῶν** αὐτὸν
and saying	καὶ λέγων
Come over to **Macedonia**	Διαβὰς εἰς **Μακεδονίαν**
and help us	βοήθησον ἡμῖν

No longer (**Μηκέτι**) drink only water, but use a little **wine** (**οἴνῳ**) for the sake of your stomach and your frequent **ailments** (**ἀσθενείας**). (ESV)

μηκέτι	no longer	22x
mēketi		S3371

οἶνος ➢ DAY 60   ἀσθένεια ➢ DAY 176

Μηκέτι ὑδροπότει, ἀλλὰ **οἴνῳ** ὀλίγῳ χρῶ διὰ τὸν στόμαχον καὶ τὰς πυκνάς σου **ἀσθενείας**.

No longer drink only water	**Μηκέτι** ὑδροπότει
but use	ἀλλὰ . . . χρῶ
a little **wine**	**οἴνῳ** ὀλίγῳ
for the sake of your stomach	διὰ τὸν στόμαχον
and your frequent **ailments**	καὶ τὰς πυκνάς σου **ἀσθενείας**

Recalling (**μεμνημένος**) your tears, I long **to see** (**ἰδεῖν**) you, so that **I may be filled** (**πληρωθῶ**) with joy. (NIV)

μιμνήσκομαι	to remember, recall, mention	22x
mimnēskomai		S3403

ὁράω ➤ 1:40   **πληρόω** ➤ 1:200

ἐπιποθῶν σε **ἰδεῖν**, **μεμνημένος** σου τῶν δακρύων, ἵνα χαρᾶς **πληρωθῶ**

Recalling	μεμνημένος
your tears	σου τῶν δακρύων
I long	ἐπιποθῶν
to see you	σε **ἰδεῖν**
so that **I may be filled**	ἵνα . . . **πληρωθῶ**
with joy	χαρᾶς

And **he took (παραλαβὼν)** them that very hour of the night and washed their **wounds (πληγῶν)**, and immediately he was baptized, he and **all (ἅπαντες)** his household. (NASB)

| πληγή | blow, wound, plague | 22x |
| *plēgē* | | S4127 |

παραλαμβάνω ➤ 1:313   **ἅπας** ➤ DAY 68

καὶ **παραλαβὼν** αὐτοὺς ἐν ἐκείνῃ τῇ ὥρᾳ τῆς νυκτὸς ἔλουσεν ἀπὸ τῶν **πληγῶν**, καὶ ἐβαπτίσθη αὐτὸς καὶ οἱ αὐτοῦ **ἅπαντες** παραχρῆμα,

And **he took** them	καὶ **παραλαβὼν** αὐτοὺς
that very hour	ἐν ἐκείνῃ τῇ ὥρᾳ
of the night	τῆς νυκτὸς
and washed their **wounds**	ἔλουσεν ἀπὸ τῶν **πληγῶν**
and immediately	καὶ . . . παραχρῆμα
he was baptized	ἐβαπτίσθη
he	αὐτὸς
and **all** his household	καὶ οἱ αὐτοῦ **ἅπαντες**

Oh, the depth of the **riches (πλούτου)** and wisdom and knowledge of God! How unsearchable are his **judgments (κρίματα)** and how inscrutable his **ways (ὁδοὶ)**! (ESV)

πλοῦτος	wealth	22x
*plou*tos		S4149

     ὁδός ➤ 1:166   **κρίμα** ➤ DAY 137

Ὦ βάθος **πλούτου** καὶ σοφίας καὶ γνώσεως θεοῦ· ὡς ἀνεξεραύνητα τὰ **κρίματα** αὐτοῦ καὶ ἀνεξιχνίαστοι αἱ **ὁδοὶ** αὐτοῦ.

Oh, the depth	Ὦ βάθος
of the **riches**	**πλούτου**
and wisdom	καὶ σοφίας
and knowledge	καὶ γνώσεως
of God!	θεοῦ
How unsearchable are	ὡς ἀνεξεραύνητα
his **judgments**	τὰ **κρίματα** αὐτοῦ
and how inscrutable	καὶ ἀνεξιχνίαστοι
his **ways!**	αἱ **ὁδοὶ** αὐτοῦ

Paul looked straight at the **Sanhedrin (συνεδρίῳ)** and said, "Brothers, I have lived my life before God in all good **conscience (συνειδήσει) to (ἄχρι)** this day." (CSB)

| **συνέδριον** | Sanhedrin, council | 22x |
| *sunedrion* | | S4892 |

ἄχρι ➤ 1:311   συνείδησις ➤ DAY 111

ἀτενίσας δὲ Παῦλος τῷ **συνεδρίῳ** εἶπεν Ἄνδρες ἀδελφοί, ἐγὼ πάσῃ **συνειδήσει** ἀγαθῇ πεπολίτευμαι τῷ θεῷ **ἄχρι** ταύτης τῆς ἡμέρας.

Paul looked straight at the **Sanhedrin**	ἀτενίσας δὲ Παῦλος τῷ **συνεδρίῳ**
and said	εἶπεν
Brothers	Ἄνδρες ἀδελφοί
I have lived my life	ἐγὼ . . . πεπολίτευμαι
before God	τῷ θεῷ
in all good **conscience**	πάσῃ **συνειδήσει** ἀγαθῇ
to this day	**ἄχρι** ταύτης τῆς ἡμέρας

And with whom was He provoked for **forty (τεσσεράκοντα)**
years? Was it not with those **who sinned (ἁμαρτήσασιν)**, whose
corpses fell in the **desert (ἐρήμῳ)**? (MLB)

| **τεσσεράκοντα** | forty | 22x |
| *tesserakonta* | | S5062 |

ἔρημος ➤ 1:334   **ἁμαρτάνω** ➤ 1:342

τίσιν δὲ προσώχθισεν **τεσσεράκοντα** ἔτη; οὐχὶ τοῖς **ἁμαρτήσασιν**,
ὧν τὰ κῶλα ἔπεσεν ἐν τῇ **ἐρήμῳ**;

And with whom	τίσιν δὲ
was He provoked	προσώχθισεν
for **forty** years?	**τεσσεράκοντα** ἔτη;
Was it not	οὐχὶ
with those **who sinned**	τοῖς **ἁμαρτήσασιν**
whose corpses	ὧν τὰ κῶλα
fell	ἔπεσεν
in the **desert**?	ἐν τῇ **ἐρήμῳ**;

When they were unable **to repay (ἀποδοῦναι), he graciously forgave (ἐχαρίσατο)** them both. So which of them **will love (ἀγαπήσει)** him more? (NASB)

| χαρίζομαι | pardon, forgive, show kindness to, grant | 22x |
| *charizomai* | | S5483 |

ἀγαπάω ➤ 1:114   ἀποδίδωμι ➤ 1:317

μὴ ἐχόντων αὐτῶν **ἀποδοῦναι** ἀμφοτέροις **ἐχαρίσατο**. τίς οὖν αὐτῶν πλεῖον **ἀγαπήσει** αὐτόν;

When they were unable	μὴ ἐχόντων αὐτῶν
to repay	**ἀποδοῦναι**
he graciously forgave	**ἐχαρίσατο**
them both	ἀμφοτέροις
So which of them	τίς οὖν αὐτῶν
will love him	**ἀγαπήσει** αὐτόν;
more?	πλεῖον

But his citizens **hated (ἐμίσουν)** him and sent a delegation **after (ὀπίσω)** him, saying, "We do not want this man **to reign (βασιλεῦσαι)** over us." (ESV)

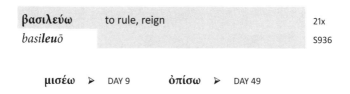

| **βασιλεύω** | to rule, reign | 21x |
| *basileuō* | | S936 |

μισέω ➤ DAY 9 **ὀπίσω** ➤ DAY 49

Οἱ δὲ πολῖται αὐτοῦ **ἐμίσουν** αὐτόν, καὶ ἀπέστειλαν πρεσβείαν **ὀπίσω** αὐτοῦ λέγοντες Οὐ θέλομεν τοῦτον **βασιλεῦσαι** ἐφ᾽ ἡμᾶς.

But his citizens	Οἱ δὲ πολῖται αὐτοῦ
hated him	**ἐμίσουν** αὐτόν
and sent a delegation	καὶ ἀπέστειλαν πρεσβείαν
after him	**ὀπίσω** αὐτοῦ
saying	λέγοντες
We do not want this man	Οὐ θέλομεν τοῦτον
to reign over us	**βασιλεῦσαι** ἐφ᾽ ἡμᾶς

Until I come, **give your attention (πρόσεχε)** to public reading, **exhortation (παρακλήσει)**, and **teaching (διδασκαλίᾳ)**. (CSB)

διδασκαλία	teaching	21x
didaskalia		S1319

παράκλησις ▷ DAY 105   **προσέχω** ▷ DAY 187

ἕως ἔρχομαι **πρόσεχε** τῇ ἀναγνώσει, τῇ **παρακλήσει**, τῇ **διδασκαλίᾳ**.

Until I come	ἕως ἔρχομαι
give your attention	**πρόσεχε**
to public reading	τῇ ἀναγνώσει
exhortation	τῇ **παρακλήσει**
and **teaching**	τῇ **διδασκαλίᾳ**

And he said to his servants, "This is John the Baptist; he **has been raised (ἠγέρθη)** from the **dead (νεκρῶν)**, and for this reason these powers **are at work (ἐνεργοῦσιν)** in him." (NRSV)

ἐνεργέω	to work, be at work, produce	21x
energeō		S1754

　　ἐγείρω　➤　1:118　　　　**νεκρός**　➤　1:129

καὶ εἶπεν τοῖς παισὶν αὐτοῦ Οὗτός ἐστιν Ἰωάνης ὁ βαπτιστής· αὐτὸς **ἠγέρθη** ἀπὸ τῶν **νεκρῶν**, καὶ διὰ τοῦτο αἱ δυνάμεις **ἐνεργοῦσιν** ἐν αὐτῷ.

And he said to his servants	καὶ εἶπεν τοῖς παισὶν αὐτοῦ
This is	Οὗτός ἐστιν
John the Baptist	Ἰωάνης ὁ βαπτιστής
he **has been raised**	αὐτὸς **ἠγέρθη**
from the **dead**	ἀπὸ τῶν **νεκρῶν**
and for this reason	καὶ διὰ τοῦτο
these powers **are at work**	αἱ δυνάμεις **ἐνεργοῦσιν**
in him	ἐν αὐτῷ

So when we could stand it **no longer (μηκέτι), we thought it best (ηὐδοκήσαμεν)** to be left **by ourselves (μόνοι)** in Athens. (NIV)

εὐδοκέω	to be well pleased, approve, consider	21x
eudokeō	good, resolve	S2106

  μόνος   ➤ 1:323   **μηκέτι**   ➤   DAY 224

Διὸ **μηκέτι** στέγοντες **ηὐδοκήσαμεν** καταλειφθῆναι ἐν Ἀθήναις **μόνοι,**

So	Διὸ
when we could stand it **no longer**	**μηκέτι** στέγοντες
we thought it best	**ηὐδοκήσαμεν**
to be left	καταλειφθῆναι
by ourselves	**μόνοι**
in Athens	ἐν Ἀθήναις

I sent you **to reap** (**θερίζειν**) that for which you **did** not **labor**
(**κεκοπιάκατε**). Others **have labored** (**κεκοπιάκασιν**), and you
have entered (**εἰσεληλύθατε**) into their labor. (ESV)

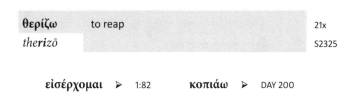

| **θερίζω** | to reap | 21x |
| *therizō* | | S2325 |

εἰσέρχομαι ➤ 1:82   κοπιάω ➤ DAY 200

ἐγὼ ἀπέστειλα ὑμᾶς **θερίζειν** ὃ οὐχ ὑμεῖς **κεκοπιάκατε**· ἄλλοι
κεκοπιάκασιν, καὶ ὑμεῖς εἰς τὸν κόπον αὐτῶν **εἰσεληλύθατε**.

I sent you	ἐγὼ ἀπέστειλα ὑμᾶς
to reap	**θερίζειν**
that for which you **did** not **labor**	ὃ οὐχ ὑμεῖς **κεκοπιάκατε**
Others **have labored**	ἄλλοι **κεκοπιάκασιν**
and you **have entered**	καὶ ὑμεῖς . . . **εἰσεληλύθατε**
into their labor	εἰς τὸν κόπον αὐτῶν

But the **things that proceed (ἐκπορευόμενα)** out of the **mouth (στόματος)** come from the heart, **and those (κἀκεῖνα)** defile the man. (NASB)

κἀκεῖνος	and he, and that	21x
kakeinos		S2548

στόμα ➤ 1:216   ἐκπορεύομαι ➤ DAY 70

τὰ δὲ **ἐκπορευόμενα** ἐκ τοῦ **στόματος** ἐκ τῆς καρδίας ἐξέρχεται, **κἀκεῖνα** κοινοῖ τὸν ἄνθρωπον.

But the **things that proceed**	τὰ δὲ **ἐκπορευόμενα**
out of the **mouth**	ἐκ τοῦ **στόματος**
come	ἐξέρχεται
from the heart	ἐκ τῆς καρδίας
and those defile	**κἀκεῖνα** κοινοῖ
the man	τὸν ἄνθρωπον

Do not **imagine (δοκεῖτε)** that I **shall accuse (κατηγορήσω)** you before the Father; your accuser is Moses, in whom you **are hoping (ἠλπίκατε)**. (MLB)

κατηγορέω	to accuse, charge, prosecute	21x
katēgoreō		S2723

　　　δοκέω ➤ 1:256　　　　**ἐλπίζω** ➤ DAY 78

μὴ **δοκεῖτε** ὅτι ἐγὼ **κατηγορήσω** ὑμῶν πρὸς τὸν πατέρα· ἔστιν ὁ κατηγορῶν ὑμῶν Μωυσῆς, εἰς ὃν ὑμεῖς **ἠλπίκατε**.

Do not **imagine** that	μὴ **δοκεῖτε** ὅτι
I **shall accuse** you	ἐγὼ **κατηγορήσω** ὑμῶν
before the Father	πρὸς τὸν πατέρα
your accuser	ὁ κατηγορῶν ὑμῶν
is Moses	ἔστιν . . . Μωυσῆς
in whom	εἰς ὃν
you **are hoping**	ὑμεῖς **ἠλπίκατε**

For the sorrow that is according to the will of God **produces (ἐργάζεται)** a **repentance (μετάνοιαν)** without regret, leading to salvation, but the sorrow of the world **produces (κατεργάζεται)** death. (NASB)

| μετάνοια | repentance, change of heart | 21x |
| *metanoia* | | S3341 |

| ἐργάζομαι | ▸ | 1:361 | κατεργάζομαι | ▸ | DAY 220 |

ἡ γὰρ κατὰ θεὸν λύπη **μετάνοιαν** εἰς σωτηρίαν ἀμεταμέλητον **ἐργάζεται·** ἡ δὲ τοῦ κόσμου λύπη θάνατον **κατεργάζεται.**

For the sorrow	ἡ γὰρ . . . λύπη
that is according to the will of God	κατὰ θεὸν
produces a **repentance**	μετάνοιαν . . . ἐργάζεται
without regret	ἀμεταμέλητον
leading to salvation	εἰς σωτηρίαν
but the sorrow of the world	ἡ δὲ τοῦ κόσμου λύπη
produces death	θάνατον **κατεργάζεται**

The Law came in so that the transgression would increase; but **where (οὗ) sin (ἁμαρτία)** increased, **grace (χάρις)** abounded all the more. (NASB)

οὗ	where, to the place where	21x
hou		S3757

   ἁμαρτία ➤ 1:91   **χάρις** ➤ 1:106

νόμος δὲ παρεισῆλθεν ἵνα πλεονάσῃ τὸ παράπτωμα· **οὗ** δὲ ἐπλεόνασεν ἡ **ἁμαρτία**, ὑπερεπερίσσευσεν ἡ **χάρις**,

The Law came in	νόμος δὲ παρεισῆλθεν
so that the transgression would increase	ἵνα πλεονάσῃ τὸ παράπτωμα
but **where sin** increased	**οὗ** δὲ ἐπλεόνασεν ἡ **ἁμαρτία**
grace abounded all the more	ὑπερεπερίσσευσεν ἡ **χάρις**

Consider (ἡγήσασθε) it **complete (Πᾶσαν)** joy, my brothers, when you become involved in all sorts of **trials (πειρασμοῖς)**.

(MLB)

πειρασμός	trial, test, testing, temptation	21x
peirasmos		S3986

    πᾶς ➤ 1:16   **ἡγέομαι** ➤ DAY 119

Πᾶσαν χαρὰν **ἡγήσασθε**, ἀδελφοί μου, ὅταν **πειρασμοῖς** περιπέσητε ποικίλοις,

Consider it	**ἡγήσασθε**
complete joy	**Πᾶσαν** χαρὰν
my brothers	ἀδελφοί μου
when you become involved in	ὅταν . . . περιπέσητε
all sorts of **trials**	**πειρασμοῖς** . . . ποικίλοις

When Jesus heard this, he said to him, "You still lack one thing.
Sell (πώλησον) everything you have and give to the **poor**
(πτωχοῖς), and you will have treasure in heaven. Then come,
follow (ἀκολούθει) me." (NIV)

πωλέω	to sell	21x
pōleō		S4453

ἀκολουθέω ➤ 1:192   **πτωχός** ➤ DAY 61

ἀκούσας δὲ ὁ Ἰησοῦς εἶπεν αὐτῷ Ἔτι ἕν σοι λείπει· πάντα ὅσα
ἔχεις **πώλησον** καὶ διάδος **πτωχοῖς**, καὶ ἕξεις θησαυρὸν ἐν [τοῖς]
οὐρανοῖς, καὶ δεῦρο **ἀκολούθει** μοι.

When Jesus heard this	ἀκούσας δὲ ὁ Ἰησοῦς
he said to him	εἶπεν αὐτῷ
You still lack one thing	Ἔτι ἕν σοι λείπει
Sell everything you have	πάντα ὅσα ἔχεις **πώλησον**
and give to the **poor**	καὶ διάδος **πτωχοῖς**
and you will have treasure in heaven	καὶ ἕξεις θησαυρὸν ἐν [τοῖς] οὐρανοῖς
Then come	καὶ δεῦρο
follow me	**ἀκολούθει** μοι

But **we have** (Ἔχομεν) this treasure in earthen **vessels (σκεύεσιν)**, so that the surpassing greatness of the **power (δυνάμεως)** will be of God and not from ourselves. (NASB)

σκεῦος	vessel, utensil, property, object	21x
skeuos		S4632

ἔχω ➤ 1:23   δύναμις ➤ 1:141

Ἔχομεν δὲ τὸν θησαυρὸν τοῦτον ἐν ὀστρακίνοις **σκεύεσιν**, ἵνα ἡ ὑπερβολὴ τῆς **δυνάμεως** ᾖ τοῦ θεοῦ καὶ μὴ ἐξ ἡμῶν·

But **we have**	Ἔχομεν δὲ
this treasure	τὸν θησαυρὸν τοῦτον
in earthen **vessels**	ἐν ὀστρακίνοις **σκεύεσιν**
so that the surpassing greatness	ἵνα ἡ ὑπερβολὴ
of the **power**	τῆς **δυνάμεως**
will be	ᾖ
of God	τοῦ θεοῦ
and not from ourselves	καὶ μὴ ἐξ ἡμῶν

Jesus **turned (στραφεὶς)** and saw her. "Take heart, **daughter (θύγατερ)**," he said, "your faith **has healed (σέσωκέν)** you." And the woman **was healed (ἐσώθη)** at that moment. (NIV)

στρέφω	to turn, change	21x
strephō		S4762

σῴζω   ➤   1:160   θυγάτηρ   ➤   DAY 120

ὁ δὲ Ἰησοῦς **στραφεὶς** καὶ ἰδὼν αὐτὴν εἶπεν Θάρσει, **θύγατερ**· ἡ πίστις σου **σέσωκέν** σε. καὶ **ἐσώθη** ἡ γυνὴ ἀπὸ τῆς ὥρας ἐκείνης.

Jesus **turned**	ὁ δὲ Ἰησοῦς **στραφεὶς**
and saw her	καὶ ἰδὼν αὐτὴν
Take heart, **daughter**	Θάρσει, **θύγατερ**
he said	εἶπεν
your faith **has healed** you	ἡ πίστις σου **σέσωκέν** σε
And the woman **was healed**	καὶ **ἐσώθη** ἡ γυνὴ
at that moment	ἀπὸ τῆς ὥρας ἐκείνης

For if you love those who love you, what **reward (μισθὸν)** do you
have? Do **not (οὐχὶ)** even the **tax collectors (τελῶναι)** do the
same? (NRSV)

τελώνης	tax collector	21x
telōnēs		S5057

οὐχί ➤ 1:292   **μισθός** ➤ DAY 103

ἐὰν γὰρ ἀγαπήσητε τοὺς ἀγαπῶντας ὑμᾶς, τίνα **μισθὸν** ἔχετε;
οὐχὶ καὶ οἱ **τελῶναι** τὸ αὐτὸ ποιοῦσιν;

For if you love	ἐὰν γὰρ ἀγαπήσητε
those who love you	τοὺς ἀγαπῶντας ὑμᾶς
what **reward**	τίνα **μισθὸν**
do you have?	ἔχετε;
Do **not** even the **tax collectors** do	οὐχὶ καὶ οἱ **τελῶναι** . . . ποιοῦσιν;
the same?	τὸ αὐτὸ

Honor (τιμήσατε) everyone. Love the brotherhood. **Fear (φοβεῖσθε)** God. **Honor (τιμᾶτε)** the **emperor (βασιλέα)**. (ESV)

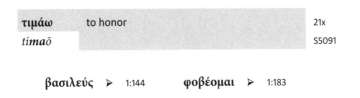

τιμάω	to honor	21x
timaō		S5091

βασιλεύς ➤ 1:144   **φοβέομαι** ➤ 1:183

πάντας **τιμήσατε**, τὴν ἀδελφότητα ἀγαπᾶτε, τὸν θεὸν **φοβεῖσθε**, τὸν **βασιλέα τιμᾶτε**.

Honor everyone	πάντας **τιμήσατε**
Love the brotherhood	τὴν ἀδελφότητα ἀγαπᾶτε
Fear God	τὸν θεὸν **φοβεῖσθε**
Honor the **emperor**	τὸν **βασιλέα τιμᾶτε**

And the men **marveled (ἐθαύμασαν)**, saying, "What sort of man is this, that even **winds (ἄνεμοι)** and sea **obey (ὑπακούουσιν)** him?" (ESV)

ὑπακούω	to obey	
hupakouō		21x
		S5219

θαυμάζω ➤ 1:348   **ἄνεμος** ➤ DAY 77

Οἱ δὲ ἄνθρωποι **ἐθαύμασαν** λέγοντες Ποταπός ἐστιν οὗτος ὅτι καὶ οἱ **ἄνεμοι** καὶ ἡ θάλασσα αὐτῷ **ὑπακούουσιν**;

And the men **marveled**	Οἱ δὲ ἄνθρωποι **ἐθαύμασαν**
saying	λέγοντες
What sort of man is this	Ποταπός ἐστιν οὗτος
that even **winds**	ὅτι καὶ οἱ **ἄνεμοι**
and sea	καὶ ἡ θάλασσα
obey him?	αὐτῷ **ὑπακούουσιν**;

So the **tribune (χιλίαρχος) dismissed (ἀπέλυσε)** the young
man, **charging (παραγγείλας)** him, "Tell no one that you have
informed me of these things." (ESV)

| **χιλίαρχος** | military commander (of hundreds of | 21x |
| *chiliarchos* | soldiers) | S5506 |

| **ἀπολύω** ➤ 1:250 | **παραγγέλλω** ➤ DAY 81 |

ὁ μὲν οὖν **χιλίαρχος ἀπέλυσε** τὸν νεανίσκον **παραγγείλας** μηδενὶ
ἐκλαλῆσαι ὅτι ταῦτα ἐνεφάνισας πρὸς ἐμέ.

So the **tribune**	ὁ μὲν οὖν **χιλίαρχος**
dismissed the young man	**ἀπέλυσε** τὸν νεανίσκον
charging him	**παραγγείλας**
Tell no one	μηδενὶ ἐκλαλῆσαι
that you have informed me of	ὅτι . . . ἐνεφάνισας πρὸς ἐμέ
these things	ταῦτα

After being baptized, Jesus came up immediately from the water; and behold, the heavens **were opened (ἠνεῴχθησαν)**, and he saw the Spirit of God **descending (καταβαῖνον) as (ὡσεὶ)** a dove and lighting on Him. (NASB)

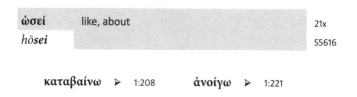

| ὡσεί | like, about | 21x |
| *hōsei* | | S5616 |

καταβαίνω ➤ 1:208   **ἀνοίγω** ➤ 1:221

βαπτισθεὶς δὲ ὁ Ἰησοῦς εὐθὺς ἀνέβη ἀπὸ τοῦ ὕδατος· καὶ ἰδοὺ **ἠνεῴχθησαν** οἱ οὐρανοί, καὶ εἶδεν πνεῦμα θεοῦ **καταβαῖνον ὡσεὶ** περιστερὰν ἐρχόμενον ἐπ᾽ αὐτόν·

After being baptized	βαπτισθεὶς δὲ
Jesus came up immediately	ὁ Ἰησοῦς εὐθὺς ἀνέβη
from the water	ἀπὸ τοῦ ὕδατος
and behold	καὶ ἰδοὺ
the heavens **were opened**	**ἠνεῴχθησαν** οἱ οὐρανοί
and he saw the Spirit of God	καὶ εἶδεν πνεῦμα θεοῦ
descending as a dove	**καταβαῖνον ὡσεὶ** περιστερὰν
and lighting on Him	ἐρχόμενον ἐπ᾽ αὐτόν

Peter went down to the men and said, "Behold, I am the one **you are looking for (ζητεῖτε)**; what is the **reason (αἰτία)** for which **you have come (πάρεστε)**?" (NASB)

αἰτία	reason, cause, charge, accusation, matter	20x
aitia		S156

ζητέω ➤ 1:150   πάρειμι ➤ DAY 202

καταβὰς δὲ Πέτρος πρὸς τοὺς ἄνδρας εἶπεν Ἰδοὺ ἐγώ εἰμι ὃν **ζητεῖτε**· τίς ἡ **αἰτία** δι᾽ ἣν **πάρεστε**;

Peter went down	καταβὰς δὲ Πέτρος
to the men	πρὸς τοὺς ἄνδρας
and said	εἶπεν
Behold	Ἰδοὺ
I am the one **you are looking for**	ἐγώ εἰμι ὃν **ζητεῖτε**
what is the **reason**	τίς ἡ **αἰτία**
for which **you have come?**	δι᾽ ἣν **πάρεστε**;

For indeed **circumcision (περιτομὴ)** is of value if **you practice (πράσσῃς)** the Law; but if you are a transgressor of the Law, your **circumcision (περιτομή)** has become **uncircumcision (ἀκροβυστία)**. (NASB)

| **ἀκροβυστία** | uncircumcision, foreskin | 20x |
| *akrobustia* | | S203 |

   πράσσω   ➤   DAY 21   **περιτομή**   ➤   DAY 42

περιτομὴ μὲν γὰρ ὠφελεῖ ἐὰν νόμον **πράσσῃς**· ἐὰν δὲ παραβάτης νόμου ᾖς, ἡ **περιτομή** σου **ἀκροβυστία** γέγονεν.

For indeed	μὲν γὰρ
circumcision is of value	**περιτομὴ** . . . ὠφελεῖ
if **you practice** the Law	ἐὰν νόμον **πράσσῃς**
but if	ἐὰν δὲ
you are a transgressor of the Law	παραβάτης νόμου ᾖς
your **circumcision**	ἡ **περιτομή** σου
has become **uncircumcision**	**ἀκροβυστία** γέγονεν

Then Peter said, "**Silver (Ἀργύριον)** or gold I do not have [lit., **is (ὑπάρχει)** not to me], but what I do have I give you. In the name of Jesus Christ of Nazareth, **walk (περιπάτει)**." (NIV)

| ἀργύριον | silver | 20x |
| *argurion* | | S694 |

περιπατέω ▷ 1:179   ὑπάρχω ▷ 1:274

εἶπεν δὲ Πέτρος Ἀργύριον καὶ χρυσίον οὐχ ὑπάρχει μοι, ὃ δὲ ἔχω τοῦτό σοι δίδωμι· ἐν τῷ ὀνόματι Ἰησοῦ Χριστοῦ τοῦ Ναζωραίου περιπάτει.

Then Peter said	εἶπεν δὲ Πέτρος
Silver or gold	**Ἀργύριον** καὶ χρυσίον
I do not have [lit., **is** not to me]	οὐχ **ὑπάρχει** μοι
but what I do have	ὃ δὲ ἔχω
I give you	τοῦτό σοι δίδωμι
In the name of Jesus Christ of Nazareth	ἐν τῷ ὀνόματι Ἰησοῦ Χριστοῦ τοῦ Ναζωραίου
walk	**περιπάτει**

Therefore we have been buried with him by **baptism** (βαπτίσματος) into death, so that, **just as (ὥσπερ)** Christ **was raised (ἠγέρθη)** from the dead by the glory of the Father, so we too might walk in newness of life. (NRSV)

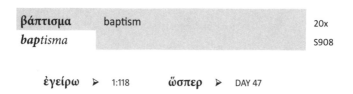

| βάπτισμα | baptism | 20x |
| *bap*tisma | | S908 |

ἐγείρω ▷ 1:118   ὥσπερ ▷ DAY 47

συνετάφημεν οὖν αὐτῷ διὰ τοῦ **βαπτίσματος** εἰς τὸν θάνατον, ἵνα **ὥσπερ ἠγέρθη** Χριστὸς ἐκ νεκρῶν διὰ τῆς δόξης τοῦ πατρός, οὕτως καὶ ἡμεῖς ἐν καινότητι ζωῆς περιπατήσωμεν.

Therefore we have been buried with him	συνετάφημεν οὖν αὐτῷ
by **baptism**	διὰ τοῦ **βαπτίσματος**
into death	εἰς τὸν θάνατον
so that, **just as** Christ **was raised** from the dead	ἵνα **ὥσπερ ἠγέρθη** Χριστὸς ἐκ νεκρῶν
by the glory of the Father	διὰ τῆς δόξης τοῦ πατρός
so we too might walk	οὕτως καὶ ἡμεῖς . . . περιπατήσωμεν
in newness of life	ἐν καινότητι ζωῆς

He who [**γε: untranslated**] did not spare his own Son, but **gave**
him **up (παρέδωκεν)** for us all—how **will he** not also, along with
him, **graciously give (χαρίσεται)** us all things? (NIV)

γέ	indeed, really, at least; (often untranslated)	20x
ge		S1065

παραδίδωμι   ➤   1:140   **χαρίζομαι**   ➤   DAY 230

ὅς **γε** τοῦ ἰδίου υἱοῦ οὐκ ἐφείσατο, ἀλλὰ ὑπὲρ ἡμῶν πάντων
παρέδωκεν αὐτόν, πῶς οὐχὶ καὶ σὺν αὐτῷ τὰ πάντα ἡμῖν
χαρίσεται;

He who did not spare his own Son	ὅς **γε** τοῦ ἰδίου υἱοῦ οὐκ ἐφείσατο
but **gave** him **up**	ἀλλὰ . . . **παρέδωκεν** αὐτόν
for us all	ὑπὲρ ἡμῶν πάντων
how **will he** not also . . . **graciously give** us	πῶς οὐχὶ καὶ . . . ἡμῖν **χαρίσεται**;
along with him	σὺν αὐτῷ
all things?	τὰ πάντα

Being then God's **offspring (γένος)**, **we ought (ὀφείλομεν)** not to think that the divine being is like gold or silver or **stone (λίθῳ)**, an image formed by the art and imagination of man. (ESV)

γένος	race, kind, offspring, descendant	20x
genos		S1085

λίθος ➤ 1:270   **ὀφείλω** ➤ DAY 51

γένος οὖν ὑπάρχοντες τοῦ θεοῦ οὐκ **ὀφείλομεν** νομίζειν χρυσῷ ἢ ἀργύρῳ ἢ **λίθῳ**, χαράγματι τέχνης καὶ ἐνθυμήσεως ἀνθρώπου, τὸ θεῖον εἶναι ὅμοιον.

Being then God's **offspring**	γένος οὖν ὑπάρχοντες τοῦ θεοῦ
we ought not to think	οὐκ **ὀφείλομεν** νομίζειν
that the divine being is like	τὸ θεῖον εἶναι ὅμοιον
gold or silver or **stone**	χρυσῷ ἢ ἀργύρῳ ἢ **λίθῳ**
an image formed	χαράγματι
by the art	τέχνης
and imagination	καὶ ἐνθυμήσεως
of man	ἀνθρώπου

Now His **parents (γονεῖς)** went to Jerusalem every year at the
Feast (ἑορτῇ) of the **Passover (πάσχα)**. (NASB)

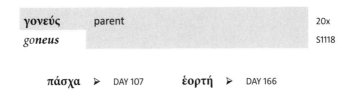

| γονεύς | parent | 20x |
| *goneus* | | S1118 |

πάσχα ➤ DAY 107   ἑορτή ➤ DAY 166

Καὶ ἐπορεύοντο οἱ **γονεῖς** αὐτοῦ κατ᾽ ἔτος εἰς Ἰερουσαλὴμ τῇ
ἑορτῇ τοῦ **πάσχα**.

Now His **parents** went	Καὶ ἐπορεύοντο οἱ **γονεῖς** αὐτοῦ
to Jerusalem	εἰς Ἰερουσαλὴμ
every year	κατ᾽ ἔτος
at the **Feast** of the **Passover**	τῇ **ἑορτῇ** τοῦ **πάσχα**

But the **centurion (ἑκατοντάρχης)**, wishing to save Paul, **kept (ἐκώλυσεν)** them from carrying out their plan. **He ordered (ἐκέλευσέν)** those who could swim to jump overboard first and make for the land. (ESV)

ἑκατοντάρχης	centurion	20x
hekatontarchēs		S1543

     κελεύω ▷ DAY 199   **κωλύω** ▷ DAY 222

ὁ δὲ **ἑκατοντάρχης** βουλόμενος διασῶσαι τὸν Παῦλον **ἐκώλυσεν** αὐτοὺς τοῦ βουλήματος, **ἐκέλευσέν** τε τοὺς δυναμένους κολυμβᾶν ἀπορίψαντας πρώτους ἐπὶ τὴν γῆν ἐξιέναι,

But the **centurion**	ὁ δὲ **ἑκατοντάρχης**
wishing to save Paul	βουλόμενος διασῶσαι τὸν Παῦλον
kept them	**ἐκώλυσεν** αὐτοὺς
from carrying out their plan	τοῦ βουλήματος
He ordered those who could swim	**ἐκέλευσέν** τε τοὺς δυναμένους κολυμβᾶν
to jump overboard first	ἀπορίψαντας πρώτους
and make for the land	ἐπὶ τὴν γῆν ἐξιέναι

For (διότι) by works of the law no human being will be justified [lit., all flesh **will** not **be justified (δικαιωθήσεται)**] in his sight, since through the law comes **knowledge (ἐπίγνωσις)** of sin. (ESV)

| **ἐπίγνωσις** | knowledge, discernment | 20x |
| *epignōsis* | | S1922 |

δικαιόω ▷ DAY 14   **διότι** ▷ DAY 194

διότι ἐξ ἔργων νόμου οὐ **δικαιωθήσεται** πᾶσα σὰρξ ἐνώπιον αὐτοῦ, διὰ γὰρ νόμου **ἐπίγνωσις** ἁμαρτίας.

For by works of the law	**διότι** ἐξ ἔργων νόμου
no human being will be justified [lit., all flesh **will** not **be justified**]	οὐ **δικαιωθήσεται** πᾶσα σὰρξ
in his sight	ἐνώπιον αὐτοῦ
since through the law comes	διὰ γὰρ νόμου
knowledge of sin	**ἐπίγνωσις** ἁμαρτίας

Preach the word; **be ready (ἐπίστηθι)** in season and out of season; reprove, **rebuke (ἐπιτίμησον)**, and exhort, with complete patience and **teaching (διδαχῇ)**. (ESV)

| ἐφίστημι | to come upon, stand by, be ready, appear | 20x |
| *ephistēmi* | | S2186 |

διδαχή ➤ DAY 92   **ἐπιτιμάω** ➤ DAY 96

κήρυξον τὸν λόγον, **ἐπίστηθι** εὐκαίρως ἀκαίρως, ἔλεγξον, **ἐπιτίμησον**, παρακάλεσον, ἐν πάσῃ μακροθυμίᾳ καὶ **διδαχῇ**.

Preach the word	κήρυξον τὸν λόγον
be ready	**ἐπίστηθι**
in season	εὐκαίρως
and out of season	ἀκαίρως
reprove	ἔλεγξον
rebuke	**ἐπιτίμησον**
and exhort	παρακάλεσον
with complete patience	ἐν πάσῃ μακροθυμίᾳ
and **teaching**	καὶ **διδαχῇ**

Then the soldiers of the **governor (ἡγεμόνος)** took Jesus into the governor's headquarters, and **they gathered (συνήγαγον)** the **whole (ὅλην)** cohort around him. (NRSV)

ἡγεμών	governor	20x
hēgemōn		S2232

　　ὅλος　➤　1:156　　　συνάγω　➤　1:278

Τότε οἱ στρατιῶται τοῦ **ἡγεμόνος** παραλαβόντες τὸν Ἰησοῦν εἰς τὸ πραιτώριον **συνήγαγον** ἐπ᾿ αὐτὸν **ὅλην** τὴν σπεῖραν.

Then the soldiers of the **governor**	Τότε οἱ στρατιῶται τοῦ **ἡγεμόνος**
took Jesus	παραλαβόντες τὸν Ἰησοῦν
into the governor's headquarters	εἰς τὸ πραιτώριον
and **they gathered**	**συνήγαγον**
the **whole** cohort	**ὅλην** τὴν σπεῖραν
around him	ἐπ᾿ αὐτὸν

The God of Abraham, **Isaac** (Ἰσαάκ) and Jacob, the God of our fathers, has glorified His **Servant** (παῖδα) Jesus, whom you delivered up and **disowned** (ἠρνήσασθε) before Pilate, when he had decided to set Him free. (MLB)

| Ἰσαάκ | Isaac | 20x |
| *Isaak* | | S2464 |

ἀρνέομαι ➤ DAY 62   παῖς ➤ DAY 201

ὁ θεὸς Ἀβραὰμ καὶ **Ἰσαὰκ** καὶ Ἰακώβ, ὁ θεὸς τῶν πατέρων ἡμῶν, ἐδόξασεν τὸν **παῖδα** αὐτοῦ Ἰησοῦν, ὃν ὑμεῖς μὲν παρεδώκατε καὶ **ἠρνήσασθε** κατὰ πρόσωπον Πειλάτου, κρίναντος ἐκείνου ἀπολύειν·

The God of Abraham, **Isaac** and Jacob	ὁ θεὸς Ἀβραὰμ καὶ **Ἰσαὰκ** καὶ Ἰακώβ
the God of our fathers	ὁ θεὸς τῶν πατέρων ἡμῶν
has glorified His **Servant** Jesus	ἐδόξασεν τὸν **παῖδα** αὐτοῦ Ἰησοῦν
whom you delivered up	ὃν ὑμεῖς μὲν παρεδώκατε
and **disowned**	καὶ **ἠρνήσασθε**
before Pilate	κατὰ πρόσωπον Πειλάτου
when he had decided	κρίναντος ἐκείνου
to set Him free	ἀπολύειν

He took the **seven (ἑπτὰ)** loaves and the **fish (ἰχθύας)**, and **He gave thanks (εὐχαριστήσας)**, broke them, and kept on giving them to the disciples, and the disciples gave them to the crowds.
(HCSB)

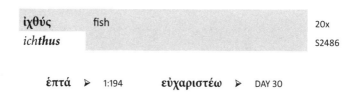

ἰχθύς	fish	20x
ichthus		S2486

ἑπτά ➤ 1:194   **εὐχαριστέω** ➤ DAY 30

ἔλαβεν τοὺς **ἑπτὰ** ἄρτους καὶ τοὺς **ἰχθύας** καὶ **εὐχαριστήσας**
ἔκλασεν καὶ ἐδίδου τοῖς μαθηταῖς οἱ δὲ μαθηταὶ τοῖς ὄχλοις.

He took the **seven** loaves	ἔλαβεν τοὺς **ἑπτὰ** ἄρτους
and the **fish**	καὶ τοὺς **ἰχθύας**
and **He gave thanks**	καὶ **εὐχαριστήσας**
broke them	ἔκλασεν
and kept on giving them to the disciples	καὶ ἐδίδου τοῖς μαθηταῖς
and the disciples gave them to the crowds	οἱ δὲ μαθηταὶ τοῖς ὄχλοις

And if (κἂν) I donate all my goods to feed the poor, **and if (κἂν)** **I give (παραδῶ)** my body in order **to boast (καυχήσωμαι)** but do not have love, I gain nothing. (HCSB)

κἂν	and if, even if	20x
kan		S2579

παραδίδωμι ➤ 1:140	**καυχάομαι** ➤ DAY 32

κἂν ψωμίσω πάντα τὰ ὑπάρχοντά μου, **κἂν παραδῶ** τὸ σῶμά μου, ἵνα **καυχήσωμαι**, ἀγάπην δὲ μὴ ἔχω, οὐδὲν ὠφελοῦμαι.

And if I donate . . . to feed the poor	**κἂν** ψωμίσω
all my goods	πάντα τὰ ὑπάρχοντά μου
and if I give my body	**κἂν παραδῶ** τὸ σῶμά μου
in order **to boast**	ἵνα **καυχήσωμαι**
but do not have love	ἀγάπην δὲ μὴ ἔχω
I gain nothing	οὐδὲν ὠφελοῦμαι

But this **I admit (ὁμολογῶ)** to you, that according to the **Way (ὁδὸν)**, which they call a sect, **I worship (λατρεύω)** the God of our ancestors, believing everything laid down according to the law or written in the prophets. (NRSV)

λατρεύω	to serve, worship	20x
latreuō		S3000

ὁδός ➤ 1:166　　　**ὁμολογέω** ➤ DAY 153

ὁμολογῶ δὲ τοῦτό σοι ὅτι κατὰ τὴν **ὁδὸν** ἣν λέγουσιν αἵρεσιν οὕτως **λατρεύω** τῷ πατρῴῳ θεῷ, πιστεύων πᾶσι τοῖς κατὰ τὸν νόμον καὶ τοῖς ἐν τοῖς προφήταις γεγραμμένοις,

But this **I admit** to you	**ὁμολογῶ** δὲ τοῦτό σοι
that according to the **Way**	ὅτι κατὰ τὴν **ὁδὸν**
which they call a sect	ἣν λέγουσιν αἵρεσιν
I worship the God of our ancestors	οὕτως **λατρεύω** τῷ πατρῴῳ θεῷ
believing everything laid down according to the law	πιστεύων πᾶσι τοῖς κατὰ τὸν νόμον
or written in the prophets	καὶ τοῖς ἐν τοῖς προφήταις γεγραμμένοις

Do you **still not (οὔπω)** understand? Don't **you remember (μνημονεύετε)** the five loaves for the five thousand, and **how many (πόσους)** basketfuls you gathered? (NIV)

μνημονεύω	to remember, mention	20x
mnēmoneuō		S3421

οὔπω ➤ DAY 104   **πόσος** ➤ DAY 140

οὔπω νοεῖτε, οὐδὲ **μνημονεύετε** τοὺς πέντε ἄρτους τῶν πεντακισχιλίων καὶ **πόσους** κοφίνους ἐλάβετε;

Do you **still not** understand?	**οὔπω** νοεῖτε
Don't **you remember**	οὐδὲ **μνημονεύετε**
the five loaves	τοὺς πέντε ἄρτους
for the five thousand	τῶν πεντακισχιλίων
and **how many** basketfuls	καὶ **πόσους** κοφίνους
you gathered?	ἐλάβετε;

He fasted (νηστεύσας) forty days and forty **nights (νύκτας)**, and afterwards **he was famished (ἐπείνασεν)**. (NRSV)

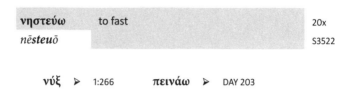

| νηστεύω | to fast | 20x |
| nēsteuō | | S3522 |

νύξ ➢ 1:266   πεινάω ➢ DAY 203

καὶ **νηστεύσας** ἡμέρας τεσσεράκοντα καὶ **νύκτας** τεσσεράκοντα ὕστερον **ἐπείνασεν**.

He fasted	καὶ **νηστεύσας**
forty days	ἡμέρας τεσσεράκοντα
and forty **nights**	καὶ **νύκτας** τεσσεράκοντα
and afterwards	ὕστερον
he was famished	**ἐπείνασεν**

And Jesus said to them, "Have you come out with **swords**
(μαχαιρῶν) and **clubs** (ξύλων) to arrest Me, **as** (Ὡς) you would
against a robber?" (NASB)

| ξύλον | wood, tree, club | 20x |
| *xulon* | | S3586 |

ὡς ➤ 1:36   μάχαιρα ➤ DAY 123

καὶ ἀποκριθεὶς ὁ Ἰησοῦς εἶπεν αὐτοῖς **Ὡς** ἐπὶ λῃστὴν ἐξήλθατε
μετὰ **μαχαιρῶν** καὶ **ξύλων** συλλαβεῖν με;

And Jesus said to them	καὶ ἀποκριθεὶς ὁ Ἰησοῦς εἶπεν αὐτοῖς
Have you come out	ἐξήλθατε
with **swords**	μετὰ **μαχαιρῶν**
and **clubs**	καὶ **ξύλων**
to arrest Me	συλλαβεῖν με;
as you would against a robber?	**Ὡς** ἐπὶ λῃστὴν

For **if (Ἐὰν) you forgive (ἀφῆτε)** others their **trespasses (παραπτώματα)**, your heavenly Father **will forgive (ἀφήσει)** you too. (MLB)

παράπτωμα	lapse, trespass, falling away	20x
paraptōma		S3900

     ἐάν   ▷   1:52   ἀφίημι   ▷   1:115

Ἐὰν γὰρ **ἀφῆτε** τοῖς ἀνθρώποις τὰ **παραπτώματα** αὐτῶν, **ἀφήσει** καὶ ὑμῖν ὁ πατὴρ ὑμῶν ὁ οὐράνιος·

For **if you forgive**	Ἐὰν γὰρ **ἀφῆτε**
others	τοῖς ἀνθρώποις
their **trespasses**	τὰ **παραπτώματα** αὐτῶν
your heavenly Father	ὁ πατὴρ ὑμῶν ὁ οὐράνιος
will forgive	**ἀφήσει**
you too	καὶ ὑμῖν

And **in the same way (ὁμοίως)** he sprinkled with the blood both
the **tent (σκηνὴν)** and all the **vessels (σκεύη)** used in worship.
(ESV)

σκηνή	tent, booth, tabernacle	20x
skēnē		S4633

ὁμοίως ➤ DAY 80   **σκεῦος** ➤ DAY 242

καὶ τὴν **σκηνὴν** δὲ καὶ πάντα τὰ **σκεύη** τῆς λειτουργίας τῷ αἵματι
ὁμοίως ἐράντισεν.

And **in the same way**	δὲ . . . **ὁμοίως**
he sprinkled	ἐράντισεν
with the blood	τῷ αἵματι
both the **tent**	καὶ τὴν **σκηνὴν**
and all the **vessels**	καὶ πάντα τὰ **σκεύη**
used in worship	τῆς λειτουργίας

For the foolishness of God is **wiser (σοφώτερον)** than men, and the **weakness (ἀσθενὲς)** of God is **stronger (ἰσχυρότερον)** than men. (ESV)

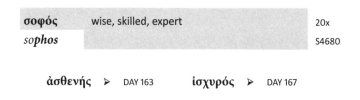

σοφός	wise, skilled, expert	20x
sophos		S4680

ἀσθενής ➢ DAY 163   **ἰσχυρός** ➢ DAY 167

ὅτι τὸ μωρὸν τοῦ θεοῦ **σοφώτερον** τῶν ἀνθρώπων ἐστίν, καὶ τὸ **ἀσθενὲς** τοῦ θεοῦ **ἰσχυρότερον** τῶν ἀνθρώπων.

For the foolishness of God	ὅτι τὸ μωρὸν τοῦ θεοῦ
is **wiser**	**σοφώτερον** . . . ἐστίν
than men	τῶν ἀνθρώπων
and the **weakness** of God	καὶ τὸ **ἀσθενὲς** τοῦ θεοῦ
is **stronger**	**ἰσχυρότερον**
than men	τῶν ἀνθρώπων

"In one **hour (ὥρᾳ) such great (τοσοῦτος) wealth (πλοῦτος)** has been brought to ruin!" Every sea captain, and all who travel by ship, the sailors, and all who earn their living from the sea, will stand far off. (NIV)

τοσοῦτος, τοσαύτη, τοσοῦτον	so great, so large, so long, so many	20x
tosoutos, tosautē, tosouton		S5118

     ὥρα   ▷   1:159   **πλοῦτος**   ▷   DAY 227

ὅτι μιᾷ **ὥρᾳ** ἠρημώθη ὁ **τοσοῦτος πλοῦτος**. καὶ πᾶς κυβερνήτης καὶ πᾶς ὁ ἐπὶ τόπον πλέων, καὶ ναῦται καὶ ὅσοι τὴν θάλασσαν ἐργάζονται, ἀπὸ μακρόθεν ἔστησαν

In one **hour**	ὅτι μιᾷ **ὥρᾳ**
such great wealth	ὁ **τοσοῦτος πλοῦτος**
has been brought to ruin!	ἠρημώθη
Every sea captain	καὶ πᾶς κυβερνήτης
and all who travel by ship	καὶ πᾶς ὁ ἐπὶ τόπον πλέων
the sailors	καὶ ναῦται
and all who earn their living from the sea	καὶ ὅσοι τὴν θάλασσαν ἐργάζονται
will stand far off	ἀπὸ μακρόθεν ἔστησαν

The two **were running (ἔτρεχον)** together; and the other disciple
ran ahead faster than Peter and came to the **tomb (μνημεῖον)**
first (πρῶτος). (NASB)

τρέχω	to run	20x
trechō		S5143

    πρῶτος ➤ 1:182   **μνημεῖον** ➤ DAY 17

ἔτρεχον δὲ οἱ δύο ὁμοῦ· καὶ ὁ ἄλλος μαθητὴς προέδραμεν
τάχειον τοῦ Πέτρου καὶ ἦλθεν **πρῶτος** εἰς τὸ **μνημεῖον**,

The two **were running**	**ἔτρεχον** δὲ οἱ δύο
together	ὁμοῦ
and the other disciple	καὶ ὁ ἄλλος μαθητὴς
ran ahead	προέδραμεν
faster than Peter	τάχειον τοῦ Πέτρου
and came . . . **first**	καὶ ἦλθεν **πρῶτος**
to the **tomb**	εἰς τὸ **μνημεῖον**

This is how one **should regard (λογιζέσθω)** us, as **servants
(ὑπηρέτας)** of Christ and stewards of the **mysteries (μυστηρίων)**
of God. (ESV)

| ὑπηρέτης | servant, attendant | 20x |
| *hupēretēs* | | S5257 |

    λογίζομαι ➤ DAY 8   **μυστήριον** ➤ DAY 124

Οὕτως ἡμᾶς **λογιζέσθω** ἄνθρωπος ὡς **ὑπηρέτας** Χριστοῦ καὶ
οἰκονόμους **μυστηρίων** θεοῦ.

This is how	Οὕτως
one **should regard** us	ἡμᾶς **λογιζέσθω** ἄνθρωπος
as **servants**	ὡς **ὑπηρέτας**
of Christ	Χριστοῦ
and stewards	καὶ οἰκονόμους
of the **mysteries** of God	**μυστηρίων** θεοῦ

God **exalted (ὕψωσεν)** this man to his **right hand (δεξιᾷ)** as ruler and **Savior (σωτῆρα)**, to give repentance to Israel and forgiveness of sins. (CSB)

| ὑψόω | to lift up, exalt, raise | 20x |
| *hupsoō* | | S5312 |

δεξιός ▷ 1:290   **σωτήρ** ▷ DAY 206

τοῦτον ὁ θεὸς ἀρχηγὸν καὶ **σωτῆρα ὕψωσεν** τῇ **δεξιᾷ** αὐτοῦ, [τοῦ] δοῦναι μετάνοιαν τῷ Ἰσραὴλ καὶ ἄφεσιν ἁμαρτιῶν·

God **exalted** this man	τοῦτον ὁ θεὸς . . . **ὕψωσεν**
to his **right hand**	τῇ **δεξιᾷ** αὐτοῦ
as ruler and **Savior**	ἀρχηγὸν καὶ **σωτῆρα**
to give repentance	[τοῦ] δοῦναι μετάνοιαν
to Israel	τῷ Ἰσραὴλ
and forgiveness of sins	καὶ ἄφεσιν ἁμαρτιῶν

that you abstain (ἀπέχεσθαι) from what has been sacrificed to
idols, and from blood, and from what has been strangled, and
from **sexual immorality (πορνείας)**. If you keep yourselves from
these, **you will do (πράξετε)** well. Farewell. (ESV)

| ἀπέχω | to receive, be away from, refrain, abstain | 19x |
| *apechō* | | S568 |

πράσσω ▷ DAY 21   πορνεία ▷ DAY 171

ἀπέχεσθαι εἰδωλοθύτων καὶ αἵματος καὶ πνικτῶν καὶ **πορνείας·**
ἐξ ὧν διατηροῦντες ἑαυτοὺς εὖ **πράξετε.** Ἔρρωσθε.

that you abstain	ἀπέχεσθαι
from what has been sacrificed to idols	εἰδωλοθύτων
and from blood	καὶ αἵματος
and from what has been strangled	καὶ πνικτῶν
and from **sexual immorality**	καὶ **πορνείας**
If you keep yourselves	διατηροῦντες ἑαυτοὺς
from these	ἐξ ὧν
you will do well	εὖ **πράξετε**
Farewell	Ἔρρωσθε

When the **harvest (καρπῶν)** time **approached (ἤγγισεν)**, he
sent his servants to the **tenants (γεωργοὺς)** to collect his **fruit
(καρποὺς)**. (NIV)

γεωργός	farmer	19x
geōrgos		S1092

  καρπός ➤ 1:247   **ἐγγίζω** ➤ 1:352

ὅτε δὲ **ἤγγισεν** ὁ καιρὸς τῶν **καρπῶν**, ἀπέστειλεν τοὺς δούλους
αὐτοῦ πρὸς τοὺς **γεωργοὺς** λαβεῖν τοὺς **καρποὺς** αὐτοῦ.

When the **harvest** time	ὅτε δὲ . . . ὁ καιρὸς τῶν **καρπῶν**
approached	**ἤγγισεν**
he sent his servants	ἀπέστειλεν τοὺς δούλους αὐτοῦ
to the **tenants**	πρὸς τοὺς **γεωργοὺς**
to collect his **fruit**	λαβεῖν τοὺς **καρποὺς** αὐτοῦ

Yet, with respect to the **promise (ἐπαγγελίαν)** of God, **he did not waver (διεκρίθη)** in unbelief but grew strong in faith, **giving (δοὺς)** glory to God. (NASB)

διακρίνω *diakrinō*	to discern, distinguish, separate, doubt, waver	19x S1252

    δίδωμι ➤ 1:43   **ἐπαγγελία** ➤ 1:299

εἰς δὲ τὴν **ἐπαγγελίαν** τοῦ θεοῦ οὐ **διεκρίθη** τῇ ἀπιστίᾳ ἀλλὰ ἐνεδυναμώθη τῇ πίστει, **δοὺς** δόξαν τῷ θεῷ

Yet, with respect to the **promise** of God	εἰς δὲ τὴν **ἐπαγγελίαν** τοῦ θεοῦ
he did not **waver**	οὐ **διεκρίθη**
in unbelief	τῇ ἀπιστίᾳ
but grew strong	ἀλλὰ ἐνεδυναμώθη
in faith	τῇ πίστει
giving glory	**δοὺς** δόξαν
to God	τῷ θεῷ

For it is by **grace (χάριτί)** you have been **saved (σεσωσμένοι)**, through faith—and this is not from yourselves, it is the **gift (δῶρον)** of God. (NIV)

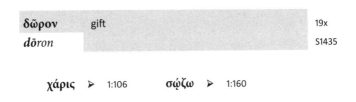

δῶρον	gift	19x
dōron		S1435

χάρις ▷ 1:106   σῴζω ▷ 1:160

τῇ γὰρ **χάριτί** ἐστε **σεσωσμένοι** διὰ πίστεως· καὶ τοῦτο οὐκ ἐξ ὑμῶν, θεοῦ τὸ **δῶρον**·

For it is by **grace**	τῇ γὰρ **χάριτί**
you have been **saved**	ἐστε **σεσωσμένοι**
through faith	διὰ πίστεως
and this is not from yourselves	καὶ τοῦτο οὐκ ἐξ ὑμῶν
it is the **gift** of God	θεοῦ τὸ **δῶρον**

I desire, then, that in every place the men should pray, **lifting up (ἐπαίροντας)** holy hands **without (χωρὶς) anger (ὀργῆς)** or argument. (NRSV)

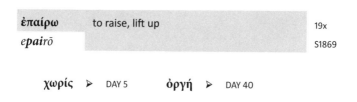

ἐπαίρω   to raise, lift up   19x
epairō   S1869

χωρίς ➤ DAY 5   **ὀργή** ➤ DAY 40

Βούλομαι οὖν προσεύχεσθαι τοὺς ἄνδρας ἐν παντὶ τόπῳ, **ἐπαίροντας** ὁσίους χεῖρας **χωρὶς ὀργῆς** καὶ διαλογισμῶν.

I desire, then	Βούλομαι οὖν
that . . . the men should pray	προσεύχεσθαι τοὺς ἄνδρας
in every place	ἐν παντὶ τόπῳ
lifting up holy hands	**ἐπαίροντας** ὁσίους χεῖρας
without anger	**χωρὶς ὀργῆς**
or argument	καὶ διαλογισμῶν

Look, I have given you the authority to trample **on (ἐπάνω)** snakes and scorpions and over all the power of the **enemy (ἐχθροῦ)**; nothing at all **will harm (ἀδικήσει)** you. (CSB)

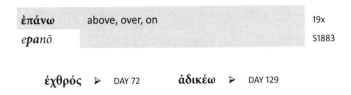

| **ἐπάνω** | above, over, on | 19x |
| *epanō* | | S1883 |

ἐχθρός ▷ DAY 72   **ἀδικέω** ▷ DAY 129

ἰδοὺ δέδωκα ὑμῖν τὴν ἐξουσίαν τοῦ πατεῖν **ἐπάνω** ὄφεων καὶ σκορπίων, καὶ ἐπὶ πᾶσαν τὴν δύναμιν τοῦ **ἐχθροῦ**, καὶ οὐδὲν ὑμᾶς οὐ μὴ **ἀδικήσει**.

Look	ἰδοὺ
I have given you the authority	δέδωκα ὑμῖν τὴν ἐξουσίαν
to trample **on**	τοῦ πατεῖν **ἐπάνω**
snakes and scorpions	ὄφεων καὶ σκορπίων
and over all	καὶ ἐπὶ πᾶσαν
the power of the **enemy**	τὴν δύναμιν τοῦ **ἐχθροῦ**
nothing at all	καὶ οὐδὲν . . . οὐ μὴ
will harm you	ὑμᾶς . . . **ἀδικήσει**

But when her owners saw that their **hope (ἐλπὶς)** of gain was gone, **they seized (ἐπιλαβόμενοι)** Paul and Silas and dragged them into the marketplace before the **rulers (ἄρχοντας)**. (ESV)

ἐπιλαμβάνομαι *epilambanomai*	to lay hold of, take hold of, seize	19x S1949

ἐλπίς   ▷   1:296   ἄρχων   ▷   DAY 27

Ἰδόντες δὲ οἱ κύριοι αὐτῆς ὅτι ἐξῆλθεν ἡ **ἐλπὶς** τῆς ἐργασίας αὐτῶν **ἐπιλαβόμενοι** τὸν Παῦλον καὶ τὸν Σίλαν εἵλκυσαν εἰς τὴν ἀγορὰν ἐπὶ τοὺς **ἄρχοντας,**

But when her owners saw that	Ἰδόντες δὲ οἱ κύριοι αὐτῆς ὅτι
their **hope** of gain was gone	ἐξῆλθεν ἡ **ἐλπὶς** τῆς ἐργασίας αὐτῶν
they seized Paul and Silas	**ἐπιλαβόμενοι** τὸν Παῦλον καὶ τὸν Σίλαν
and dragged them into the marketplace	εἵλκυσαν εἰς τὴν ἀγορὰν
before the **rulers**	ἐπὶ τοὺς **ἄρχοντας**

But **you have come (προσεληλύθατε)** to **Mount (ὄρει)** Zion
and to the city of the living God, the **heavenly (ἐπουρανίῳ)**
Jerusalem, and to innumerable angels in festal gathering. (NRSV)

| ἐπουράνιος | heavenly | 19x |
| *epouranios* | | S2032 |

προσέρχομαι ➤ 1:197   **ὄρος** ➤ 1:255

ἀλλὰ **προσεληλύθατε** Σιὼν **ὄρει** καὶ πόλει θεοῦ ζῶντος,
Ἰερουσαλὴμ **ἐπουρανίῳ**, καὶ μυριάσιν ἀγγέλων, πανηγύρει

But **you have come**	ἀλλὰ **προσεληλύθατε**
to **Mount** Zion	Σιὼν **ὄρει**
and to the city	καὶ πόλει
of the living God	θεοῦ ζῶντος
the **heavenly** Jerusalem	Ἰερουσαλὴμ **ἐπουρανίῳ**
and to innumerable angels	καὶ μυριάσιν ἀγγέλων
in festal gathering	πανηγύρει

And they persevered in the apostles' **teaching (διδαχῇ)** and in **fellowship (κοινωνία)**, in the breaking of bread and in **prayers (προσευχαῖς)**. (MLB)

κοινωνία	fellowship	19x
koinōnia		S2842

προσευχή ▷ DAY 44   διδαχή ▷ DAY 92

ἦσαν δὲ προσκαρτεροῦντες τῇ **διδαχῇ** τῶν ἀποστόλων καὶ τῇ **κοινωνίᾳ**, τῇ κλάσει τοῦ ἄρτου καὶ ταῖς **προσευχαῖς**.

And they persevered	ἦσαν δὲ προσκαρτεροῦντες
in the apostles' **teaching**	τῇ **διδαχῇ** τῶν ἀποστόλων
and in **fellowship**	καὶ τῇ **κοινωνίᾳ**
in the breaking of bread	τῇ κλάσει τοῦ ἄρτου
and in **prayers**	καὶ ταῖς **προσευχαῖς**

He said, "In a certain **city (πόλει)** there was a **judge (Κριτής) who** neither **feared (φοβούμενος)** God nor had respect for people."
(NRSV)

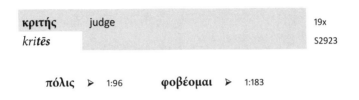

| κριτής | judge | 19x |
| *kritēs* | | S2923 |

πόλις ▷ 1:96   **φοβέομαι** ▷ 1:183

λέγων **Κριτής** τις ἦν ἔν τινι **πόλει** τὸν θεὸν μὴ **φοβούμενος** καὶ ἄνθρωπον μὴ ἐντρεπόμενος.

He said	λέγων
In a certain **city**	ἔν τινι **πόλει**
there was a **judge**	**Κριτής** τις ἦν
who neither **feared** God	τὸν θεὸν μὴ **φοβούμενος**
nor had respect for people	καὶ ἄνθρωπον μὴ ἐντρεπόμενος

But the disciples [lit., they] **understood (συνῆκαν)** none of these things, and the meaning of this **statement (ῥῆμα)** was **hidden (κεκρυμμένον)** from them, and they did not comprehend the things that were said. (NASB)

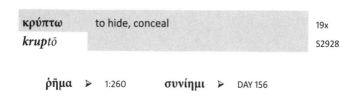

| **κρύπτω** | to hide, conceal | 19x |
| *kruptō* | | S2928 |

ῥῆμα ➤ 1:260   συνίημι ➤ DAY 156

Καὶ αὐτοὶ οὐδὲν τούτων **συνῆκαν**, καὶ ἦν τὸ **ῥῆμα** τοῦτο **κεκρυμμένον** ἀπ᾽ αὐτῶν, καὶ οὐκ ἐγίνωσκον τὰ λεγόμενα.

But the disciples [lit., they] **understood**	Καὶ αὐτοὶ . . . **συνῆκαν**
none of these things	οὐδὲν τούτων
and the meaning of this **statement**	καὶ . . . τὸ **ῥῆμα** τοῦτο
was **hidden** from them	ἦν . . . **κεκρυμμένον** ἀπ᾽ αὐτῶν
and they did not comprehend	καὶ οὐκ ἐγίνωσκον
the things that were said	τὰ λεγόμενα

Therefore, if anyone is in Christ, he is a **new (καινὴ) creation (κτίσις)**; old things **have passed away (παρῆλθεν)**, and look, **new things (καινά)** have come. (HCSB)

κτίσις	creation, creature	19x
ktisis		S2937

καινός ➤ 1:362   **παρέρχομαι** ➤ DAY 106

ὥστε εἴ τις ἐν Χριστῷ, **καινὴ κτίσις**· τὰ ἀρχαῖα **παρῆλθεν**, ἰδοὺ γέγονεν **καινά**·

Therefore	ὥστε
if anyone is in Christ	εἴ τις ἐν Χριστῷ
he is a **new creation**	**καινὴ κτίσις**
old things **have passed away**	τὰ ἀρχαῖα **παρῆλθεν**
and look	ἰδοὺ
new things have come	γέγονεν **καινά**

Our fathers had the **tent (σκηνὴ)** of **witness (μαρτυρίου)** in the wilderness, just as he who spoke to Moses directed him to make it, according to the pattern that **he had seen (ἑωράκει)**. (ESV)

μαρτύριον	witness, evidence	19x
marturion		S3142

ὁράω	▷	1:40	σκηνή	▷	DAY 268

Ἡ **σκηνὴ** τοῦ **μαρτυρίου** ἦν τοῖς πατράσιν ἡμῶν ἐν τῇ ἐρήμῳ, καθὼς διετάξατο ὁ λαλῶν τῷ Μωυσῇ ποιῆσαι αὐτὴν κατὰ τὸν τύπον ὃν **ἑωράκει**,

Our fathers had	ἦν τοῖς πατράσιν ἡμῶν
the **tent** of **witness**	Ἡ **σκηνὴ** τοῦ **μαρτυρίου**
in the wilderness	ἐν τῇ ἐρήμῳ
just as he who spoke to Moses	καθὼς . . . ὁ λαλῶν τῷ Μωυσῇ
directed him	διετάξατο
to make it	ποιῆσαι αὐτὴν
according to the pattern	κατὰ τὸν τύπον
that **he had seen**	ὃν **ἑωράκει**

When they bring you before the synagogues and the **rulers (ἀρχὰς)** and the authorities, do not **worry about (μεριμνήσητε)** how or what you are to speak in your defense, or what **you are to say (εἴπητε)**. (NASB)

μεριμνάω *merimnaō*	to be anxious about, be concerned about, care for	19x S3309

    λέγω ➤ 1:9   **ἀρχή** ➤ 1:281

Ὅταν δὲ εἰσφέρωσιν ὑμᾶς ἐπὶ τὰς συναγωγὰς καὶ τὰς **ἀρχὰς** καὶ τὰς ἐξουσίας, μὴ **μεριμνήσητε** πῶς [ἢ τί] ἀπολογήσησθε ἢ τί **εἴπητε·**

When they bring you	Ὅταν δὲ εἰσφέρωσιν ὑμᾶς
before the synagogues	ἐπὶ τὰς συναγωγὰς
and the **rulers**	καὶ τὰς **ἀρχὰς**
and the authorities	καὶ τὰς ἐξουσίας
do not **worry about**	μὴ **μεριμνήσητε**
how or what you are to speak in your defense	πῶς [ἢ τί] ἀπολογήσησθε
or what **you are to say**	ἢ τί **εἴπητε**

And no one puts **new (νέον)** wine into **old (παλαιούς)** wineskins; otherwise the **new (νέος)** wine will burst the skins and it **will be spilled out (ἐκχυθήσεται)**, and the skins will be ruined. (NASB)

| παλαιός | old | 19x |
| *palaios* | | S3820 |

ἐκχέω   ➤   DAY 132   νέος   ➤   DAY 183

καὶ οὐδεὶς βάλλει οἶνον **νέον** εἰς ἀσκοὺς **παλαιούς·** εἰ δὲ μήγε, ῥήξει ὁ οἶνος ὁ **νέος** τοὺς ἀσκούς, καὶ αὐτὸς **ἐκχυθήσεται** καὶ οἱ ἀσκοὶ ἀπολοῦνται·

And no one puts	καὶ οὐδεὶς βάλλει
new wine	οἶνον **νέον**
into **old** wineskins	εἰς ἀσκοὺς **παλαιούς**
otherwise	εἰ δὲ μήγε
the **new** wine will burst	ῥήξει ὁ οἶνος ὁ **νέος**
the skins	τοὺς ἀσκούς
and it **will be spilled out**	καὶ αὐτὸς **ἐκχυθήσεται**
and the skins will be ruined	καὶ οἱ ἀσκοὶ ἀπολοῦνται

When they found Him **across (πέραν)** the sea, they asked Him, "Rabbi, **when (πότε)** did You get **here (ὧδε)**?" (MLB)

πότε	at what time? when?	19x
pote		S4219

ὧδε ➤ 1:267   πέραν ➤ DAY 204

καὶ εὑρόντες αὐτὸν **πέραν** τῆς θαλάσσης εἶπον αὐτῷ Ῥαββεί, **πότε ὧδε** γέγονας;

When they found Him	καὶ εὑρόντες αὐτὸν
across the sea	**πέραν** τῆς θαλάσσης
they asked Him	εἶπον αὐτῷ
Rabbi	Ῥαββεί
when	**πότε**
did You get	γέγονας;
here?	**ὧδε**

After listening to the king, they went on their way. And behold, the **star (ἀστὴρ)** that they had seen when it rose **went before (προῆγεν)** them until it came to rest over the place where the **child (παιδίον)** was. (ESV)

προάγω *proagō*	to lead forth, precede, go before	19x S4254

παιδίον	➤	1:302	ἀστήρ	➤	DAY 177

οἱ δὲ ἀκούσαντες τοῦ βασιλέως ἐπορεύθησαν, καὶ ἰδοὺ ὁ **ἀστὴρ** ὃν εἶδον ἐν τῇ ἀνατολῇ **προῆγεν** αὐτούς, ἕως ἐλθὼν ἐστάθη ἐπάνω οὗ ἦν τὸ **παιδίον**.

After listening to the king	οἱ δὲ ἀκούσαντες τοῦ βασιλέως
they went on their way	ἐπορεύθησαν
And behold	καὶ ἰδοὺ
the **star** that they had seen	ὁ **ἀστὴρ** ὃν εἶδον
when it rose	ἐν τῇ ἀνατολῇ
went before them	**προῆγεν** αὐτούς
until it came to rest over	ἕως ἐλθὼν ἐστάθη ἐπάνω
the place where the **child** was	οὗ ἦν τὸ **παιδίον**

Then he said to me, "Do not seal up the words of the **prophecy (προφητείας)** of this **book (βιβλίου)**, for the **time (καιρὸς)** is near." (MLB)

| προφητεία | prophecy, declaration | 19x |
| *prophēteia* | | S4394 |

καιρός ➤ 1:199   **βιβλίον** ➤ DAY 53

Καὶ λέγει μοι Μὴ σφραγίσῃς τοὺς λόγους τῆς **προφητείας** τοῦ **βιβλίου** τούτου, ὁ **καιρὸς** γὰρ ἐγγύς ἐστιν.

Then he said to me	Καὶ λέγει μοι
Do not seal up	Μὴ σφραγίσῃς
the words	τοὺς λόγους
of the **prophecy**	τῆς **προφητείας**
of this **book**	τοῦ **βιβλίου** τούτου
for the **time**	ὁ **καιρὸς** γὰρ
is near	ἐγγύς ἐστιν

And he said, "**Truly (Ἀληθῶς)**, I tell you, this **poor (πτωχὴ) widow (χήρα)** has put in more than all of them." (ESV)

ἀληθῶς	truly	18x
alēthōs		S230

πτωχός ➤ DAY 61　　　χήρα ➤ DAY 158

καὶ εἶπεν Ἀληθῶς λέγω ὑμῖν ὅτι ἡ **χήρα** αὕτη ἡ **πτωχὴ** πλεῖον πάντων ἔβαλεν·

And he said	καὶ εἶπεν
Truly	**Ἀληθῶς**
I tell you	λέγω ὑμῖν ὅτι
this **poor widow**	ἡ **χήρα** αὕτη ἡ **πτωχὴ**
has put in	ἔβαλεν
more than all of them	πλεῖον πάντων

So they **were sent off** (ἀπολυθέντες) and went down to **Antioch** (Ἀντιόχειαν). When **they gathered** the congregation **together** (συναγαγόντες), they delivered the letter. (NRSV)

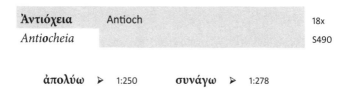

| Ἀντιόχεια | Antioch | 18x |
| *Antiocheia* | | S490 |

| ἀπολύω | ▷ | 1:250 | συνάγω | ▷ | 1:278 |

Οἱ μὲν οὖν **ἀπολυθέντες** κατῆλθον εἰς Ἀντιόχειαν, καὶ **συναγαγόντες** τὸ πλῆθος ἐπέδωκαν τὴν ἐπιστολήν·

So they **were sent off**	Οἱ μὲν οὖν **ἀπολυθέντες**
and went down to **Antioch**	κατῆλθον εἰς **Ἀντιόχειαν**
When **they gathered** the congregation **together**	καὶ **συναγαγόντες** τὸ πλῆθος
they delivered the letter	ἐπέδωκαν τὴν ἐπιστολήν

But **rejoice (χαίρετε)** insofar as you are sharing Christ's sufferings, so that **you may** also **be glad (χαρῆτε)** and shout for joy when his glory is revealed [lit., in the **revealing (ἀποκαλύψει)** of his **glory (δόξης)**]. (NRSV)

ἀποκάλυψις	revelation, unveiling	18x
apokalupsis		S602

δόξα ▷ 1:95   **χαίρω** ▷ 1:228

ἀλλὰ καθὸ κοινωνεῖτε τοῖς τοῦ Χριστοῦ παθήμασιν **χαίρετε**, ἵνα καὶ ἐν τῇ **ἀποκαλύψει** τῆς **δόξης** αὐτοῦ **χαρῆτε** ἀγαλλιώμενοι.

But **rejoice**	ἀλλὰ . . . **χαίρετε**
insofar as	καθὸ
you are sharing	κοινωνεῖτε
Christ's sufferings	τοῖς τοῦ Χριστοῦ παθήμασιν
so that **you may** also **be glad**	ἵνα καὶ . . . **χαρῆτε**
and shout for joy	ἀγαλλιώμενοι
when his glory is revealed [lit., in the **revealing** of his **glory**]	ἐν τῇ **ἀποκαλύψει** τῆς **δόξης** αὐτοῦ

Let no one deceive you in any [lit., **no (μηδένα)**] way. For that day will not come [lit., For], unless the rebellion comes first, and the man of lawlessness **is revealed (ἀποκαλυφθῇ)**, the son of **destruction (ἀπωλείας)**. (ESV)

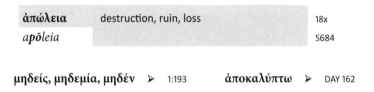

| ἀπώλεια | destruction, ruin, loss | 18x |
| *apōleia* | | S684 |

μηδείς, μηδεμία, μηδέν ➤ 1:193 **ἀποκαλύπτω** ➤ DAY 162

μή τις ὑμᾶς ἐξαπατήσῃ κατὰ **μηδένα** τρόπον· ὅτι ἐὰν μὴ ἔλθῃ ἡ ἀποστασία πρῶτον καὶ **ἀποκαλυφθῇ** ὁ ἄνθρωπος τῆς ἀνομίας, ὁ υἱὸς τῆς **ἀπωλείας**,

Let no one deceive you	μή τις ὑμᾶς ἐξαπατήσῃ
in any [lit., **no**] way	κατὰ **μηδένα** τρόπον
For that day will not come [lit., For]	ὅτι
unless the rebellion comes first	ἐὰν μὴ ἔλθῃ ἡ ἀποστασία πρῶτον
and the man of lawlessness **is revealed**	καὶ **ἀποκαλυφθῇ** ὁ ἄνθρωπος τῆς ἀνομίας
the son of **destruction**	ὁ υἱὸς τῆς **ἀπωλείας**

and will come out **to deceive (πλανῆσαι)** the nations which are in the four corners of the earth, Gog and Magog, to gather them together for the war; the **number (ἀριθμὸς)** of them is like the sand of the **seashore (θαλάσσης)**. (NASB)

ἀριθμός	number	18x
arithmos		S706

       θάλασσα ➤ 1:188   **πλανάω** ➤ DAY 20

καὶ ἐξελεύσεται **πλανῆσαι** τὰ ἔθνη τὰ ἐν ταῖς τέσσαρσι γωνίαις τῆς γῆς, τὸν Γὼγ καὶ Μαγώγ, συναγαγεῖν αὐτοὺς εἰς τὸν πόλεμον, ὧν ὁ **ἀριθμὸς** αὐτῶν ὡς ἡ ἄμμος τῆς **θαλάσσης**.

and will come out	καὶ ἐξελεύσεται
to deceive the nations	**πλανῆσαι** τὰ ἔθνη
which are in the four corners of the earth	τὰ ἐν ταῖς τέσσαρσι γωνίαις τῆς γῆς
Gog and Magog	τὸν Γὼγ καὶ Μαγώγ
to gather them together	συναγαγεῖν αὐτοὺς
for the war	εἰς τὸν πόλεμον
the **number** of them	ὧν ὁ **ἀριθμὸς** αὐτῶν
is like the sand of the **seashore**	ὡς ἡ ἄμμος τῆς **θαλάσσης**

We do not want you **to be unaware (ἀγνοεῖν)**, brothers and sisters, of the **affliction (θλίψεως)** we experienced in **Asia (Ἀσίᾳ)**; for we were so utterly, unbearably crushed that we despaired of life itself. (NRSV)

Ἀσία	Asia (the Roman province)	18x
Asia		S773

 θλῖψις ➤ 1:339   **ἀγνοέω** ➤ DAY 209

Οὐ γὰρ θέλομεν ὑμᾶς **ἀγνοεῖν**, ἀδελφοί, ὑπὲρ τῆς **θλίψεως** ἡμῶν τῆς γενομένης ἐν τῇ **Ἀσίᾳ**, ὅτι καθ' ὑπερβολὴν ὑπὲρ δύναμιν ἐβαρήθημεν, ὥστε ἐξαπορηθῆναι ἡμᾶς καὶ τοῦ ζῆν·

We do not want you **to be unaware**	Οὐ γὰρ θέλομεν ὑμᾶς **ἀγνοεῖν**
brothers and sisters	ἀδελφοί
of the **affliction** we experienced	ὑπὲρ τῆς **θλίψεως** ἡμῶν τῆς γενομένης
in **Asia**	ἐν τῇ **Ἀσίᾳ**
for we were . . . crushed	ὅτι . . . ἐβαρήθημεν
so utterly	καθ' ὑπερβολὴν
unbearably	ὑπὲρ δύναμιν
that we despaired	ὥστε ἐξαπορηθῆναι ἡμᾶς
of life itself	καὶ τοῦ ζῆν

And the scribes and the Pharisees began to question, saying, "Who is this who speaks **blasphemies (βλασφημίας)**? Who can **forgive (ἀφεῖναι)** sins but God **alone (μόνος)**?" (ESV)

βλασφημία	blasphemy	18x
blasphēmia		S988

ἀφίημι ➢ 1:115   μόνος ➢ 1:323

καὶ ἤρξαντο διαλογίζεσθαι οἱ γραμματεῖς καὶ οἱ Φαρισαῖοι λέγοντες Τίς ἐστιν οὗτος ὃς λαλεῖ **βλασφημίας**; τίς δύναται ἁμαρτίας **ἀφεῖναι** εἰ μὴ **μόνος** ὁ θεός;

And the scribes and the Pharisees	καὶ . . . οἱ γραμματεῖς καὶ οἱ Φαρισαῖοι
began to question	ἤρξαντο διαλογίζεσθαι
saying	λέγοντες
Who is this	Τίς ἐστιν οὗτος
who speaks **blasphemies**?	ὃς λαλεῖ **βλασφημίας**;
Who can	τίς δύναται
forgive sins	ἁμαρτίας **ἀφεῖναι**
but God **alone**?	εἰ μὴ **μόνος** ὁ θεός;

Don't **worry (μεριμνᾶτε)** about anything, but in everything, through prayer and **petition (δεήσει)** with thanksgiving, **let** your requests **be made known (γνωριζέσθω)** to God. (HCSB)

δέησις	prayer, petition	18x
deēsis		S1162

γνωρίζω ▷ DAY 145   μεριμνάω ▷ DAY 287

μηδὲν **μεριμνᾶτε**, ἀλλ᾽ ἐν παντὶ τῇ προσευχῇ καὶ τῇ **δεήσει** μετ᾽ εὐχαριστίας τὰ αἰτήματα ὑμῶν **γνωριζέσθω** πρὸς τὸν θεόν·

Don't **worry** about anything	μηδὲν **μεριμνᾶτε**
but in everything	ἀλλ᾽ ἐν παντὶ
through prayer	τῇ προσευχῇ
and **petition**	καὶ τῇ **δεήσει**
with thanksgiving	μετ᾽ εὐχαριστίας
let your requests **be made known**	τὰ αἰτήματα ὑμῶν **γνωριζέσθω**
to God	πρὸς τὸν θεόν

This greeting is in **my own (ἐμῇ)** hand—Paul. **Remember (μνημονεύετέ)** my imprisonment [lit., **chains (δεσμῶν)**]. Grace be with you. (HCSB)

δεσμός	chain, bond	18x
desmos		S1199

ἐμός ➤ 1:217   **μνημονεύω** ➤ DAY 264

Ὁ ἀσπασμὸς τῇ **ἐμῇ** χειρὶ Παύλου. **μνημονεύετέ** μου τῶν **δεσμῶν**. ἡ χάρις μεθ᾽ ὑμῶν.

This greeting	Ὁ ἀσπασμὸς
is in **my own** hand	τῇ **ἐμῇ** χειρὶ
Paul	Παύλου
Remember	**μνημονεύετέ**
my imprisonment [lit., **chains**]	μου τῶν **δεσμῶν**
Grace be with you	ἡ χάρις μεθ᾽ ὑμῶν

No one after **lighting (ἅψας)** a lamp hides it under a **jar (σκεύει)**, or puts it under a bed, but puts it on a lampstand, so that those **who enter (εἰσπορευόμενοι)** may see the light. (NRSV)

εἰσπορεύομαι	to journey in(to), go in(to)	18x
eisporeuomai		S1531

ἅπτω ▷ DAY 26   σκεῦος ▷ DAY 242

Οὐδεὶς δὲ λύχνον **ἅψας** καλύπτει αὐτὸν **σκεύει** ἢ ὑποκάτω κλίνης τίθησιν, ἀλλ᾽ ἐπὶ λυχνίας τίθησιν, ἵνα οἱ **εἰσπορευόμενοι** βλέπωσιν τὸ φῶς.

No one after **lighting** a lamp	Οὐδεὶς δὲ λύχνον **ἅψας**
hides it under a **jar**	καλύπτει αὐτὸν **σκεύει**
or puts it under a bed	ἢ ὑποκάτω κλίνης τίθησιν
but puts it on a lampstand	ἀλλ᾽ ἐπὶ λυχνίας τίθησιν
so that those **who enter**	ἵνα οἱ **εἰσπορευόμενοι**
may see the light	βλέπωσιν τὸ φῶς

Now a **large (ἱκανῶν)** herd of pigs was feeding there on the **hillside (ὄρει)**, and they begged him to **let (ἐπιτρέψῃ)** them enter these. So **he gave** them **permission (ἐπέτρεψεν)**. (ESV)

ἐπιτρέπω	to allow, permit	18x
epitrepō		S2010

ὄρος ▷ 1:255   **ἱκανός** ▷ DAY 6

Ἦν δὲ ἐκεῖ ἀγέλη χοίρων **ἱκανῶν** βοσκομένη ἐν τῷ **ὄρει**· καὶ παρεκάλεσαν αὐτὸν ἵνα **ἐπιτρέψῃ** αὐτοῖς εἰς ἐκείνους εἰσελθεῖν· καὶ **ἐπέτρεψεν** αὐτοῖς.

Now a **large** herd of pigs	δὲ . . . ἀγέλη χοίρων **ἱκανῶν**
was feeding there	Ἦν . . . ἐκεῖ . . . βοσκομένη
on the **hillside**	ἐν τῷ **ὄρει**
and they begged him	καὶ παρεκάλεσαν αὐτὸν
to **let** them	ἵνα **ἐπιτρέψῃ** αὐτοῖς
enter these	εἰς ἐκείνους εἰσελθεῖν
So **he gave** them **permission**	καὶ **ἐπέτρεψεν** αὐτοῖς

And all the people in the **synagogue (συναγωγῇ) were filled
(ἐπλήσθησαν)** with **rage (θυμοῦ)** as they heard these things.
(NASB)

θυμός	wrath, rage, anger	18x
thumos		S2372

    συναγωγή ➤ 1:284   **πίμπλημι** ➤ DAY 186

καὶ **ἐπλήσθησαν** πάντες **θυμοῦ** ἐν τῇ **συναγωγῇ** ἀκούοντες
ταῦτα,

And all the people	καὶ . . . πάντες
in the **synagogue**	ἐν τῇ **συναγωγῇ**
were filled	**ἐπλήσθησαν**
with **rage**	**θυμοῦ**
as they heard these things	ἀκούοντες ταῦτα

The former **preach (καταγγέλλουσιν)** Christ out of selfish ambition, not sincerely, supposing that they can stir up **trouble (θλίψιν)** for me while I am in **chains (δεσμοῖς)**. (NIV)

καταγγέλλω *katangellō*	to announce, proclaim	18x S2605

θλῖψις ▷ 1:339   δεσμός ▷ DAY 300

οἱ δὲ ἐξ ἐριθίας τὸν χριστὸν **καταγγέλλουσιν**, οὐχ ἁγνῶς, οἰόμενοι **θλίψιν** ἐγείρειν τοῖς **δεσμοῖς** μου.

The former **preach** Christ	οἱ δὲ ... τὸν χριστὸν **καταγγέλλουσιν**
out of selfish ambition	ἐξ ἐριθίας
not sincerely	οὐχ ἁγνῶς
supposing that they can stir up **trouble**	οἰόμενοι **θλίψιν** ἐγείρειν
for me while I am in **chains**	τοῖς **δεσμοῖς** μου

When Judas, His betrayer, saw that **He was condemned**
(**κατεκρίθη**), he felt remorse and **returned (ἔστρεψεν)** the thirty
pieces of silver (ἀργύρια) to the chief priests and elders. (MLB)

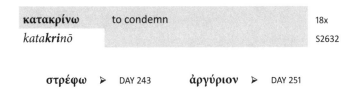

| **κατακρίνω** | to condemn | 18x |
| *katakrinō* | | S2632 |

στρέφω   ➤   DAY 243   **ἀργύριον**   ➤   DAY 251

Τότε ἰδὼν Ἰούδας ὁ παραδοὺς αὐτὸν ὅτι **κατεκρίθη** μεταμεληθεὶς
ἔστρεψεν τὰ τριάκοντα **ἀργύρια** τοῖς ἀρχιερεῦσιν καὶ
πρεσβυτέροις

When Judas . . . saw	Τότε ἰδὼν Ἰούδας
His betrayer	ὁ παραδοὺς αὐτὸν
that **He was condemned**	ὅτι **κατεκρίθη**
he felt remorse	μεταμεληθεὶς
and **returned**	**ἔστρεψεν**
the thirty **pieces of silver**	τὰ τριάκοντα **ἀργύρια**
to the chief priests and elders	τοῖς ἀρχιερεῦσιν καὶ πρεσβυτέροις

He has filled **the hungry (πεινῶντας)** with **good things (ἀγαθῶν)**
but has sent the rich away **empty (κενούς)**. (NIV)

| κενός | empty, vain, foolish, worthless | 18x |
| kenos | | S2756 |

ἀγαθός ➤ 1:164   πεινάω ➤ DAY 203

πεινῶντας ἐνέπλησεν **ἀγαθῶν** καὶ πλουτοῦντας ἐξαπέστειλεν
κενούς.

He has filled	ἐνέπλησεν
the hungry	**πεινῶντας**
with **good things**	**ἀγαθῶν**
but has sent . . . away	καὶ . . . ἐξαπέστειλεν
the rich	πλουτοῦντας
empty	**κενούς**

One of the **rulers (ἄρχων) inquired of (ἐπηρώτησέν)** Him, "Good Teacher, what shall I do **to inherit (κληρονομήσω)** eternal life?" (MLB)

κληρονομέω	to inherit	18x
klēronomeō		S2816

ἐπερωτάω ▶ 1:286   ἄρχων ▶ DAY 27

Καὶ **ἐπηρώτησέν** τις αὐτὸν **ἄρχων** λέγων Διδάσκαλε ἀγαθέ, τί ποιήσας ζωὴν αἰώνιον **κληρονομήσω**;

One of the **rulers**	τις . . . **ἄρχων**
inquired of Him	Καὶ **ἐπηρώτησέν** . . . αὐτὸν . . . λέγων
Good Teacher	Διδάσκαλε ἀγαθέ
what shall I do	τί ποιήσας
to inherit	**κληρονομήσω**;
eternal life?	ζωὴν αἰώνιον

Behold, I tell you a **mystery (μυστήριον); we will** not **all sleep**
(πάντες . . . κοιμηθησόμεθα), but we will **all (πάντες)** be
changed. (NASB)

| κοιμάομαι | to sleep, fall asleep | 18x |
| *koimaomai* | | S2837 |

πᾶς ➤ 1:16   μυστήριον ➤ DAY 124

ἰδοὺ **μυστήριον** ὑμῖν λέγω· **πάντες** οὐ **κοιμηθησόμεθα πάντες** δὲ
ἀλλαγησόμεθα,

Behold	ἰδοὺ
I tell you a **mystery**	**μυστήριον** ὑμῖν λέγω
we will not **all sleep**	**πάντες** οὐ **κοιμηθησόμεθα**
but we will **all** be changed	**πάντες** δὲ ἀλλαγησόμεθα

And he (κἀκεῖνος) answers from within, "Do not bother me
[lit., do not cause me **troubles (κόπους)**]; the door has already
been locked, and my children are with me in bed; I cannot **get up
(ἀναστὰς)** and give you anything." (NRSV)

κόπος	trouble, toil, labor	18x
kopos		S2873

ἀνίστημι ➤ 1:155 κἀκεῖνος ➤ DAY 236

κἀκεῖνος ἔσωθεν ἀποκριθεὶς εἴπῃ Μή μοι **κόπους** πάρεχε· ἤδη ἡ
θύρα κέκλεισται, καὶ τὰ παιδία μου μετ' ἐμοῦ εἰς τὴν κοίτην εἰσίν·
οὐ δύναμαι **ἀναστὰς** δοῦναί σοι.

And he answers	**κἀκεῖνος** . . . ἀποκριθεὶς εἴπῃ
from within	ἔσωθεν
Do not bother me [lit., do not cause me **troubles**]	Μή μοι **κόπους** πάρεχε
the door has already been locked	ἤδη ἡ θύρα κέκλεισται
and my children are with me	καὶ τὰ παιδία μου μετ' ἐμοῦ . . . εἰσίν
in bed	εἰς τὴν κοίτην
I cannot **get up**	οὐ δύναμαι **ἀναστὰς**
and give you anything	δοῦναί σοι

I assure you, the present **generation (γενεὰ) will** not **pass on (παρέλθῃ) until (μέχρις** οὗ) all this takes place. (MLB)

| μέχρι | until, as far as | 18x |
| *mechri* | | S3360 |

γενεά ▷ 1:344   παρέρχομαι ▷ DAY 106

ἀμὴν λέγω ὑμῖν ὅτι οὐ μὴ **παρέλθῃ** ἡ **γενεὰ** αὕτη **μέχρις** οὗ ταῦτα πάντα γένηται.

I assure you	ἀμὴν λέγω ὑμῖν ὅτι
the present **generation**	ἡ **γενεὰ** αὕτη
will not **pass on**	οὐ μὴ **παρέλθῃ**
until all this	**μέχρις** οὗ ταῦτα πάντα
takes place	γένηται

Paul [lit., he] entered the synagogue and spoke boldly over a period of **three (τρεῖς) months (μῆνας)**, arguing and **persuading (πείθων)** them about the kingdom of God. (CSB)

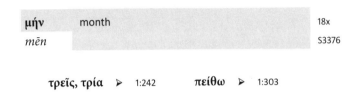

| μήν | month | 18x |
| *mēn* | | S3376 |

τρεῖς, τρία ➤ 1:242   **πείθω** ➤ 1:303

Εἰσελθὼν δὲ εἰς τὴν συναγωγὴν ἐπαρρησιάζετο ἐπὶ **μῆνας τρεῖς** διαλεγόμενος καὶ **πείθων** περὶ τῆς βασιλείας τοῦ θεοῦ.

Paul [lit., he] entered the synagogue	Εἰσελθὼν δὲ εἰς τὴν συναγωγὴν
and spoke boldly	ἐπαρρησιάζετο
over a period of **three months**	ἐπὶ **μῆνας τρεῖς**
arguing	διαλεγόμενος
and **persuading** them	καὶ **πείθων**
about the kingdom of God	περὶ τῆς βασιλείας τοῦ θεοῦ

Nor can they **prove (παραστῆσαι)** to you the charges of which **they now accuse (νυνὶ κατηγοροῦσίν)** me. (NASB)

| νυνί
nuni | now | 18x
S3570 |

παρίστημι ➤ 1:365   κατηγορέω ➤ DAY 237

οὐδὲ **παραστῆσαι** δύνανταί σοι περὶ ὧν **νυνὶ κατηγοροῦσίν** μου.

Nor can they	οὐδὲ . . . δύνανταί
prove	**παραστῆσαι**
to you	σοι
the charges of which	περὶ ὧν
they . . . accuse	**κατηγοροῦσίν**
now	**νυνὶ**
me	μου

In him the whole **structure (οἰκοδομὴ)** is joined together and **grows (αὔξει)** into a holy **temple (ναὸν)** in the Lord. (NRSV)

οἰκοδομή *oikodomē*	structure, building; encouragement, building up	18x S3619

ναός ➤ 1:336   **αὐξάνω** ➤ DAY 192

ἐν ᾧ πᾶσα **οἰκοδομὴ** συναρμολογουμένη **αὔξει** εἰς **ναὸν** ἅγιον ἐν κυρίῳ,

In him	ἐν ᾧ
the whole **structure**	πᾶσα **οἰκοδομὴ**
is joined together	συναρμολογουμένη
and **grows**	**αὔξει**
into a holy **temple**	εἰς **ναὸν** ἅγιον
in the Lord	ἐν κυρίῳ

He put before (παρέθηκεν) them another parable: "The kingdom of heaven is like a man **who sowed (σπείραντι)** good seed in his **field (ἀγρῷ).**" (MLB)

παρατίθημι	to set before, serve, deposit, entrust	18x
paratithēmi		S3908

σπείρω ▷ 1:304　　　**ἀγρός** ▷ DAY 34

Ἄλλην παραβολὴν **παρέθηκεν** αὐτοῖς λέγων Ὡμοιώθη ἡ βασιλεία τῶν οὐρανῶν ἀνθρώπῳ **σπείραντι** καλὸν σπέρμα ἐν τῷ **ἀγρῷ** αὐτοῦ.

He put before them	**παρέθηκεν** αὐτοῖς λέγων
another parable	Ἄλλην παραβολὴν
The kingdom of heaven	ἡ βασιλεία τῶν οὐρανῶν
is like	Ὡμοιώθη
a man **who sowed**	ἀνθρώπῳ **σπείραντι**
good seed	καλὸν σπέρμα
in his **field**	ἐν τῷ **ἀγρῷ** αὐτοῦ

"And now, behold, the hand of the Lord is upon you, and you
will be blind and unable to see the sun for a time." **Immediately
(παραχρῆμα)** mist and **darkness (σκότος)** fell upon him, and he
went about **seeking (ἐζήτει)** people to lead him by the hand. (ESV)

παραχρῆμα	immediately		18x
parachrēma			S3916

ζητέω ➤ 1:150   **σκότος** ➤ DAY 99

καὶ νῦν ἰδοὺ χεὶρ Κυρίου ἐπὶ σέ, καὶ ἔσῃ τυφλὸς μὴ βλέπων τὸν
ἥλιον ἄχρι καιροῦ. **παραχρῆμα** δὲ ἔπεσεν ἐπ᾽ αὐτὸν ἀχλὺς καὶ
σκότος, καὶ περιάγων **ἐζήτει** χειραγωγούς.

And now, behold	καὶ νῦν ἰδοὺ
the hand of the Lord is upon you	χεὶρ Κυρίου ἐπὶ σέ
and you will be blind	καὶ ἔσῃ τυφλὸς
and unable to see the sun	μὴ βλέπων τὸν ἥλιον
for a time	ἄχρι καιροῦ
Immediately mist and **darkness**	**παραχρῆμα** δὲ . . . ἀχλὺς καὶ **σκότος**
fell upon him	ἔπεσεν ἐπ᾽ αὐτὸν
and he went about	καὶ περιάγων
seeking people to lead him by the hand	**ἐζήτει** χειραγωγούς

When he saw the **crowds** (ὄχλους), he had compassion on them, because they were harassed and helpless, like **sheep** (πρόβατα) without a **shepherd** (ποιμένα). (NIV)

ποιμήν	shepherd, ruler		18x
poimēn			S4166

ὄχλος ➤ 1:90   **πρόβατον** ➤ DAY 43

Ἰδὼν δὲ τοὺς **ὄχλους** ἐσπλαγχνίσθη περὶ αὐτῶν ὅτι ἦσαν ἐσκυλμένοι καὶ ἐριμμένοι ὡσεὶ **πρόβατα** μὴ ἔχοντα **ποιμένα**.

When he saw the **crowds**	Ἰδὼν δὲ τοὺς **ὄχλους**
he had compassion	ἐσπλαγχνίσθη
on them	περὶ αὐτῶν
because they were harassed	ὅτι ἦσαν ἐσκυλμένοι
and helpless	καὶ ἐριμμένοι
like **sheep**	ὡσεὶ **πρόβατα**
without a **shepherd**	μὴ ἔχοντα **ποιμένα**

Or what king, going out to encounter another king in **war**
(**πόλεμον**), **will** not **sit down** (**καθίσας**) first and deliberate
whether he is able with ten **thousand** (**χιλιάσιν**) to meet him who
comes against him with twenty **thousand** (**χιλιάδων**)? (ESV)

πόλεμος	war, battle	18x
polemos		S4171

καθίζω　▷　1:327　　**χιλιάς**　▷　DAY 208

ἢ τίς βασιλεὺς πορευόμενος ἑτέρῳ βασιλεῖ συνβαλεῖν εἰς **πόλεμον**
οὐχὶ **καθίσας** πρῶτον βουλεύσεται εἰ δυνατός ἐστιν ἐν δέκα
χιλιάσιν ὑπαντῆσαι τῷ μετὰ εἴκοσι **χιλιάδων** ἐρχομένῳ ἐπ᾽ αὐτόν;

Or what king	ἢ τίς βασιλεὺς
going out to encounter	πορευόμενος . . . συνβαλεῖν
another king in **war**	ἑτέρῳ βασιλεῖ . . . εἰς **πόλεμον**
will not **sit down** first	οὐχὶ **καθίσας** πρῶτον
and deliberate	βουλεύσεται
whether he is able	εἰ δυνατός ἐστιν
with ten **thousand**	ἐν δέκα **χιλιάσιν**
to meet him who comes against him	ὑπαντῆσαι τῷ . . . ἐρχομένῳ ἐπ᾽ αὐτόν;
with twenty **thousand**?	μετὰ εἴκοσι **χιλιάδων**

"Lord," he said, "**have mercy on (ἐλέησόν)** my son, because he has seizures and suffers terribly. He **often (πολλάκις)** falls into the fire and **often (πολλάκις)** into the **water (ὕδωρ)**." (CSB)

πολλάκις	often, frequently	18x
pollakis		S4178

ὕδωρ ➤ 1:218   **ἐλεέω** ➤ DAY 71

καὶ λέγων Κύριε, **ἐλέησόν** μου τὸν υἱόν, ὅτι σεληνιάζεται καὶ κακῶς ἔχει, **πολλάκις** γὰρ πίπτει εἰς τὸ πῦρ καὶ **πολλάκις** εἰς τὸ **ὕδωρ**·

Lord	Κύριε
he said	καὶ λέγων
have mercy on my son	**ἐλέησόν** μου τὸν υἱόν
because he has seizures	ὅτι σεληνιάζεται
and suffers terribly	καὶ κακῶς ἔχει
He **often** falls	**πολλάκις** γὰρ πίπτει
into the fire	εἰς τὸ πῦρ
and **often** into the **water**	καὶ **πολλάκις** εἰς τὸ **ὕδωρ**

And who of you by **being worried (μεριμνῶν)** can **add (προσθεῖναι) a single (ἕνα)** hour [lit., cubit] to his life? (NASB)

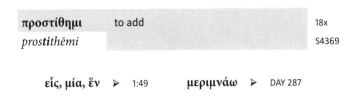

| προστίθημι | to add | 18x |
| *pros**ti**thēmi* | | S4369 |

εἷς, μία, ἕν   ➤   1:49   μεριμνάω   ➤   DAY 287

τίς δὲ ἐξ ὑμῶν **μεριμνῶν** δύναται **προσθεῖναι** ἐπὶ τὴν ἡλικίαν αὐτοῦ πῆχυν **ἕνα**;

And who of you	τίς δὲ ἐξ ὑμῶν
by **being worried**	**μεριμνῶν**
can	δύναται
add	**προσθεῖναι**
a single hour [lit., cubit]	πῆχυν **ἕνα**;
to his life?	ἐπὶ τὴν ἡλικίαν αὐτοῦ

Blessed (Μακάριοι) are those who wash their robes, that they may have the right to the **tree (ξύλον)** of life and to enter through the **gates (πυλῶσιν)** into the city. (MLB)

πυλών	gate, entrance, passage	18x
pulōn		S4440

μακάριος   ▷   1:308   ξύλον   ▷   DAY 266

Μακάριοι οἱ πλύνοντες τὰς στολὰς αὐτῶν, ἵνα ἔσται ἡ ἐξουσία αὐτῶν ἐπὶ τὸ **ξύλον** τῆς ζωῆς καὶ τοῖς **πυλῶσιν** εἰσέλθωσιν εἰς τὴν πόλιν.

Blessed are those who wash	**Μακάριοι** οἱ πλύνοντες
their robes	τὰς στολὰς αὐτῶν
that they may have the right	ἵνα ἔσται ἡ ἐξουσία αὐτῶν
to the **tree** of life	ἐπὶ τὸ **ξύλον** τῆς ζωῆς
and to enter through the **gates**	καὶ τοῖς **πυλῶσιν** εἰσέλθωσιν
into the city	εἰς τὴν πόλιν

Yet we do speak wisdom among those who are **mature (τελείοις)**;
a wisdom, however, not of this **age (αἰῶνος)** nor of the rulers
of this **age (αἰῶνος)**, who **are passing away (καταργουμένων)**.
(NASB)

τέλειος	complete, mature, perfect	18x
teleios		S5046

αἰών ▷ 1:136   καταργέω ▷ DAY 136

Σοφίαν δὲ λαλοῦμεν ἐν τοῖς **τελείοις**, σοφίαν δὲ οὐ τοῦ
αἰῶνος τούτου οὐδὲ τῶν ἀρχόντων τοῦ **αἰῶνος** τούτου τῶν
καταργουμένων·

Yet we do speak wisdom	Σοφίαν δὲ λαλοῦμεν
among those who are **mature**	ἐν τοῖς **τελείοις**
a wisdom, however	σοφίαν δὲ
not of this **age**	οὐ τοῦ **αἰῶνος** τούτου
nor of the rulers	οὐδὲ τῶν ἀρχόντων
of this **age**	τοῦ **αἰῶνος** τούτου
who **are passing away**	τῶν **καταργουμένων**

And **she gave birth to** (ἔτεκεν) her firstborn son and wrapped him in swaddling cloths and laid him in a manger, **because** (**διότι**) there was no **place** (**τόπος**) for them in the inn. (ESV)

τίκτω	to give birth to, bear	18x
tiktō		S5088

τόπος ➤ 1:180   διότι ➤ DAY 194

καὶ **ἔτεκεν** τὸν υἱὸν αὐτῆς τὸν πρωτότοκον, καὶ ἐσπαργάνωσεν αὐτὸν καὶ ἀνέκλινεν αὐτὸν ἐν φάτνῃ, **διότι** οὐκ ἦν αὐτοῖς **τόπος** ἐν τῷ καταλύματι.

And **she gave birth to**	καὶ **ἔτεκεν**
her firstborn son	τὸν υἱὸν αὐτῆς τὸν πρωτότοκον
and wrapped him in swaddling cloths	καὶ ἐσπαργάνωσεν αὐτὸν
and laid him in a manger	καὶ ἀνέκλινεν αὐτὸν ἐν φάτνῃ
because	**διότι**
there was no **place** for them	οὐκ ἦν αὐτοῖς **τόπος**
in the inn	ἐν τῷ καταλύματι

For he is not a Jew who is one **outwardly** (ἐν τῷ **φανερῷ**), nor is
circumcision (**περιτομή**) that which is **outward** (ἐν τῷ **φανερῷ**)
in the **flesh** (**σαρκὶ**). (NASB)

φανερός	manifest, clear, visible	18x
phaneros		S5318

     σάρξ ➤ 1:110   **περιτομή** ➤ DAY 42

οὐ γὰρ ὁ ἐν τῷ **φανερῷ** Ἰουδαῖός ἐστιν, οὐδὲ ἡ ἐν τῷ **φανερῷ** ἐν
σαρκὶ περιτομή·

For he is not a Jew	οὐ γὰρ . . . Ἰουδαῖός ἐστιν
who is one **outwardly**	ὁ ἐν τῷ **φανερῷ**
nor is **circumcision**	οὐδὲ . . . **περιτομή**
that which is **outward**	ἡ ἐν τῷ **φανερῷ**
in the **flesh**	ἐν **σαρκὶ**

Then one of the **four (τεσσάρων)** living creatures gave to the seven angels seven **golden (χρυσᾶς)** bowls filled with the **wrath (θυμοῦ)** of God, who lives for ever and ever. (NIV)

χρυσοῦς	golden	18x
chrusous		S5552

τέσσαρες ▷ DAY 13   θυμός ▷ DAY 303

καὶ ἓν ἐκ τῶν **τεσσάρων** ζῴων ἔδωκεν τοῖς ἑπτὰ ἀγγέλοις ἑπτὰ φιάλας **χρυσᾶς** γεμούσας τοῦ **θυμοῦ** τοῦ θεοῦ τοῦ ζῶντος εἰς τοὺς αἰῶνας τῶν αἰώνων.

Then one of the **four** living creatures	καὶ ἓν ἐκ τῶν **τεσσάρων** ζῴων
gave to the seven angels	ἔδωκεν τοῖς ἑπτὰ ἀγγέλοις
seven **golden** bowls	ἑπτὰ φιάλας **χρυσᾶς**
filled with the **wrath** of God	γεμούσας τοῦ **θυμοῦ** τοῦ θεοῦ
who lives for ever and ever	τοῦ ζῶντος εἰς τοὺς αἰῶνας τῶν αἰώνων

But as servants of God we commend ourselves in every way: by great **endurance** (ὑπομονῇ), in **afflictions** (θλίψεσιν), **hardships** (ἀνάγκαις), calamities, . . . (ESV)

ἀνάγκη	necessity, obligation, compulsion, distress	17x
ananke		S318

θλῖψις ➤ 1:339   **ὑπομονή** ➤ DAY 76

ἀλλ᾽ ἐν παντὶ συνιστάνοντες ἑαυτοὺς ὡς θεοῦ διάκονοι· ἐν **ὑπομονῇ** πολλῇ, ἐν **θλίψεσιν**, ἐν **ἀνάγκαις**, ἐν στενοχωρίαις,

But as servants of God	ἀλλ᾽ . . . ὡς θεοῦ διάκονοι
we commend ourselves	συνιστάνοντες ἑαυτοὺς
in every way	ἐν παντὶ
by great **endurance**	ἐν **ὑπομονῇ** πολλῇ
in **afflictions**	ἐν **θλίψεσιν**
hardships	ἐν **ἀνάγκαις**
calamities	ἐν στενοχωρίαις

Now we who are strong **have an obligation (Ὀφείλομεν) to bear (βαστάζειν)** the weaknesses of those without strength, and not **to please (ἀρέσκειν)** ourselves. (CSB)

ἀρέσκω	to please, serve	17x
areskō		S700

ὀφείλω   ➤   DAY 51   βαστάζω   ➤   DAY 130

Ὀφείλομεν δὲ ἡμεῖς οἱ δυνατοὶ τὰ ἀσθενήματα τῶν ἀδυνάτων βαστάζειν, καὶ μὴ ἑαυτοῖς ἀρέσκειν.

Now we who are strong	δὲ ἡμεῖς οἱ δυνατοὶ
have an obligation	**Ὀφείλομεν**
to bear	**βαστάζειν**
the weaknesses	τὰ ἀσθενήματα
of those without strength	τῶν ἀδυνάτων
and not **to please** ourselves	καὶ μὴ ἑαυτοῖς **ἀρέσκειν**

This is my blood of the **covenant (διαθήκης)**, which **is poured out (ἐκχυννόμενον)** for many for the **forgiveness (ἄφεσιν)** of sins. (NIV)

| ἄφεσις | forgiveness, remission, sending away, letting go | 17x |
| *aphesis* | | S859 |

διαθήκη ➤ DAY 64   **ἐκχέω** ➤ DAY 132

τοῦτο γάρ ἐστιν τὸ αἷμά μου τῆς **διαθήκης** τὸ περὶ πολλῶν **ἐκχυννόμενον** εἰς **ἄφεσιν** ἁμαρτιῶν·

This is my blood	τοῦτο γάρ ἐστιν τὸ αἷμά μου
of the **covenant**	τῆς **διαθήκης**
which **is poured out**	τὸ . . . **ἐκχυννόμενον**
for many	περὶ πολλῶν
for the **forgiveness** of sins	εἰς **ἄφεσιν** ἁμαρτιῶν

But he said to them, "You give them something to eat." They said,
"We have no more than five loaves and two fish—unless we are to
go and **buy (ἀγοράσωμεν) food (βρώματα)** for all these **people
(λαὸν)**." (ESV)

| βρῶμα | food | 17x |
| *brōma* | | S1033 |

λαός ➤ 1:116   ἀγοράζω ➤ DAY 88

εἶπεν δὲ πρὸς αὐτούς Δότε αὐτοῖς φαγεῖν ὑμεῖς. οἱ δὲ εἶπαν
Οὐκ εἰσὶν ἡμῖν πλεῖον ἢ ἄρτοι πέντε καὶ ἰχθύες δύο, εἰ μήτι
πορευθέντες ἡμεῖς **ἀγοράσωμεν** εἰς πάντα τὸν **λαὸν** τοῦτον
βρώματα.

But he said to them	εἶπεν δὲ πρὸς αὐτούς
You give them something to eat	Δότε αὐτοῖς φαγεῖν ὑμεῖς
They said	οἱ δὲ εἶπαν
We have no more than	Οὐκ εἰσὶν ἡμῖν πλεῖον ἢ
five loaves and two fish	ἄρτοι πέντε καὶ ἰχθύες δύο
unless we are to go	εἰ μήτι πορευθέντες ἡμεῖς
and **buy food**	**ἀγοράσωμεν** . . . **βρώματα**
for all these **people**	εἰς πάντα τὸν **λαὸν** τοῦτον

He then asked another, "**How much (πόσον)** do you owe?" And he replied, "A **hundred (Ἑκατὸν)** sacks of wheat." To him he said, "**Take (Δέξαι)** your bill and write eighty." (MLB)

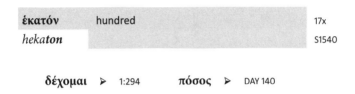

| **ἑκατόν** | hundred | 17x |
| *hekaton* | | S1540 |

δέχομαι ➤ 1:294   **πόσος** ➤ DAY 140

ἔπειτα ἑτέρῳ εἶπεν Σὺ δὲ **πόσον** ὀφείλεις; ὁ δὲ εἶπεν **Ἑκατὸν** κόρους σίτου· λέγει αὐτῷ **Δέξαι** σου τὰ γράμματα καὶ γράψον ὀγδοήκοντα.

He . . . asked another	ἑτέρῳ εἶπεν
then	ἔπειτα
How much do you owe?	Σὺ δὲ **πόσον** ὀφείλεις;
And he replied	ὁ δὲ εἶπεν
A **hundred** sacks of wheat	**Ἑκατὸν** κόρους σίτου
To him he said	λέγει αὐτῷ
Take your bill	**Δέξαι** σου τὰ γράμματα
and write eighty	καὶ γράψον ὀγδοήκοντα

As many as (ὅσους) I love, **I rebuke (ἐλέγχω)** and discipline. So be zealous and **repent (μετανόησον).** (CSB)

ἐλέγχω	to rebuke, reprove, expose	17x
elenchō		S1651

    ὅσος ➤ 1:153   **μετανοέω** ➤ DAY 57

ἐγὼ **ὅσους** ἐὰν φιλῶ **ἐλέγχω** καὶ παιδεύω· ζήλευε οὖν καὶ **μετανόησον**.

As many as	**ὅσους** ἐὰν
I love	ἐγὼ . . . φιλῶ
I rebuke	**ἐλέγχω**
and discipline	καὶ παιδεύω
So be zealous	ζήλευε οὖν
and **repent**	καὶ **μετανόησον**

So **He left (ἀφεὶς)** them, **embarked (ἐμβὰς)** again and crossed to the **other side (πέραν)**. (MLB)

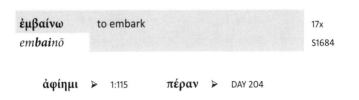

ἐμβαίνω	to embark	17x
embainō		S1684

ἀφίημι ➤ 1:115   **πέραν** ➤ DAY 204

καὶ **ἀφεὶς** αὐτοὺς πάλιν **ἐμβὰς** ἀπῆλθεν εἰς τὸ **πέραν**.

So **He left** them	καὶ **ἀφεὶς** αὐτοὺς
embarked again	πάλιν **ἐμβὰς**
and crossed	ἀπῆλθεν
to the **other side**	εἰς τὸ **πέραν**

Her **parents (γονεῖς) were amazed (ἐξέστησαν)**; but He **instructed (παρήγγειλεν)** them to tell no one what had happened. (MLB)

ἐξίστημι	to astonish, amaze, be out of one's mind	17x
existēmi		S1839

παραγγέλλω ▷ DAY 81   **γονεύς** ▷ DAY 255

καὶ **ἐξέστησαν** οἱ **γονεῖς** αὐτῆς· ὁ δὲ **παρήγγειλεν** αὐτοῖς μηδενὶ εἰπεῖν τὸ γεγονός.

Her **parents**	καὶ . . . οἱ **γονεῖς** αὐτῆς
were amazed	**ἐξέστησαν**
but He **instructed** them	ὁ δὲ **παρήγγειλεν** αὐτοῖς
to tell no one	μηδενὶ εἰπεῖν
what had happened	τὸ γεγονός

The **next day (ἐπαύριον) He decided (ἠθέλησεν)** to leave for Galilee. Jesus found Philip and told him, "**Follow (Ἀκολούθει) Me!**" (HCSB)

ἐπαύριον	tomorrow, the next day	17x
epaurion		S1887

θέλω ➤ 1:78   **ἀκολουθέω** ➤ 1:192

Τῇ **ἐπαύριον ἠθέλησεν** ἐξελθεῖν εἰς τὴν Γαλιλαίαν. καὶ εὑρίσκει Φίλιππον καὶ λέγει αὐτῷ ὁ Ἰησοῦς **Ἀκολούθει** μοι.

The **next day**	Τῇ **ἐπαύριον**
He decided	**ἠθέλησεν**
to leave for Galilee	ἐξελθεῖν εἰς τὴν Γαλιλαίαν
Jesus found Philip	καὶ εὑρίσκει Φίλιππον . . . ὁ Ἰησοῦς
and told him	καὶ λέγει αὐτῷ
Follow Me!	**Ἀκολούθει** μοι

They arrested [lit., **they laid (ἐπέβαλον) hands (χεῖρας)** on] the apostles and **put (ἔθεντο)** them in the public jail. (NIV)

| ἐπιβάλλω | to throw upon, place upon, lay | 17x |
| *epiballō* | | S1911 |

χείρ ▷ 1:88   τίθημι ▷ 1:170

καὶ **ἐπέβαλον** τὰς **χεῖρας** ἐπὶ τοὺς ἀποστόλους καὶ **ἔθεντο** αὐτοὺς ἐν τηρήσει δημοσίᾳ.

They arrested [lit., **they laid hands** on]	καὶ **ἐπέβαλον** τὰς **χεῖρας** ἐπὶ
the apostles	τοὺς ἀποστόλους
and **put** them	καὶ **ἔθεντο** αὐτοὺς
in the public jail	ἐν τηρήσει δημοσίᾳ

You too, be **ready (ἕτοιμοι)**; for the Son of Man is coming at an [lit., at **that (ᾗ)**] hour that **you do** not **expect (δοκεῖτε).** (NASB)

ἕτοιμος	ready, prepared	17x
*het*oimos		S2092

    ὅς, ἥ, ὅ ➢ 1:12   **δοκέω** ➢ 1:256

καὶ ὑμεῖς γίνεσθε **ἕτοιμοι**, ὅτι ᾗ ὥρᾳ οὐ **δοκεῖτε** ὁ υἱὸς τοῦ ἀνθρώπου ἔρχεται.

You too	καὶ ὑμεῖς
be **ready**	γίνεσθε **ἕτοιμοι**
for the Son of Man is coming	ὅτι . . . ὁ υἱὸς τοῦ ἀνθρώπου ἔρχεται
at an [lit., at **that**] hour	ᾗ ὥρᾳ
that **you do** not **expect**	οὐ **δοκεῖτε**

The kingdom of heaven is **like (Ὁμοία) treasure (θησαυρῷ)
hidden (κεκρυμμένῳ)** in a field, which someone found and **hid
(ἔκρυψεν)**; then in his joy he goes and sells all that he has and
buys that field. (NRSV)

θησαυρός	treasure, storehouse	17x
thēsauros		S2344

ὅμοιος	➤	1:364	κρύπτω	➤	DAY 284

Ὁμοία ἐστὶν ἡ βασιλεία τῶν οὐρανῶν **θησαυρῷ κεκρυμμένῳ** ἐν
τῷ ἀγρῷ, ὃν εὑρὼν ἄνθρωπος **ἔκρυψεν**, καὶ ἀπὸ τῆς χαρᾶς αὐτοῦ
ὑπάγει καὶ πωλεῖ ὅσα ἔχει καὶ ἀγοράζει τὸν ἀγρὸν ἐκεῖνον.

The kingdom of heaven is **like**	Ὁμοία ἐστὶν ἡ βασιλεία τῶν οὐρανῶν
treasure hidden in a field	**θησαυρῷ κεκρυμμένῳ** ἐν τῷ ἀγρῷ
which someone found	ὃν εὑρὼν ἄνθρωπος
and **hid**	**ἔκρυψεν**
then in his joy	καὶ ἀπὸ τῆς χαρᾶς αὐτοῦ
he goes	ὑπάγει
and sells all that he has	καὶ πωλεῖ ὅσα ἔχει
and buys that field	καὶ ἀγοράζει τὸν ἀγρὸν ἐκεῖνον

If we put bits into the **mouths (στόματα)** of **horses (ἵππων)** so that they **obey (πείθεσθαι)** us, we guide their whole bodies as well. (ESV)

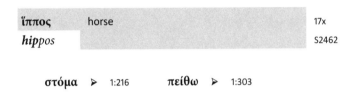

| ἵππος | horse | 17x |
| *hippos* | | S2462 |

στόμα ➤ 1:216   **πείθω** ➤ 1:303

εἰ δὲ τῶν **ἵππων** τοὺς χαλινοὺς εἰς τὰ **στόματα** βάλλομεν εἰς τὸ **πείθεσθαι** αὐτοὺς ἡμῖν, καὶ ὅλον τὸ σῶμα αὐτῶν μετάγομεν.

If we put	εἰ δὲ . . . βάλλομεν
bits	τοὺς χαλινοὺς
into the **mouths** of **horses**	τῶν **ἵππων** . . . εἰς τὰ **στόματα**
so that they **obey** us	εἰς τὸ **πείθεσθαι** αὐτοὺς ἡμῖν
we guide	μετάγομεν
their whole bodies	ὅλον τὸ σῶμα αὐτῶν
as well	καὶ

The **following day** (ἐπαύριον) he entered **Caesarea** (Καισαρίαν).
Now Cornelius was expecting them and had called together his
relatives and close **friends** (φίλους). (CSB)

Καισάρεια	Caesarea	17x
Kaisareia		S2542

φίλος ▷ DAY 113   **ἐπαύριον** ▷ DAY 333

τῇ δὲ **ἐπαύριον** εἰσῆλθεν εἰς τὴν **Καισαρίαν**· ὁ δὲ Κορνήλιος ἦν
προσδοκῶν αὐτοὺς συγκαλεσάμενος τοὺς συγγενεῖς αὐτοῦ καὶ
τοὺς ἀναγκαίους **φίλους**.

The **following day**	τῇ δὲ **ἐπαύριον**
he entered **Caesarea**	εἰσῆλθεν εἰς τὴν **Καισαρίαν**
Now Cornelius	ὁ δὲ Κορνήλιος
was expecting them	ἦν προσδοκῶν αὐτοὺς
and had called together	συγκαλεσάμενος
his relatives	τοὺς συγγενεῖς αὐτοῦ
and close **friends**	καὶ τοὺς ἀναγκαίους **φίλους**

This fellow **said (ἔφη)**, "I am able **to destroy (καταλῦσαι)** the temple of God and **rebuild (οἰκοδομῆσαι)** it in three days." (NIV)

καταλύω	to destroy, demolish, tear down	17x
kataluō		S2647

φημί ➤ 1:249   **οἰκοδομέω** ➤ DAY 10

Οὗτος ἔφη Δύναμαι **καταλῦσαι** τὸν ναὸν τοῦ θεοῦ καὶ διὰ τριῶν ἡμερῶν **οἰκοδομῆσαι**.

This fellow **said**	Οὗτος **ἔφη**
I am able	Δύναμαι
to destroy	**καταλῦσαι**
the temple of God	τὸν ναὸν τοῦ θεοῦ
and **rebuild** it	καὶ . . . **οἰκοδομῆσαι**
in three days	διὰ τριῶν ἡμερῶν

Let us hold fast (κατέχωμεν) the confession of our **hope (ἐλπίδος)** without wavering, for he who promised is **faithful (πιστὸς)**. (ESV)

κατέχω *katechō*	to hold fast, hold back, detain	17x S2722

πιστός ➤ 1:245   ἐλπίς ➤ 1:296

κατέχωμεν τὴν ὁμολογίαν τῆς **ἐλπίδος** ἀκλινῆ, **πιστὸς** γὰρ ὁ ἐπαγγειλάμενος·

Let us hold fast	κατέχωμεν
the confession	τὴν ὁμολογίαν
of our **hope**	τῆς **ἐλπίδος**
without wavering	ἀκλινῆ
for he who promised	γὰρ ὁ ἐπαγγειλάμενος
is **faithful**	**πιστὸς**

He became **as much (τοσούτῳ) greater (κρείττων)** than the angels as the name **He inherited (κεκληρονόμηκεν)** was superior to theirs. (MLB)

κρείττων	better	17x
kreittōn		S2909

      τοσοῦτος, τοσαύτη, τοσοῦτον   ➤   DAY 270

      κληρονομέω   ➤   DAY 307

τοσούτῳ κρείττων γενόμενος τῶν ἀγγέλων ὅσῳ διαφορώτερον παρ᾽ αὐτοὺς **κεκληρονόμηκεν** ὄνομα.

He became	γενόμενος
as much	**τοσούτῳ**
greater	**κρείττων**
than the angels	τῶν ἀγγέλων
as	ὅσῳ
the name **He inherited**	**κεκληρονόμηκεν** ὄνομα
was superior to theirs	διαφορώτερον παρ᾽ αὐτοὺς

But when His brothers **had gone up (ἀνέβησαν)** to the **feast (ἑορτήν)**, then **He** Himself also **went up (ἀνέβη)**, not publicly, but as if, in **secret (κρυπτῷ)**. (NASB)

κρυπτός	hidden, secret	17x
kruptos		S2927

ἀναβαίνω ➤ 1:206   ἑορτή ➤ DAY 166

Ὡς δὲ **ἀνέβησαν** οἱ ἀδελφοὶ αὐτοῦ εἰς τὴν **ἑορτήν**, τότε καὶ αὐτὸς **ἀνέβη**, οὐ φανερῶς ἀλλὰ ὡς ἐν **κρυπτῷ**.

But when His brothers **had gone up**	Ὡς δὲ **ἀνέβησαν** οἱ ἀδελφοὶ αὐτοῦ
to the **feast**	εἰς τὴν **ἑορτήν**
then	τότε
He Himself also **went up**	καὶ αὐτὸς **ἀνέβη**
not publicly	οὐ φανερῶς
but as if	ἀλλὰ ὡς
in **secret**	ἐν **κρυπτῷ**

All the **crowds (ὄχλοι) were amazed (ἐξίσταντο)** and said, "**Can (Μήτι)** this be the Son of David?" (NRSV)

| μήτι | if not, unless; (used in questions in which a | 17x |
| *mēti* | negative answer is expected) | S3385 |

ὄχλος ▷ 1:90   ἐξίστημι ▷ DAY 332

Καὶ **ἐξίσταντο** πάντες οἱ **ὄχλοι** καὶ ἔλεγον **Μήτι** οὗτός ἐστιν ὁ υἱὸς Δαυείδ;

All the **crowds**	Καὶ . . . πάντες οἱ **ὄχλοι**
were amazed	**ἐξίσταντο**
and said	καὶ ἔλεγον
Can this be	**Μήτι** οὗτός ἐστιν
the Son of David?	ὁ υἱὸς Δαυείδ;

But when you **fast (νηστεύων)**, anoint your head and **wash (νίψαι)** your **face (πρόσωπόν)**. (MLB)

| νίπτω | to wash | 17x |
| *niptō* | | S3538 |

πρόσωπον ➤ 1:231   νηστεύω ➤ DAY 265

σὺ δὲ **νηστεύων** ἄλειψαί σου τὴν κεφαλὴν καὶ τὸ **πρόσωπόν** σου **νίψαι**,

But when you **fast**	σὺ δὲ **νηστεύων**
anoint	ἄλειψαί
your head	σου τὴν κεφαλὴν
and **wash**	καὶ . . . **νίψαι**
your **face**	τὸ **πρόσωπόν** σου

Yet **not even (οὐδὲ)** Titus, who was with me, was compelled
to be circumcised (περιτμηθῆναι), even though he was a
Greek (Ἕλλην). (NIV)

περιτέμνω	to circumcise	17x
peritemnō		S4059

οὐδέ　➤　1:119　　　Ἕλλην　➤　DAY 196

ἀλλ᾽ **οὐδὲ** Τίτος ὁ σὺν ἐμοί, Ἕλλην ὤν, ἠναγκάσθη
περιτμηθῆναι·

Yet **not even** Titus	ἀλλ᾽ **οὐδὲ** Τίτος
who was with me	ὁ σὺν ἐμοί
was compelled	ἠναγκάσθη
to be circumcised	**περιτμηθῆναι**
even though he was a **Greek**	Ἕλλην ὤν

until (μέχρι) we all attain to the unity of the faith and of the **knowledge (ἐπιγνώσεως)** of the Son of God, to mature manhood, to the measure of the stature of the **fullness (πληρώματος)** of Christ. (ESV)

| πλήρωμα *plērōma* | fullness, fulfillment, completion | 17x S4138 |

| ἐπίγνωσις ▷ DAY 257 | μέχρι ▷ DAY 310 |

μέχρι καταντήσωμεν οἱ πάντες εἰς τὴν ἑνότητα τῆς πίστεως καὶ τῆς **ἐπιγνώσεως** τοῦ υἱοῦ τοῦ θεοῦ, εἰς ἄνδρα τέλειον, εἰς μέτρον ἡλικίας τοῦ **πληρώματος** τοῦ χριστοῦ,

until we all attain	**μέχρι** καταντήσωμεν οἱ πάντες
to the unity	εἰς τὴν ἑνότητα
of the faith	τῆς πίστεως
and of the **knowledge** of the Son of God	καὶ τῆς **ἐπιγνώσεως** τοῦ υἱοῦ τοῦ θεοῦ
to mature manhood	εἰς ἄνδρα τέλειον
to the measure	εἰς μέτρον
of the stature	ἡλικίας
of the **fullness** of Christ	τοῦ **πληρώματος** τοῦ χριστοῦ

You have heard that it was said, "Love your **neighbor (πλησίον)** and **hate (μισήσεις)** your **enemy (ἐχθρόν)**." (MLB)

πλησίον	near, neighboring, neighbor	17x
plēsion		S4139

μισέω ➤ DAY 9   **ἐχθρός** ➤ DAY 72

Ἠκούσατε ὅτι ἐρρέθη Ἀγαπήσεις τὸν **πλησίον** σου καὶ **μισήσεις** τὸν **ἐχθρόν** σου.

You have heard that	Ἠκούσατε ὅτι
it was said	ἐρρέθη
Love	Ἀγαπήσεις
your **neighbor**	τὸν **πλησίον** σου
and **hate**	καὶ **μισήσεις**
your **enemy**	τὸν **ἐχθρόν** σου

And the rain fell, and the **floods (ποταμοὶ)** came, and the **winds (ἄνεμοι)** blew and beat on that house, but **it did** not **fall (ἔπεσεν)**, because it had been founded on the rock. (ESV)

ποταμός	river	17x
potamos		S4215

πίπτω ▷ 1:191   ἄνεμος ▷ DAY 77

καὶ κατέβη ἡ βροχὴ καὶ ἦλθαν οἱ **ποταμοὶ** καὶ ἔπνευσαν οἱ **ἄνεμοι** καὶ προσέπεσαν τῇ οἰκίᾳ ἐκείνῃ, καὶ οὐκ **ἔπεσεν**, τεθεμελίωτο γὰρ ἐπὶ τὴν πέτραν.

And the rain fell	καὶ κατέβη ἡ βροχὴ
and the **floods** came	καὶ ἦλθαν οἱ **ποταμοὶ**
and the **winds** blew	καὶ ἔπνευσαν οἱ **ἄνεμοι**
and beat on that house	καὶ προσέπεσαν τῇ οἰκίᾳ ἐκείνῃ
but **it did** not **fall**	καὶ οὐκ **ἔπεσεν**
because it had been founded	τεθεμελίωτο γὰρ
on the rock	ἐπὶ τὴν πέτραν

I, Jesus, have sent My angel to testify to you these things for the churches. I am the **root (ῥίζα)** and the **descendant (γένος)** of David, the bright morning **star (ἀστὴρ)**. (NASB)

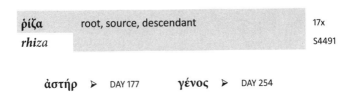

| ῥίζα | root, source, descendant | 17x |
| *rhiza* | | S4491 |

ἀστήρ   ▷   DAY 177   γένος   ▷   DAY 254

Ἐγὼ Ἰησοῦς ἔπεμψα τὸν ἄγγελόν μου μαρτυρῆσαι ὑμῖν ταῦτα ἐπὶ ταῖς ἐκκλησίαις. ἐγώ εἰμι ἡ **ῥίζα** καὶ τὸ **γένος** Δαυείδ, ὁ **ἀστὴρ** ὁ λαμπρός, ὁ πρωινός.

I, Jesus	Ἐγὼ Ἰησοῦς
have sent	ἔπεμψα
My angel	τὸν ἄγγελόν μου
to testify to you these things	μαρτυρῆσαι ὑμῖν ταῦτα
for the churches	ἐπὶ ταῖς ἐκκλησίαις
I am the **root**	ἐγώ εἰμι ἡ **ῥίζα**
and the **descendant** of David	καὶ τὸ **γένος** Δαυείδ
the bright morning **star**	ὁ **ἀστὴρ** ὁ λαμπρός, ὁ πρωινός

But when the disciples saw him walking on the sea, **they were terrified** (ἐταράχθησαν), and said, "It is a ghost!" and **they cried out** (ἔκραξαν) in **fear** (φόβου). (ESV)

ταράσσω	to disturb, trouble	17x
tarassō		S5015

κράζω ➤ 1:282   **φόβος** ➤ 1:326

οἱ δὲ μαθηταὶ ἰδόντες αὐτὸν ἐπὶ τῆς θαλάσσης περιπατοῦντα **ἐταράχθησαν** λέγοντες ὅτι Φάντασμά ἐστιν, καὶ ἀπὸ τοῦ **φόβου** **ἔκραξαν**.

But when the disciples saw him	οἱ δὲ μαθηταὶ ἰδόντες αὐτὸν
walking	περιπατοῦντα
on the sea	ἐπὶ τῆς θαλάσσης
they were terrified	**ἐταράχθησαν**
and said	λέγοντες ὅτι
It is a ghost!	Φάντασμά ἐστιν
and **they cried out**	καὶ . . . **ἔκραξαν**
in **fear**	ἀπὸ τοῦ **φόβου**

But Jesus, **aware of (γνοὺς)** their malice, said, "Why **are you putting** me **to the test (πειράζετε)**, you **hypocrites (ὑποκριταί)**?"
(NRSV)

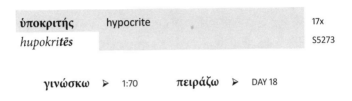

| ὑποκριτής | hypocrite | 17x |
| *hupokritēs* | | S5273 |

γινώσκω ▷ 1:70   πειράζω ▷ DAY 18

γνοὺς δὲ ὁ Ἰησοῦς τὴν πονηρίαν αὐτῶν εἶπεν Τί με **πειράζετε**, **ὑποκριταί**;

But Jesus	δὲ ὁ Ἰησοῦς
aware of	**γνοὺς**
their malice	τὴν πονηρίαν αὐτῶν
said	εἶπεν
Why **are you putting** me **to the test**	Τί με **πειράζετε**
you **hypocrites?**	**ὑποκριταί**;

After those days **were over (τελειωσάντων)**, as they **were returning (ὑποστρέφειν)**, the boy Jesus **stayed behind (ὑπέμεινεν)** in Jerusalem, but his parents did not know it. (CSB)

ὑπομένω *hupomenō*	to endure, remain behind	17x S5278

ὑποστρέφω   ▷   DAY 52   τελειόω   ▷   DAY 207

καὶ **τελειωσάντων** τὰς ἡμέρας, ἐν τῷ **ὑποστρέφειν** αὐτοὺς **ὑπέμεινεν** Ἰησοῦς ὁ παῖς ἐν Ἰερουσαλήμ, καὶ οὐκ ἔγνωσαν οἱ γονεῖς αὐτοῦ.

After those days **were over**	καὶ **τελειωσάντων** τὰς ἡμέρας
as they **were returning**	ἐν τῷ **ὑποστρέφειν** αὐτοὺς
the boy Jesus **stayed behind**	**ὑπέμεινεν** Ἰησοῦς ὁ παῖς
in Jerusalem	ἐν Ἰερουσαλήμ
but his parents	καὶ . . . οἱ γονεῖς αὐτοῦ
did not know it	οὐκ ἔγνωσαν

For the wages of sin is **death (θάνατος)**, but the **gift (χάρισμα)** of God is eternal **life (ζωὴ)** in Christ Jesus our Lord. (MLB)

χάρισμα	gift, endowment	17x
charisma		S5486

ζωή ➤ 1:125   **θάνατος** ➤ 1:138

τὰ γὰρ ὀψώνια τῆς ἁμαρτίας **θάνατος**, τὸ δὲ **χάρισμα** τοῦ θεοῦ **ζωὴ** αἰώνιος ἐν Χριστῷ Ἰησοῦ τῷ κυρίῳ ἡμῶν.

For the wages	τὰ γὰρ ὀψώνια
of sin	τῆς ἁμαρτίας
is **death**	**θάνατος**
but the **gift** of God	τὸ δὲ **χάρισμα** τοῦ θεοῦ
is eternal **life**	**ζωὴ** αἰώνιος
in Christ Jesus	ἐν Χριστῷ Ἰησοῦ
our Lord	τῷ κυρίῳ ἡμῶν

The **former (πρῶτον)** narrative I composed, **O (ὦ)** Theophilus, regarding all that Jesus **began (ἤρξατο)** to do and to teach . . . (MLB)

ὦ	O!		17x
ō			S5599

πρῶτος ▷ 1:182   **ἄρχω** ▷ 1:201

Τὸν μὲν **πρῶτον** λόγον ἐποιησάμην περὶ πάντων, **ὦ** Θεόφιλε, ὧν **ἤρξατο** Ἰησοῦς ποιεῖν τε καὶ διδάσκειν

The **former** narrative	Τὸν μὲν **πρῶτον** λόγον
I composed	ἐποιησάμην
O Theophilus	**ὦ** Θεόφιλε
regarding all	περὶ πάντων
that Jesus **began**	ὧν **ἤρξατο** Ἰησοῦς
to do	ποιεῖν
and to teach	τε καὶ διδάσκειν

In the same way ('Ωσαύτως) the Spirit also helps our **weakness**
(**ἀσθενείᾳ**); for we do not know how **to pray (προσευξώμεθα)** as
we should, but the Spirit Himself intercedes for us with groanings
too deep for words. (NASB)

ὡσαύτως	likewise, in the same way	17x
hōsautōs		S5615

προσεύχομαι ➤ 1:198　　**ἀσθένεια** ➤ DAY 176

'Ωσαύτως δὲ καὶ τὸ πνεῦμα συναντιλαμβάνεται τῇ **ἀσθενείᾳ**
ἡμῶν· τὸ γὰρ τί **προσευξώμεθα** καθὸ δεῖ οὐκ οἴδαμεν, ἀλλὰ αὐτὸ
τὸ πνεῦμα ὑπερεντυγχάνει στεναγμοῖς ἀλαλήτοις,

In the same way	'Ωσαύτως δὲ
the Spirit also helps	καὶ τὸ πνεῦμα συναντιλαμβάνεται
our **weakness**	τῇ **ἀσθενείᾳ** ἡμῶν
for we do not know	γὰρ . . . οὐκ οἴδαμεν
how **to pray**	τὸ . . . τί **προσευξώμεθα**
as we should	καθὸ δεῖ
but the Spirit Himself intercedes for us	ἀλλὰ αὐτὸ τὸ πνεῦμα ὑπερεντυγχάνει
with groanings	στεναγμοῖς
too deep for words	ἀλαλήτοις

I **do** not **nullify (ἀθετῶ)** the grace of God, for if **righteousness (δικαιοσύνη)** were through the law, **then (ἄρα)** Christ died for no purpose. (ESV)

ἀθετέω	to annul, set aside, ignore, reject	16x
atheteō		S114

δικαιοσύνη ➤ 1:187   **ἄρα / ἄρα** ➤ 1:310

Οὐκ **ἀθετῶ** τὴν χάριν τοῦ θεοῦ· εἰ γὰρ διὰ νόμου **δικαιοσύνη**, **ἄρα** Χριστὸς δωρεὰν ἀπέθανεν.

I **do** not **nullify**	Οὐκ **ἀθετῶ**
the grace of God	τὴν χάριν τοῦ θεοῦ
for if **righteousness**	εἰ γὰρ . . . **δικαιοσύνη**
were through the law	διὰ νόμου
then Christ died	**ἄρα** Χριστὸς . . . ἀπέθανεν
for no purpose	δωρεὰν

Eat anything that **is sold (πωλούμενον)** in the meat market without **asking questions (ἀνακρίνοντες)** for **conscience' (συνείδησιν)** sake. (NASB)

ἀνακρίνω	to examine, inquire into	16x
anakrinō		S350

συνείδησις ▷ DAY 111   πωλέω ▷ DAY 241

Πᾶν τὸ ἐν μακέλλῳ **πωλούμενον** ἐσθίετε μηδὲν **ἀνακρίνοντες** διὰ τὴν **συνείδησιν,**

Eat	ἐσθίετε
anything	Πᾶν
that **is sold**	τὸ . . . **πωλούμενον**
in the meat market	ἐν μακέλλῳ
without **asking questions**	μηδὲν **ἀνακρίνοντες**
for **conscience'** sake	διὰ τὴν **συνείδησιν**

At the time of the **banquet (δείπνου)** he sent his servant to tell those **who had been invited (κεκλημένοις)**, "Come, for everything is now **ready (ἕτοιμά)**." (NIV)

δεῖπνον	dinner, supper, banquet	16x
deipnon		S1173

καλέω ➤ 1:112   **ἕτοιμος** ➤ DAY 335

καὶ ἀπέστειλεν τὸν δοῦλον αὐτοῦ τῇ ὥρᾳ τοῦ **δείπνου** εἰπεῖν τοῖς **κεκλημένοις** Ἔρχεσθε ὅτι ἤδη **ἕτοιμά** ἐστιν.

At the time of the **banquet**	τῇ ὥρᾳ τοῦ **δείπνου**
he sent his servant	καὶ ἀπέστειλεν τὸν δοῦλον αὐτοῦ
to tell	εἰπεῖν
those **who had been invited**	τοῖς **κεκλημένοις**
Come	Ἔρχεσθε
for	ὅτι
everything is . . . **ready**	**ἕτοιμά** ἐστιν
now	ἤδη

Remember (μιμνήσκεσθε) the prisoners (δεσμίων), as though you were in prison with them, and the mistreated, as though yourselves were suffering bodily [lit., were in **body (σώματι)**].
(HCSB)

δέσμιος	bound, captive, prisoner	16x
desmios		S1198

σῶμα ➤ 1:117   μιμνήσκομαι ➤ DAY 225

μιμνήσκεσθε τῶν δεσμίων ὡς συνδεδεμένοι, τῶν κακουχουμένων ὡς καὶ αὐτοὶ ὄντες ἐν σώματι.

Remember	μιμνήσκεσθε
the **prisoners**	τῶν **δεσμίων**
as though	ὡς
you were in prison with them	συνδεδεμένοι
and the mistreated	τῶν κακουχουμένων
as though	ὡς
you yourselves were suffering bodily [lit., were in **body**]	καὶ αὐτοὶ ὄντες ἐν **σώματι**

"**Show (Δείξατέ)** me a **denarius (δηνάριον)**. Whose **likeness (εἰκόνα)** and inscription does it have?" They said, "Caesar's." (ESV)

δηνάριον	denarius	16x
dēnarion		S1220

δείκνυμι ▷ DAY 91   **εἰκών** ▷ DAY 195

Δείξατέ μοι **δηνάριον**· τίνος ἔχει **εἰκόνα** καὶ ἐπιγραφήν; οἱ δὲ εἶπαν Καίσαρος.

Show me	**Δείξατέ** μοι
a **denarius**	**δηνάριον**
Whose **likeness**	τίνος . . . **εἰκόνα**
and inscription	καὶ ἐπιγραφήν;
does it have?	ἔχει
They said	οἱ δὲ εἶπαν
Caesar's	Καίσαρος

As the people were in expectation, and all **were questioning (διαλογιζομένων)** in their **hearts (καρδίαις)** concerning John, **whether (μήποτε)** he might be the Christ, . . . (ESV)

διαλογίζομαι *dialogizomai*	to reason (with), debate (with), consider	16x S1260

καρδία ➤ 1:102   **μήποτε** ➤ DAY 182

Προσδοκῶντος δὲ τοῦ λαοῦ καὶ **διαλογιζομένων** πάντων ἐν ταῖς **καρδίαις** αὐτῶν περὶ τοῦ Ἰωάνου, **μήποτε** αὐτὸς εἴη ὁ χριστός,

As the people were in expectation	Προσδοκῶντος δὲ τοῦ λαοῦ
and all **were questioning**	καὶ **διαλογιζομένων** πάντων
in their **hearts**	ἐν ταῖς **καρδίαις** αὐτῶν
concerning John	περὶ τοῦ Ἰωάνου
whether	**μήποτε**
he might be	αὐτὸς εἴη
the Christ	ὁ χριστός

But going ahead to the **ship (πλοῖον)**, we **set sail (ἀνήχθημεν)** for Assos, intending to take Paul aboard there, for so he had **arranged (διατεταγμένος)**, intending himself to go by land. (ESV)

διατάσσω	to command	16x
diatassō		S1299

πλοῖον ▷ 1:241   **ἀνάγω** ▷ DAY 190

Ἡμεῖς δὲ προελθόντες ἐπὶ τὸ **πλοῖον ἀνήχθημεν** ἐπὶ τὴν Ἄσσον, ἐκεῖθεν μέλλοντες ἀναλαμβάνειν τὸν Παῦλον, οὕτως γὰρ **διατεταγμένος** ἦν μέλλων αὐτὸς πεζεύειν.

But going ahead to the **ship**	δὲ προελθόντες ἐπὶ τὸ **πλοῖον**
we **set sail** for Assos	Ἡμεῖς . . . **ἀνήχθημεν** ἐπὶ τὴν Ἄσσον
intending	μέλλοντες
to take Paul aboard	ἀναλαμβάνειν τὸν Παῦλον
there	ἐκεῖθεν
for so he had **arranged**	οὕτως γὰρ **διατεταγμένος** ἦν
intending himself	μέλλων αὐτὸς
to go by land	πεζεύειν

For **I was hungry (ἐπείνασα)** and you gave me something to eat, **I was thirsty (ἐδίψησα)** and you gave me something to drink, I was a stranger and **you invited** me **in (συνηγάγετέ)**. (NIV)

διψάω　　to thirst　　　　　　　　　　16x
dipsaō　　　　　　　　　　　　　　　S1372

　　συνάγω　▷　1:278　　　**πεινάω**　▷　DAY 203

ἐπείνασα γὰρ καὶ ἐδώκατέ μοι φαγεῖν, **ἐδίψησα** καὶ ἐποτίσατέ με, ξένος ἤμην καὶ **συνηγάγετέ** με,

For **I was hungry**	**ἐπείνασα** γὰρ
and you gave me something to eat	καὶ ἐδώκατέ μοι φαγεῖν
I was thirsty	**ἐδίψησα**
and you gave me something to drink	καὶ ἐποτίσατέ με
I was a stranger	ξένος ἤμην
and **you invited** me **in**	καὶ **συνηγάγετέ** με

Reaching out (ἐκτείνας) His hand **He touched (ἥψατο)** him saying, "I am willing. **Be cleansed (καθαρίσθητι)**." And instantly his leprosy **was cleansed (ἐκαθερίσθη)**. (MLB)

ἐκτείνω	to stretch out, stretch forth	16x
ekteinō		S1614

ἅπτω ➤ DAY 26   καθαρίζω ➤ DAY 79

καὶ **ἐκτείνας** τὴν χεῖρα **ἥψατο** αὐτοῦ λέγων Θέλω, **καθαρίσθητι·** καὶ εὐθέως **ἐκαθερίσθη** αὐτοῦ ἡ λέπρα.

Reaching out His hand	καὶ **ἐκτείνας** τὴν χεῖρα
He touched him	**ἥψατο** αὐτοῦ
saying	λέγων
I am willing	Θέλω
Be cleansed	**καθαρίσθητι**
And instantly	καὶ εὐθέως
his leprosy	αὐτοῦ ἡ λέπρα
was cleansed	**ἐκαθερίσθη**

But **each** (Ἕκαστος) in his own order: Christ, the firstfruits;
afterward (ἔπειτα), at his **coming** (παρουσίᾳ), those who belong
to Christ. (CSB)

ἔπειτα	then, thereafter, afterward	16x
epeita		S1899

ἕκαστος ➤ 1:203   **παρουσία** ➤ DAY 185

Ἕκαστος δὲ ἐν τῷ ἰδίῳ τάγματι· ἀπαρχὴ Χριστός, **ἔπειτα** οἱ τοῦ
χριστοῦ ἐν τῇ **παρουσίᾳ** αὐτοῦ·

But **each**	Ἕκαστος δὲ
in his own order	ἐν τῷ ἰδίῳ τάγματι
Christ	Χριστός
the firstfruits	ἀπαρχὴ
afterward	**ἔπειτα**
at his **coming**	ἐν τῇ **παρουσίᾳ** αὐτοῦ
those who belong to Christ	οἱ τοῦ χριστοῦ

Index of Scripture References

8:54	DAY 4	7:10	DAY 342	19:32	DAY 146
8:56	DAY 332	7:42	DAY 138	20:13	DAY 362
9:13	DAY 328	9:30	DAY 108	21:20	DAY 140
10:19	DAY 279	12:6	DAY 130	21:37	DAY 94
11:7	DAY 309	12:20	DAY 196	23:1	DAY 228
12:11	DAY 287	15:13	DAY 113	23:8	DAY 153
12:40	DAY 335	16:20	DAY 151	23:16	DAY 159
12:42	DAY 219	16:25	DAY 82	23:22	DAY 247
13:1	DAY 202	16:33	DAY 125	23:35	DAY 199
13:24	DAY 16	19:30	DAY 127	24:13	DAY 312
13:27	DAY 160	20:4	DAY 271	24:14	DAY 263
14:1	DAY 27	21:15	DAY 172	25:10	DAY 129
14:17	DAY 358			25:12	DAY 95
14:18	DAY 88	**Acts**		26:9	DAY 29
14:31	DAY 317	1:1	DAY 354	27:20	DAY 73
15:8	DAY 26	1:12	DAY 93	27:43	DAY 256
15:25	DAY 34	2:6	DAY 100	28:3	DAY 83
16:7	DAY 329	2:42	DAY 282	28:10	DAY 190
16:22	DAY 61	3:6	DAY 251		
17:2	DAY 110	3:13	DAY 260	**Romans**	
17:12	DAY 131	3:18	DAY 12	2:25	DAY 250
17:15	DAY 148	5:18	DAY 334	2:28	DAY 323
17:27	DAY 117	5:31	DAY 273	3:20	DAY 257
18:2	DAY 283	6:2	DAY 180	3:31	DAY 136
18:18	DAY 307	7:25	DAY 156	4:5	DAY 14
18:22	DAY 241	7:44	DAY 286	4:20	DAY 276
18:34	DAY 284	8:6	DAY 46	5:3	DAY 32
19:12	DAY 128	8:28	DAY 67	5:5	DAY 132
19:14	DAY 231	9:12	DAY 23	5:20	DAY 239
20:24	DAY 360	9:18	DAY 174	6:4	DAY 252
21:3	DAY 292	10:21	DAY 249	6:23	DAY 353
22:13	DAY 15	10:24	DAY 338	7:9	DAY 5
22:26	DAY 119	13:11	DAY 315	8:18	DAY 162
23:9	DAY 6	13:45	DAY 186	8:26	DAY 355
23:32	DAY 175	15:29	DAY 274	8:32	DAY 253
23:48	DAY 52	15:30	DAY 293	8:35	DAY 123
24:45	DAY 184	15:32	DAY 31	9:1	DAY 111
		16:1	DAY 188	11:20	DAY 157
John		16:9	DAY 223	11:33	DAY 227
1:43	DAY 333	16:19	DAY 280	12:12	DAY 44
3:26	DAY 204	16:28	DAY 21	12:19	DAY 40
4:38	DAY 235	16:33	DAY 226	13:12	DAY 134
4:46	DAY 63	17:29	DAY 254	14:21	DAY 60
5:35	DAY 85	18:10	DAY 194	15:1	DAY 326
5:45	DAY 237	19:6	DAY 126		
6:25	DAY 289	19:8	DAY 311